The Logic of English Prepositions

Intuitively Understand and Feel English like a Native Speaker

By J. Daniel Moore

The Logic of English Prepositions: Intuitively Understand and
Feel English like a Native Speaker

The author can be contacted at: jdanielmooreauthor@gmail.com

Contents

This book is dedicated to my grandparents. Thank you for all of your love and support. I love you.

This book wouldn't be possible without the feedback of my students and friends. In particular, I thank those students who participated in the early stages of what has now become this book and who allowed me to successfully test my ideas with them.

Introduction

"A language simultaneously obliges us and allows us to experience the world in a certain way."
-Mihalis Eleftheriou, founder of *Language Transfer*

(Note: this book is not associated with *Language Transfer* or it's founder in any way.)

Every language has it's own personality. A language is a living thing that lives through its speakers. Just like a person changes and grows over time, languages do the same, but more slowly. Each language has its own boundaries and ways that it likes to look at the world. This doesn't mean that a speaker of one language can't learn how to think in another language, it's just that if you really want to learn a language well and be able to think in it and feel it, you have to understand that language's personality and how it looks at the world. This affects everything in a language, including prepositions, articles, perceptions of time and space, uses of verb tenses, and more, and there's increasing scientific evidence to support this idea.

Let's look at an example. Spanish and German both use something that's called "grammatical gender", which means that some words in the language are "masculine" (male, related to "man") and some words are "feminine" (female, related to "woman"). It doesn't matter what the word is. English uses "biological gender", which basically means that things that aren't male or female in the real world are called "it" because they don't have a real world, biological gender. For example, a chair can't be a man or a woman, but in Spanish the word "chair" is feminine.

Language researchers wanted to know if the grammatical gender in other languages affected the perception of native speakers. So the researchers asked native Spanish speakers and native German speakers (who were all fluent in English) to describe different objects using English. One of the English words that the Spanish and German speakers had to describe was the word "bridge". In Spanish, the word "bridge" is masculine. They described the English word "bridge" using the words "big", "dangerous", "strong", "sturdy", and "towering". These are all words that you might often associate with men. However, in German, the word "bridge" is feminine. What words did they use? "Beautiful", "elegant", "fragile" (easy to break), "pretty", and "slender" (skinny). Interesting. It seems that a person's native language can affect how they perceive things. 1

This is just one small example, but here's the most important point: it's possible to perceive one thing in many different ways. It's possible to perceive a bridge as either "sturdy" or "fragile", "dangerous" or "pretty", etc… All of these words can describe a bridge, depending on how you want to look at it. The personality of every language determines the ways that native speakers are likely to perceive things at a basic level (meaning subconsciously), but it doesn't mean that a Spanish speaker can't think of a bridge as "beautiful" or that a German speaker can't think of a bridge as "sturdy". There are many different ways to look at things and that's one reason that languages are so different from each other. The purpose of this book is to help you discover and feel how the English language looks at the world. This book is only about prepositions, but prepositions are one of the most important parts of a language because they contain a lot of a language's personality.

This is a book about prepositions, so let's look at an example that uses them. In English, the verb "to depend" uses the preposition "on". In Spanish, the verb "depender" uses the preposition "de". The English word for "de" is usually "of". So, if we literally translate "depender de" into English, we get "to depend of". A native English speaker would never say that. It works in Spanish, but not in English. Why? Because the English language has it's own personality, and so does the Spanish language. This book will help to teach you the personality of the English language and how it looks at the world. How? With logic. Specifically, the logic that the English language applies to its prepositions.

I'm sure that your English teachers in the past told you that "there's no logic to prepositions" and that "you simply have to memorize them". I'm an English teacher (ESL/EFL) and I used to think this, too. However, I'm also a language learner. In 2017, I was teaching myself German. I already had an intermediate level in Spanish, and in both of these languages, I hated prepositions. I was always making mistakes and I couldn't seem to figure out why these languages use prepositions so differently compared to English.

One day, I was talking to a friend (who's a native German speaker) about the different meanings of the German preposition "auf". This preposition has meanings related to time, space, etc…, but the translations into English include "on", "up", "at", and even "for", depending on the context. I started to notice something interesting: it seemed that at least some of the dictionary definitions were closely connected, but some of those connections were abstract. I started to wonder if *all* of the dictionary definitions were connected in some way. So, I started with the simplest and easiest definitions and tried to find any connections. From that point, I started looking at other definitions that seemed different, but I tried to connect them to the easier definitions in a logical way. I wanted to make sure that I wasn't just imagining the connections, but that I was actually finding connections that do exist inside the German language itself. So I asked my German friend questions about certain definitions so that I could see if it were possible to connect all the definitions in a way that still made sense from the perspective of a native German speaker. At first, he told me not to try because there wasn't any logic that connected them and I just had to memorize how to use them. But I wanted to try anyway. A couple of weeks later, I had to stop learning German for a little while, but before I had stopped, it seemed that my idea was working. It seemed that there actually might be a hidden logic that connects all the different dictionary definitions, so I decided to start thinking about how we use prepositions in English.

7

The more I thought about it, the more it became very clear that English prepositions are extremely logical, and I've found no exceptions, even when a preposition is used as a noun or a verb (though I have found a few cases that are difficult to explain). But why do English teachers say that there isn't any logic? Let's imagine a farm that grows a lot of different plants. On the surface, you see all the leaves and branches of the plants (the "in" plant, the "on" plant, the "to" plant, etc...). These leaves and branches are the different dictionary definitions that seem to be disconnected and random. These "surface meanings" are what native speakers are consciously aware of. However, under the ground we find the root of each plant. The root is the logic that all the dictionary definitions are based on. This underground level is part of the subconscious mind, which means that native speakers aren't consciously aware of it. Just like on a real farm, the roots of two or more plants can touch and connect sometimes. We'll see many special connections between prepositions – for example, the extremely important connection between "at", "on", and "in".

Prepositions aren't just little grammar words. They're critically important and hold a lot of meaning, and mastering them will allow you to think more like a native speaker. Think about it this way: we know that languages slowly change as time passes, but the speakers of a language don't just randomly apply words to new contexts. There's a logical reason why words are applied to new contexts. When this happens, we get an extension of the original meaning (which might be more abstract), or we get an entirely new meaning. Either way, the new meaning is usually based on the original logic of the word in some way. The best example of this change in English is phrasal verbs. In fact, phrasal verbs can't exist if there's no logic, especially because sometimes native English speakers spontaneously create phrasal verbs to fit very specific contexts. This is only possible if there's a logic and a feeling that we can then apply in new ways to fit the context.

It's important to remember that although prepositions are logical, there's no single book or other resource that will magically solve your language learning problems. The good news is that this book is <u>not</u> about grammar rules or memorizing definitions. It's about how English prepositions feel and how the English language applies logic to them. I highly recommend that you get my other book, *The Logic of English Prepositions Workbook*, which has exercises with detailed answers that help you apply what you learn in this book. You don't have to buy the workbook, but you <u>do</u> have to apply what you learn in some way. It will take some time, creative thinking, and active practice, but this book will allow you to learn these things more easily and you'll start thinking like a native speaker much faster than normal. As with any skill, I can give you the tools, but ***<u>you</u>*** have to put in the work. In other words, you have to take the knowledge in this book and make it part of your active ability by speaking and writing. You **will** make mistakes. It's an unavoidable and natural part of learning any skill, but this book will also help you understand <u>why</u> you make those mistakes.

As a final note, this book is not for everyone. A few of my students didn't like the approach and some people will probably say that I'm wrong and that there is no logic. However, this approach has worked very well for many of my students (both intermediate and advanced) because it helps you get inside the English language in a way that allows you to start intuitively feeling the language like a native speaker does. I hope you enjoy the information in this book, as well as the method that I've developed in order to help you learn and understand it.

-J. Daniel Moore

How to Use this Book

The main part of this book is a guide through the logic (and feeling) of seventeen prepositions. Most of the prepositions that we'll look at are the small ones, like "in", "on", "to", "at", and "for", and almost all of them are extremely common. We'll look at example sentences with detailed explanations of how the logic applies in each sentence. We usually use these words as prepositions, but sometimes we can use them as verbs, adverbs, etc…, so I've included some of those in the example sentences.

There are six sections for each preposition. You can use this book any way that you want, but I recommend that you do <u>not</u> skip any section because this process is designed to help you learn better in a way that's based on scientific principles of learning. Section A has example sentences without explanations. However, for some people it's easier to look at the logic first (section B), and then go through the example sentences. Again, I don't recommend this, but do whatever works for you.

Section A shows **example sentences divided into groups**. Each group is for a different surface meaning of the preposition. This is similar to what you find in the dictionary, but without definitions. However, there are some dictionary definitions that are closely related so I put them into the same group. The point of this section is to introduce you to all of the different uses and to help you to better remember, categorize, and feel how the logic can be applied in different ways. In this section, the groups aren't labeled, but they are labeled in the explanation section (section C). This is because you will remember the material better if you try to discover the label by yourself first. A label can be "time", "space", "process", "cause", etc… After you look at each group, compare all of the groups and try to find a key idea that describes logic. Here's an example of group one from the preposition "in":

1)

My birthday is in May.
My family goes on vacation in the summer.
I was born in 1990.
I don't like to get up early in the morning.
"Do you know this man?" "No. I've never seen him in my life."
I'll be home in two days.
In time, you will understand.
The bus arrived in time.

Section B gives you the **Key Idea or Key Ideas** that describe the logic. You will also find a more detailed explanation of the logic, as well as any important notes. This includes useful notes about the etymology of the preposition ("etymology" means "the history of words"; all etymology notes are based on information from the *Online Etymology Dictionary*). Again, you can skip section A and look at this section first, but I don't recommend doing that. Some prepositions are very complicated and their logic deals with more than one key idea. If there's more than one key idea, each key idea is just a different aspect of the logic. Continuing our example with the preposition "in":

B) The Logic

Key Idea(s): "container"
"in" is a one-way preposition
Explanation of the logic: The preposition "in"...
Etymology notes: The preposition "in"...

Section C gives you the **labels for each group** that you saw in section A and **detailed explanations of every example sentence** from section A. This is the main section for each preposition and it's the section that will teach you how to understand and feel the logic. Whenever possible, I also give you alternative ways to say the same sentence. These alternatives usually use other prepositions that you can use in the same context.

Section D shows a table. This table has **examples of verbs that often use that preposition**, excluding phrasal verbs.

Section E gives you some example sentences that use **phrasal verbs**. After each sentence is a detailed explanation of what that phrasal verb means and how it connects to the logic. For some phrasal verbs, I give you more than one example to show how the logic can apply to the same verb-preposition combination in different contexts and with different meanings.

Lastly, section F gives you **idioms** that use the preposition. After each sentence is a detailed explanation of what that idiom means and how it connects to the logic.

Important Terms

There are some special terms (words) that you need to know. These terms will help you to more easily understand everything in this book. You don't have to memorize any of these because we'll apply them in specific examples and contexts later. You can always come back here later to check what these terms mean.

The Logic: This is the underlying key idea of a preposition that is logical and allows you to "feel" it. Sometimes, there are two separate or slightly separate ideas behind the logic. In the explanations of the example sentences, I also provide synonyms or more specific versions of the key idea(s) when it's useful (for example, "end point" → specific version: "destination"). This will help you understand things more easily. Remember that the logic can be applied in different and specific ways, but the key idea doesn't change.

Look at the picture below. This is a picture of an important part of the logic, which is that the logic of a preposition has a core and an area around the core. Many times, the surface meanings of a preposition will fit into the core of the logic. These are very clear and it's easy to see how it works. Sometimes, however, the surface meaning will be somewhere outside the core. The farther away from the center it is, the more abstract the connection. So, sometimes it might seem difficult to connect a sentence to the logic, but I try to explain the examples in a way that's easy to understand.

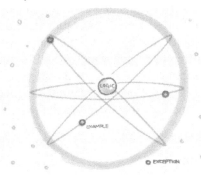

One-way Preposition: A→ B. This is the most common way that prepositions function and it's what you would expect based on the normal flow of a sentence (left to right). In other words, the word "way" in this context means "direction". A→ B. For example, "The keys (A) are <u>on</u> the table (B)". So, "one-way" just means that the meaning of the preposition applies from left to right, like normal.

Two-way Preposition: There are a few prepositions that I call "two-way" prepositions. One-way prepositions go from left to right in meaning, but the meaning of two-way prepositions can apply in two opposite directions: left to right and right to left, depending on the context. This happens with some prepositions that don't have an opposite word (examples of opposites are: to/from, up/down, etc...).

For example, the preposition "of" doesn't have an opposite and goes in two directions: "A→ B" OR "A ←B". In many cases, the preposition "of" is a "part", meaning that A is part of B. This is the normal sentence flow and goes left to right. In other cases, the preposition "of" describes some content. For example, "The table (A) is made of wood (B)". The table isn't part of the wood; the wood is the content of the table, meaning that the table consists of/is made of/is composed of wood. So in this case, the meaning of the preposition "of" is applied from right to left (A ← B). This is because the word "wood" (B) is on the right side of the sentence and the word "table" (A) is on the left side of the sentence. We read the sentence from left to right, but the meaning of the preposition is applied from right to left. If that sounds confusing, don't worry. This is all explained in a very clear way using example sentences for each two-way preposition.

Category words: The idea of "category words" is very important, and not just for prepositions, but for language in general. A category word is a word that represents the highest level category, like in a hierarchy. For example, the word "thing" is a general word that's not specific. It's also a category word. You can use the word "thing" to refer to a vehicle, an animal, etc... Starting with the word "thing", we can create other categories. For example: thing → vehicle → car. We can get more specific and say "my car", or "Toyota". Another example: thing → animal → cat. We're not only creating categories, but hierarchies, which will help you remember things more easily. We'll see how this idea applies to specific prepositions later.

Collocations and Chunks: A "chunk" of language is a group of words inside a sentence. This is a concept that some linguists use when studying language. The complete idea of "chunks" is a little complicated, but the basic idea is simple: words don't usually work alone. For example, if you say, "It depends on what time he arrives", this isn't a bunch of individual words that are put together. Your brain processes these words and concepts as small groups/chunks. You can think of this like building blocks that you can fit together to create different sentences. If we divide our example sentence into chunks, it might look like this: "It depends on what time he arrives." Notice that "depend on" is part of the same chunk. This is because the

15

verb "to depend" always uses the preposition "on". "What time" is one idea, and "he arrives" is another idea. We can change these chunks to get new sentences. For example, "I don't know what time he arrives; It depends on if he arrives (or "if he arrives"); It depends on what time he leaves." Each one of these pieces is like a single concept or idea.

Ok, we know what a chunk is, but what's a "collocation"? A collocation is simply two or more words that we often use together. In other words, they're special chunks. A chunk is just a group of words, but a collocation is a group of words that often go together. For example, "fast food", "make a mistake", and "loud and clear". Idioms are also special collocations/chunks because we don't usually change the words in an idiom. A collocation can be as simple as a verb combined with a preposition that we commonly use with that verb. This can be a phrasal verb, or it can be the preposition that the verb prefers to use most of the time. For example, "depend on". This isn't a phrasal verb, as we'll see next.

Phrasal verbs: I define a phrasal verb as "a preposition in action". This means that the whole unit (verb + preposition) is like one big word that creates a new meaning. This is because the specific action of the verb is being added to the specific logic of the preposition. A good example is the phrasal verb "move on", which we'll see later. So I define "phrasal verb" a little differently than other people. The reason is because most students try to learn phrasal verbs in a random way that makes it harder to learn. My definition helps you think about things in a clearer and more understandable way. However, the most important thing is that it doesn't matter how we define what a phrasal verb is because the logic always applies. Let's make things a little clearer. There are three ways that we use prepositions:

First, we have the easiest and most basic category: *a regular preposition that's used normally*. "The keys are on the table." There's nothing special here and it's definitely not a phrasal verb. Also in this category are the prepositions that are always or almost always used with certain verbs. For example, "depend on". In this case, "on" is just the preposition that we use with the verb "to depend". There's a logical reason that we use them together, but we'll see that later.

Second, there's what I call *"false" phrasal verbs*. There are two types of false phrasal verbs.

1) Disconnected from the verb: For example, "I like to go on rides at the amusement park" → Go where? "on rides". In this case, the preposition is attached to the word "rides", not the verb "to go". This works because of chunks. "I like to go" is one idea, "on rides" is another idea, and "at the amusement park" is another idea. Remember, we often group words together based on their relationship to each other.

2) Connected to the verb: Most resources will tell you that these are phrasal verbs, but they're not. For example, "Finish up your dinner before it gets cold." In this case, the preposition is connected to the verb, but there's no change in meaning. Most of the time, you can use the preposition, but we don't need it because the meaning doesn't change. Why do we use it if we don't need it? The specific reason depends on the preposition and the context. Don't worry about this right now. Everything will be explained later. Throughout this book, I put prepositions (and some other words) that we don't need in parentheses → "Finish (up) your dinner before it gets cold."

Lastly, we have *"true phrasal verbs"* or *"real phrasal verbs"*. This means that the meaning of the verb is changed. Usually, the meaning changes completely, but sometimes the meaning only changes a little bit. For example, "bring up". This phrasal verb has a few different meanings, but the most common is "to mention". In this case, we need the preposition "up" because the verb "to bring" by itself can't mean "to mention". Many phrasal verbs are just a different way to say a regular verb (like "to mention"). Many phrasal verbs also have more than one meaning. This is why learning the logic and feeling of each

17

preposition is so useful. In fact, I have students who have started naturally and spontaneously using phrasal verbs that they had never learned before. Sometimes they try and fail, though, which is part of the learning process.

Remember, in all three of these categories, *the logic of a preposition will always apply*. It doesn't matter if it's a phrasal verb or not. I simply give you these three categories so you can better understand this book and the English language as a whole.

Connections: Any English teacher will tell you that the purpose of prepositions is to show the relationship between two or more things. However, prepositions also have connections to other prepositions. This is an extremely important idea that will help you feel the prepositions. In this book, "connection" means that part of the logic of one preposition connects with part of the logic of another preposition. The point where they connect is a specific meaning/dictionary definition. Remember the image of the farm. Connections happen "under the surface" (the roots connect). There are three types of connections: "touch", "overlap", and "special connection". When two or more prepositions "touch" or "overlap", the result is a shared meaning "above the surface". When two or more prepositions have a "special connection", they do NOT share a meaning, but they are clearly and logically connected in a special way. This means that special connections are only "under the surface" because we're only talking about where the roots connect.

Touch: "Touch" means that two prepositions share a meaning, but they're usually not interchangeable. "Not interchangeable" means that you can't change the preposition without changing the rest of the sentence. This is because it will either change the meaning of the sentence or make the sentence grammatically incorrect. Sometimes, two or more prepositions "touch", depending on the context and meaning. The points that "touch" are two dictionary definitions. When this happens, you CANNOT use the two prepositions interchangeably. The logic of both prepositions <u>can</u> apply if you're just applying general logic,

18

but the English language only applies one of them (more on this later). Sometimes, both prepositions work, but you have to change the sentence a little if you want to use the other preposition. We'll see specific examples throughout the book.

Overlap: "Overlap" means that two or more prepositions ARE interchangeable in a certain context. This is because you can apply the logic of each preposition in a way that results in the same meaning/dictionary definition. You can simply change the preposition and leave the rest of the sentence the same. For example, "I was surprised at/by/with his skill". The meaning doesn't change, but using one preposition or another might sometimes give the sentence a slightly different feel because the logic of each preposition is different. All that happens is that the logic overlaps (AND English allows the prepositions to be interchangeable) in this particular meaning and context. It's important to note that when two prepositions overlap, the meaning is the same, but the feeling is usually a little different. This is because each preposition has its own feeling, but we can apply the logic in the same context and get the same meaning. In a way, all we're doing is looking at the sentence from a slightly different angle that doesn't change the meaning. Again, we'll see specific examples throughout the book.

Note: one of the most difficult parts of learning prepositions is knowing when prepositions overlap, just touch, or are simply not applied to a certain context at all. Unfortunately, this is one of those things that you have to "get used to", but as long as you practice a lot, this book will help make the process much easier. Just remember, you have to try to apply what you learn in speaking and writing, make mistakes, and learn from them. The more you practice, the faster you'll improve.

Special Connection: Don't forget that all connections happen "under the surface". "Touch" and "overlap" are about the meanings, which are "above the surface", but "special connections" stays "under the surface". So what is a special connection? A special connection is a logical relationship between two prepositions, often in time or space. The easiest and most basic examples are the connections like: "to" and "from", "up" and "down", "in" and "out". But it's not just opposites. We have a very special connection with the prepositions "at" (very specific), "on" (less specific), and "in" anything larger/less specific than "on") when talking about time and space. For example, "It happened at 2." "It happened on Monday." "It happened in June/in 2010/in the 1990's/in the 2nd century". We can see that each period of time gets larger and less specific. We'll see specific examples of this later in the book.

Positive state/active state and negative state/inactive state: These concepts are probably the most abstract and hard to define in the entire book. They also have many different applications "above the surface", which we'll call "surface meanings". Read the following explanation, but if it's confusing, don't worry about it too much. It will become clearer and clearer as you read the rest of the book.

Some prepositions deal with the ideas of existence and non-existence. Sometimes it's more appropriate and useful to use the terms "existence" and "non-existence" (or more specific versions, like "aware" and "unaware"), but with some prepositions it's better to use the terms "positive state" or "active state" and "negative state" or "inactive state". These ideas are very closely related to the ideas of "existence" and "non-existence".

Don't think of the word "positive" as "good" or the word "negative" as "bad". We're not making a judgment about what's "good", so it's like a "neutral positive". For example, imagine a light. When you turn the light on, the light is active. We can also say that the light is in a "positive state". The logic of the preposition "on" is a little complicated, but it's always a "positive state/active state" (and usually also a "surface" or "platform", but that doesn't apply in this case). It's very clear that a light that's turned on isn't "good", it's just active. The problem is that the idea of "active" doesn't always fit perfectly,

20

so we need the help of a more general concept or category word: "positive state".

Another example: if you're sitting in traffic and the light is red, you have to stop, which might feel "bad" or "negative", but remember, we're not judging. The red light is <u>on</u>. So, the red light is in a positive state/active state. Even though "existence" and "positive state" are closely related, the reason the word "existence" doesn't work as well as "positive state" in this case is because the physical body of the red light exists even if the light is off. So it's better to talk about a "positive state/active state" here. The idea of a "negative state" is also neutral. You can think of these positive state and negative state like computer data: a "1" (positive) vs a "0" (negative). Or you can think of the science terms used when talking about protons and electrons: "positive charge" and "negative charge". The point is that we're not saying that something is "good" or "bad", just "positive/active" or "negative/inactive". Again, all of this will be much clearer when we talk about the specific prepositions that use these ideas.

FINAL NOTE ABOUT THE LOGIC: One thing you have to always remember is that just because the logic of a particular preposition works in a certain context does <u>not</u> always mean that it will be correct. Things might "touch" or seem to "overlap", but in a certain context we simply don't say things that way in English. Things can be logical from a general view, but the English language – like any other language – has its own flavor and preferences about how the logic is applied (remember, every language has it's own "personality", just like a person). Also remember that there are cases where the logic overlaps and sometimes English uses both prepositions to mean the same thing, but sometimes it only uses one. You will learn more about this with specific examples and explanations later in the book.

IMPORTANT NOTE ABOUT TRANSLATIONS: The words in your native language are not English words. There might be close or even exact translations between two languages, but the

21

words are not the same. For example, in many cases the Spanish preposition "de" is the same as the English preposition "of". However, "de" is spelled differently and pronounced differently, and there are times when "de" is used in Spanish, but we don't translate it into English as "of". The two words may be similar between the two languages, but "de" has it's uses, logic, and meanings in the Spanish language and "of" has it's own uses, logic, and meanings in the English language. So, you have to learn how the English language views things, which is the main goal of this book. Languages are complicated, living creatures, but this book will help you see, feel, and understand things from the perspective of the English language, exactly like a native speaker does.

IMPORTANT NOTE ABOUT PARENTHESES ( ): There are many cases in English where we can omit words. These are usually grammar words and we can omit them because the context makes the meaning clear. For example, when we say "in order to" (which is about a purpose), we usually just say "to" because the meaning of "to" in this case is usually clearly implied by the context. For example: "I practice English everyday (in order) to improve". An example of a word that's not a preposition is the word "that" (used to connect two parts of a sentence). For example, "I think (that) he's right". In this book, I usually mark such cases – especially prepositions – by putting the words in parentheses ( ) → (in order) to. However, not all parentheses that I use in this book are for this purpose. Sometimes, parentheses just add extra information (like this, which is the real purpose of parentheses).

OF

A) Read the following sentences. If you don't understand a sentence, highlight it or underline it. You can use Google Translate to check the meaning of a sentence, but be careful. Prepositions can cause problems for it and the translation might not be accurate. You can use a site like italki or Lang-8 if you want to ask a native speaker. When you finish the first group, think about what the preposition "of" means in those sentences. Repeat this process after each group. Then try to find a common idea that all of the groups share. When you finish, continue to the next section. If you want to look at the logic first and then read the sentences, go to the next section first and then return here. I don't recommend that (especially if your English level is lower-intermediate), but you can do it if it works better for you.

1)

The last page of the book is blank.
Today is the first of June.
I've never been north of Los Angeles.
He got 17 out of 20 on his test.
I like the color of the sky at sunset.

What does the word "of" mean in this group?

2)

This table is made of wood.
This is a picture of a dog. (Note: not possession)
I've always thought of him as an interesting person.
I've always dreamed of living by the ocean.
I like the idea of learning many languages.

What does the word "of" mean in this group?

3)

I drank five cups of coffee.
A lot of people are at the beach.
He died of a heart attack.
I'm afraid of spiders.
She has the voice of an angel.

What does the word "of" mean in this group?

4)

There's a discount of 20 percent on all purchases.
I only got 2 hours of sleep last night.

What does the word "of" mean in this group?

B) The Logic

Note: The numbers below are for the logic, not the example sentence groups.

Key Idea(s): 1) part; 2) content

"Part" is a category word and includes specific ideas like "characteristic" and "aspect", or more specific words like "day", "page", and "points"

"Content" includes "composition", "consist of", "made of", "composed of", etc…

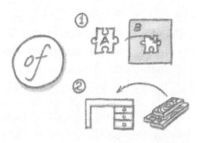

"of" is a two-way preposition

Explanation of the logic: we use the preposition "of" when we're talking about a part/characteristic of something, or when talking about what something is made of/composed of/consists of. Sometimes, you can apply both parts of the logic (meaning that the preposition "of" means both "part" and "content" in the same sentence). The preposition "of" isn't very complicated, but if your language has a similar preposition, be careful. The exact use can be a little tricky. It's also useful to know that there are times when we omit the preposition "of" because it's implied and simply works in the background. Remember, I'll usually put the preposition "of" in parentheses so that you know when this happens. For example: "a couple (of) dogs". However, I don't do it in this chapter because I don't want to cause confusion.

NOTE: The dictionary says that one of the meanings of the preposition "of" is "possession". This is true because "above the surface" the logic can apply to the idea of "possession", but I want you to forget that for now because it causes a lot of confusion. I added an extra section (section G) that gives you some information about this problem. I'll tell you when the idea of possession can be applied to an example sentence in section C, but this is only for reference so that you can understand things more easily. In sentences that use the idea of "possession", it's usually not the main idea in relation to the logic.

Another possible "surface meaning" of the preposition "of" is "origin" (which can either be "part" or "content"), but that's not the main idea in English, so I recommend that you ignore that idea. However, I will note when we can apply the idea of "origin". Again, this is only for reference because "origin" is not the main idea. The preposition in English that means "origin" is "from". For both "possession" and "origin", I separate those details in the explanations and mark them "REFERENCE". If you want to avoid the complication and confusion, you can skip that part.

Etymology notes: In Old English, the meaning was different, but it changed in Middle English. The change happened because people started using the preposition "of" as a translation for the Latin preposition "de". This is why the preposition "of" often translates to the preposition "de" (or a similar word) in Spanish and other Romance languages (languages that come from Latin). Just remember, "of" is "of". It might be very similar to a preposition in your language, but that doesn't matter. It's an English word with it's own purpose and uses. 2

Now, go back to the example sentences and try to see how the logic applies. Ask yourself: "How is 'of' a part?" or "How is 'of' showing 'content' or showing what something is made of/composed of/consists of?"

C) Detailed Explanations of the Example Sentences.

1) *Part*

The last page of the book is blank. This one is extremely simple. A book has a first page, a last page, and many other pages. Each of these pages is like one individual piece/part of the book. So "page" is a more specific version of the word "part".

ALTERNATIVES: "The book's last page is blank." REFERENCE: As you can see, this is possession, so "last page of the book" can mean possession.

Today is the first of June. June has 30 days, and the first day is one of them. So the first day is one part of June. "Day" is a more specific word for "part" in this case. 30 days of the month = 30 parts of the month

ALTERNATIVES: "Today is June first." This is the more common way to say it.

I've never been north of Los Angeles. Note that this sentence does NOT mean the north part of Los Angeles. Instead, it means any location that is in the direction "north" starting from Los Angeles (such as San Francisco, Oregon, or Canada). If you want to talk about the north part of Los Angeles, we say, "I've never been <u>to</u> the north of Los Angeles" or "I've never been to north Los Angeles". Now we're talking about the top area of the city on a map. This can be very confusing because the preposition "to" can have two slightly different meanings in this context. Don't worry about that right now. We'll look at the preposition "to" soon. In the example sentence, "north of Los Angeles" means any and all areas that are northward from Los Angeles on a map.

So, how does the example sentence mean a "part"? It's a little abstract. We're looking at all the area outside of Los Angeles (the rest of the world, or the rest of the country, at least), and based on that area, we're talking about the part of it that is specifically northward from where Los Angeles is.

REFERENCE: Lastly, you can look at this example as "origin", but it's very abstract and it might be confusing. Starting <u>from</u> Los Angeles, we're talking about any area that is out side of the city and northward. Notice the preposition "from".

He got 17 out of 20 on his test. The test has 20 questions, so there are 20 points in total. He answered 17 questions correctly. In this case, the word "point" is a specific word for "part", so each point is one part of the total score. His score is 17 parts out of the total 20 parts. Note: we'll talk about "out of" later when we see the preposition "out".

REFERENCE: This sentence can be an "origin". It's like saying, "Starting <u>from</u> 20 possible points, he answered 17 correctly". Note that we don't say it that way in English, but the idea is there. The ideas of "out of" and "from" are very similar. Again, this is why I recommend that you ignore the "origin" idea.

I like the color of the sky at sunset. This one is more abstract than the other examples, but it's the same idea. "Color" is a part or aspect of the sky. (The sky has color, size (the big sky), etc...).

REFERENCE: This sentence is a perfect example of why thinking about the preposition "of" as "possession" or "origin" can be confusing. You can look at this sentence as "possession" (the sky's color → the color belongs to the sky); or you can look at this sentence as an "origin" (the color comes from the sky).

ALTERNATIVES: "I like the sky's color at sunset." "I like the sky at sunset."

2) *Content*

This table is made of wood. If we try to say that the table is "part" of the wood, that doesn't make any sense. Here, we're talking about the material that something is made out of. The wood is the "content" or "material" of the table. It's what the table consists OF or is composed OF. Wood is the composition of the table. All of these are different ways to talk about the same idea. Please note that normally when we talk about the "contents of a table", we actually mean what's inside the drawers of the

28

table. This is because "content(s)" is usually used with the meaning "to contain". In this case, the concept of "content" applies, but it's very abstract. In normal language, it makes more sense to use the words "made of", and that's also the most common way to say this sentence.

REFERENCE: You can look at this as an "origin". The wood came from a tree, and then the table came from the wood. Notice the preposition "from". As I said, "from" is an origin, not "of", but they can touch, and sometimes they overlap.

ALTERNATIVES: This table is made from wood: We saw in some previous examples that we can apply the idea of "origin". The preposition that is about an "origin" is the preposition "from". So it makes sense that in this example sentence, the prepositions "of" and "from" connect in some way. In fact, they overlap, which means we can change the word "of" to the word "from" and the meaning in this context is the same. Notice that in the first group, "from" and "of" didn't overlap, they only touched sometimes. But group two is about the content/composition of something or what something is made of, so we can use the preposition "from" to look at the sentence in a slightly different way. This is a very good example of the difference between "touch" and "overlap". The preposition "from" isn't about a "part", but it can be about "content". However, we'll see in the other example sentences that even in this group, "of" and "from" don't always overlap. This is the most difficult part of prepositions: context. Prepositions have meaning, so just like with any other word, the context determines what prepositions you can and can't use.

This table is made out of wood: You can also add the preposition "out" before the preposition "of". This isn't always possible, but we saw in a previous example in group one that we can use "out of" when talking about an amount. This context is different, but the idea still works. Very abstract, but think of it this way: we "extract" the table from the wood. Obviously, this isn't really what happens, but in English, we can apply the concept in a way that is abstract and not literal. As I said, this will be clearer later when we talk about the preposition "out".

This table is made with wood: The logic of the preposition "with" is simple: "together". This example sentence is very simple. What did you use to make the table? Wood. So, you brought together the idea of the table and the physical wood and then you used the wood (in order) to create the table and make it real instead of just an idea. The exact meaning of the preposition "with" in this case is "using". You can reword the sentence and say, "This table is made using wood". This works because when we talk about the material that we use (in order) to make something, we use the preposition "with".

This is a picture of a dog. (Note: not possession) I put the note about possession because that's a common mistake that some students make. This is one of the reasons why I recommend that you don't think about the preposition "of" as "possession". If you wanted to talk about the idea of "possession", you can say, "This is my dog's picture", which means that the picture belongs to your dog. Ok, how does the logic apply? Is "picture" a part of "dog"? Kind of, but not really. It's clear that the dog is in the picture, which means that the dog is the content of the picture. This is the same as putting a toy inside (of) a box: we say that the toy is the content of the box.

I've always thought of him as an interesting person. This one is a little difficult and more abstract. The key is this: "him as an interesting person" is a single idea. My "thought" is not part of him, but "him as an interesting person" (which is a chunk) is the content of my thought. In other words, when I think of him, the idea "interesting person" appears in my mind. Notice in this case that we have a verb ("thought") + "of" + a noun or pronoun ("him").

NOTE: Most of the time, we use the preposition "about" with the verb "to think". "Think about" and "think of" are extremely close. The preposition "about" is "a scope". For example, if I tell you to think about trees, I want you to focus your thoughts specifically on trees and not anything else. We'll see more about this later. As we know, when we say "think of", we're talking about the content of your thoughts. The next two example sentences work the same way.

I've always dreamed of living by the ocean. The word "dream" in this context doesn't mean a dream that you have while you sleep. It means something that you really want to do. In this case, "living by the ocean" is one chunk, and it's the content of my dream. So in this case, we have a verb ("dreamed") + "of" + a second verb ("living"). In other words, when we use the preposition "of" with a verb after it, that action/verb is the content of the action/verb that's before the preposition "of".

I like the idea of learning many languages. Lastly, we have another verb after the preposition "of", but this time, there's a noun before the preposition "of". This works exactly the same way. There's an idea, and the content of the idea is "learning many language", which is a chunk. So, we have a noun ("idea") + "of" + a verb/action ("learning").

3) *Part AND Content*

Sometimes, a sentence can use both directions of the logic at the same time.

I drank five cups of coffee. Imagine you have a big pot of coffee. You take one cup of it. That's one "part" of the total amount of coffee in the pot. So here, "cup" is a specific word for "part". Specifically, the size of the part is the amount that a cup holds. This sentence is also about content (A←B). What's in the cup? Coffee. The content OF the cup is coffee. In this case, we're not saying what the cup is made of. A cup is basically just

31

an empty space and you can fill that empty space with some sort of content.

A lot of people are at the beach. "A lot" means "a large amount". Although you might be able to look at "amount" as a characteristic of "people", this sentence is clearly talking about content. We can ask, "A lot of what?" What is the <u>content</u> of the amount? Trees? Buildings? In this case, it's people. However, you can look at each person like a part of the total. Remember when we talked about the test that had 20 points total? The total amount of points was 20. Each point was part of the total. So, the "amount" is made of "people" AND each person is part of the total amount.

ALTERNATIVES: "Many people are at the beach". You're probably wondering why we say "a lot of" and not "many of". Well, we say both, but it depends on the context. We use "many X" when we're talking about the total number of that thing. We use "many of X" when we're talking about a large amount of the total. This is less than "most of X" but more than "some of X". For example, "Many of the people (that are) at the beach are tall". We're talking about a specific group of the people that are at the beach, but not all of the people that are at the beach. So, we use "of", because we're talking about a part of the whole. But when we say "many people" we're just saying that there is a large number of people as a whole. In fact, when we say "many of the people", there might only be 15 people at the beach, and we're talking about maybe 9 of them. But when we say "many people", the number is bigger (let's say 30 or 50).

He died of a heart attack. Another difficult one. In the dictionary, you'll find this example labeled as "the cause of something", which is true, but it's also really confusing. So, where's the part and where's the content in this sentence? A heart attack has a beginning, middle, and end – all parts – as well as a result (did he survive or not). It's easy to see that death ("he died") is the result, which means that this is the "part" of the

32

heart attack that we're talking about. However, in an abstract way we can also say that the heart attack is the "content" of his death. In other words, his death is made of a heart attack. How did he die? Car crash? Stabbing? No, a heart attack.

ALTERNATIVES: "He died from a heart attack." There are a few different prepositions that you can use to talk about a "result". Sometimes, it's a little complicated. For example, we can use the preposition "from" in this sentence. That might seem strange because the preposition "from" is an "origin". However, the idea of "origin" can mean a "basis", or, more specifically, a "cause", which is a specific type of "basis", and "basis" is a specific type of "origin". This is a good example of the hierarchies I mentioned in the introduction. Each step gets less abstract: origin → basis → cause. Because we're talking about a "cause", the idea of "effect" or "result" is naturally connected. From the heart attack (the cause), the effect/result is death. We'll see more about this later in the book when we talk about the preposition "from".

Note that we CANNOT say, "He died with a heart attack". The logic can apply, but this is a good point about the different ways that the logic of a preposition apply. It depends on the context, which is a big reason why prepositions are so difficult to master. In this context, if we use the preposition "with", it sounds like "heart attack" is something outside of him, like another person: "He died with his wife". This is because the logic of "with" is "together". Although "together" can mean "using" or "having", when we talk about dying, it sounds like he's together with another person or thing. It can also mean that he died in a certain position: "He died with a smile on his face". In this case, we're using the idea of "having", but it's a position that he has, not the result of his death. Basically, we can't use "with" to mean a "result" and that's the main reason why we can't use it in the sentence, "He died of a heart attack".

I'm afraid of spiders. My fear is not "part" of "spiders". Spiders are just spiders. However, spiders are the content of my fear. I might have other fears, but we're specifically talking about spiders in this case. Now, this sentence is a little weird. Notice that if I have more than one fear, we can say that the spiders are one "part" of my fear. So, in this case we also have a "part", but "part" goes the opposite direction than normal (Normally, "part" is A → B and "content" is A ← B, but in this case, "part" and "content" are both A ← B). Notice that we can say, "ONE OF the things ('parts') that I'm afraid OF is spiders". This is a strange and rare example where the logic goes in the opposite direction, but the main point is this: the logic still works perfectly fine.

She has the voice of an angel. "Voice" is part of "angel". This is because an angel has a voice, an appearance (how it looks), a height, wings, and more. All of these things are part of the angel. But how is this sentence about "content"? Well, if someone has the voice of an angel, we can say that their voice is angelic (angel-like). So, an angelic sound or quality is the "content" of her voice in an abstract way. You might see that this angelic quality can be a "part" of her voice, which is true. Just like in the previous sentence, the idea of a "part" can go both directions. Again, the important thing is that the logic still works.

REFERENCE: Obviously, this sentence does talk about "possession" because the voice belongs to an angel. However, it doesn't really belong to an actual angel. We're just saying that her voice sounds like an angel's voice.

ALTERNATIVES: "She has an angel's voice." Saying it this way is less common.
"Her voice is angelic."/"She sounds like an angel"

4) *Part AND Content + Implied Information*

This group is the most difficult because the sentences include implied information. "Implied information" is information that's not said in the sentence, but that's implied by the context. This adds an extra step. Instead of just A → B or A ← B, we also have a C. Let's look at a couple of specific examples.

There's a discount of 20 percent on all purchases. In this case, "20 percent" is the content of the discount. But "discount" clearly isn't a part of "20 percent". What's going on here? Well, that's the implied information. We're saying "20 percent", which implies a total price. So, 20 percent is the "part". Specifically, it's part of the total price. What we're really saying is: "There's a discount of 20 percent of the total price on all purchases." In this sentence, it's more like A ← B + B → C. Put another way: A ← B → C (B is the content of A (20 percent is the content of the discount), but B is also a part of C (The amount that is discounted (removed) from the total is part of the original total). If the total price is $10, then 20 percent is $2, meaning that $2 is the content of the discount because it's the specific amount that will be removed from the total (This is A ← B). However, at the same time, $2 is part of the original $10 (This is B → C). Another way to think about it: imagine you have a pie with ten pieces ("parts") and you take two pieces ("parts"), leaving 8 pieces ("parts").

ALTERNATIVES: "There's a 20 percent discount on all purchases." If we say it this way, we're using "20 percent" like an adjective to describe "discount".

I only got 2 hours of sleep last night. Can you see it? The A, B, and C are moved around a little bit, but it's the same idea. "Sleep" is the "content" of the two hours. In other words, those two hours (A) consist of sleeping (B). So, we have the normal A ← B. And how is this a "part"? Well, each hour of the night is a part of the night. More specifically, we're talking about hours that are used for sleeping. Most people sleep between 7 and 9 hours every night. So, the total number of hours is the implied information and then we remove two of those hours because those are the hours that you were sleeping. In the previous example, it was B→ C. In this case, it's A→ C because we're removing the two hours (A) from the implied total number of hours (C). Again, it's like a pizza with ten pieces. The exact connection between A, B, and C might change, but the idea is the same.

ALTERNATIVES: "I only slept (for) two hours last night." The preposition "for" in this case is a duration/length of time.

D) Some verbs that often use the preposition "of"

To be made of	To consist of	To be composed of
To dream of	To think of	To know of
To speak of	To take care of	To die of

E) **Phrasal verbs.**

There are no phrasal verbs that use the preposition "of". "Of" is simply a basic connector between two things that shows the relationship of either "part" or "content". However, there are some cases where "of" is used to connect a phrasal verb to an object.

My two-year-old son has grown out of his baby clothes. We use "of" with the preposition "out" in this sentence because "to grow out of" means that the physical size of your body is now too large to fit inside of the old clothes. Outside and inside are "parts", so your body is now on the "outside" of that size because you can't fit inside of it. This might make more sense if you remember that the logic of the preposition "in" is a "container". Because the clothes physically go around your body, they're like a container for your body.

36

My brother dropped out of school when he was fourteen. When you're attending a school as a student, we say that you are "in" school. So you can "drop out" and stop going. Again, "inside" and "outside" are parts, and the logic of "in" is a "container". In this case, the container is very abstract. The container is the process of attending school. The verb "to drop" is similar to the verb "to fall". Imagine you have a box (which is a container) and inside the box are some papers. If you turn the box upside down (put the top of the box on the floor), then the papers will fall out of the box. We have a similar idea here. If you drop out, your aren't inside of the box (attending school), you're outside of it.

Another way to think about this is that "going to school" is the content that you're dropping. It's a little hard to see here, but we have a similar sentence, "I dropped out of my math class". In this case, it's easier to see that the math class is the content that I'm dropping, like physically dropping something on the floor or letting something fall out of a box.

We own too much stuff. Let's try to get rid of some things. "To get rid of" can mean a couple different things depending on the context, but it basically means to remove something. Usually, it means "to throw something away" (put it in the trash). In this sentence, "some things" is the content that you want to get rid of. A more specific example: "Get rid of your toys". What is it that I'm throwing away? The toys.

We ran out of food and didn't have any money (in order) to buy more. We'll talk more about the phrasal verb "to run out" later. It means that there's no more of something. If you run out of food, it means that you have no food. But you can run out of many different things: shampoo, beer, toothpaste, etc... The food is the content of "run out". In other words, it's the thing (content) that you don't have anymore.

ALTERNATIVES: The exact alternative depends on the specific details, but a basic alternative is: "We ate all of the food".

F) Examples of idioms that use the preposition "of", with detailed explanations.

I'll be glad to see the back of him! This means that you really want someone to leave and you'll be glad (happy) when they do. Why "the back of him"? Because when someone leaves/walks away from you, you see their back. We use "of" because he has a front side, a back side, a left side, and a right side. We only care about his back side, which is a "part".

ALTERNATIVES: One possible alternative is: "I'll be happy when he leaves."

My job allows me to make a lot of money and still have time for my family. I get the best of both worlds! It's very common that if you get something good in one area of your life, you have to sacrifice some other part of your life. This often happens when a parent works a lot. The person makes a lot of money and can give their family what they need and want, but that person doesn't get to spend much time with them. If you make a lot of money AND you can often spend time with your family, then you don't have to sacrifice anything. Instead, you get all of the benefits, which means you have "the best of both worlds" (the

38

word "world" in this context isn't literal; world 1 = work and world 2 = family).

We use the preposition "of" because there can be good things and bad things in each "world", and you're getting the good things from both. So "the best" means the things (parts) that are good, and those things (parts) come from both worlds. Of course, you probably also get bad things from both worlds because nothing's perfect, but the point of this phrase is to say that you don't have to sacrifice and choose one world or the other world.

Tom: "How's Mary?"
Alex: "She's fine." (Mary enters the room.) "Speak of the devil."

"Speak of the devil" is a really interesting idiom. We're not talking about "the devil" or "a devil" from a religion. It's a strange thing to say because it doesn't matter how you feel about the person, so it's not a negative sentence. We use this when you're talking about someone and then they appear or arrive, as if saying their name made them appear in front of you. In the past, people believed that this is something that Satan (the devil in Christianity) might do when you say his name. We're just extending the this idea to mean that someone unexpectedly appears while you're talking about them.

How does the logic apply? Simple. "the devil" (Mary) is the content of the words that you speak. There's an interesting connection here between the prepositions "about" and "of". Both of these prepositions can be used to talk about a topic. This is one of the uses of the preposition "about", but the preposition "of" isn't often used this way. In this case, however, "the devil" (Mary) is actually the topic of the sentence, and a "topic" can be a more specific word for "content". So it's possible to have this hierarchy: content → topic.

ALTERNATIVES: "Speaking of Mary(, here she is)." This sentence means exactly the same thing, and the logic works the same way. The only difference is that this sentence isn't an idiom. You might wonder why we say "speak of" in the idiom and "speaking of" in the alternative sentence. In 99 percent of cases, we have to use the "-ing" form (present continuous) after a preposition. So in the alternative sentence, which isn't an idiom, we say "speaking". But for some reason the idiom just uses "speak". It's an idiom and occasionally idioms break grammar rules. The important point here is that the logic of the preposition "of" still works.

G) The preposition **"Of"** and **Possession**

In English, it's sometimes confusing to know when you should use the word "of" and when you should use a possessive word, such as "my", "his", or "Tom's". This can be really difficult if your native language doesn't separate these two ideas. Generally, you can think of it this way: use the preposition "of" when you're talking about a part/characteristic of something, or when you're talking about what something is made of/composed of/consists of (the content). Use a possessive word when you're talking about ownership/possession. For example:

Which is correct? John's car is blue. -OR- The car of John is blue.

In this case, "John's car is blue" is correct. He owns the car, but it is NOT part of him and he's definitely NOT made of the car. It can be confusing because the car IS part of John's possessions, but in English, "the car of John" doesn't work. Notice that we're talking about a person. The general grammar rule is that if you're talking about a person, an animal, a country, or an organization, we use the possessive form (meaning: 's, "my", "his", etc...). In other words, things that are alive or things that are an extension of humans (countries, etc...). This is because only living things can own/possess other things. Note: This is a very useful rule that will work most of the time, but in real life there are always exceptions, especially in English and especially because of the French and Latin influence on English.

Which is correct? This is a picture of my family. -OR- This is my family's picture.

In this case, BOTH are correct, but the meaning is different. The first sentence means that the my family is the content of the picture. The second sentence means that my family OWNS the picture. In that case, the content of the picture doesn't matter. It could be a picture of a city, for example, but it's a picture that my family owns. Again, we see that if we want to talk about possession and we're talking about a living thing ("family", which is a group of people), we use the possessive form to show possession. If we say "a picture of X", "picture" is not a living thing, so the main idea is not about possession.

Lastly, let's take a quick look at the use of the preposition "of" when talking about an amount (quantity). This isn't about possession, but it's useful to know so I added it here. There are some words of quantity that <u>always</u> use the preposition "of". For example:

A lot of people are learning English. / Lots of people are learning English.

There are other words of quantity that <u>sometimes</u> use the preposition of, depending on what the specific meaning of the sentence. For example:

A few people are talking. → In this case, we're just counting the number of people who are talking (three).

A few <u>of them</u> are talking. → In this case, we are saying that there are more than three people, but only three of them are talking.

"A few students are talking." VS "A few <u>of the students</u> are talking." The sentence, "A few students are talking" is exactly the same as "A few people are talking". "A few of the students are talking" is the same as "A few of them are talking".

Don't worry too much about all of these small details. With time, exposure, and practice, you'll start to feel what sounds good and what doesn't. Unfortunately, this is one point where the logic of prepositions can't help very much. Just remember that even if something means "possession" when you use the preposition "of", the idea of "possession" usually isn't the main idea. Also remember that we generally use the possessive form ('s or words like "my") with living things and we use the preposition "of" with non-living things. The main idea of the preposition "of" is always a "part", "content", or both.

ON

A) Example Sentences. Remember to follow the instructions in section A from previous prepositions.

1)

The book is on the table.
There's a picture (that's hanging) on the wall.
(Giving directions:) The library is on the right (side).
They live on Main street.

What does the word "on" mean in this group?

2)

(playing ping-pong:) I missed and the ball hit me on my chest.
You should put a coat on.
That man doesn't have anything on!

What does the word "on" mean in this group?

3)

He loves being on stage.
He's on the 3rd floor.
I'm working on a new book. (I'm writing a new book.)
He's working on the roof.
This book is on Gandhi.

What does the word "on" mean in this group?

4)

She's talking on the phone.
He's always on his computer.
You can find me on Facebook.
Is the file on your computer?
What's on TV tonight? (What program is showing?)

What does the word "on" mean in this group?

5)

It's easy to reach the beach on foot.
I saw two people (who were) on horseback.
She's on the bus.

What does the word "on" mean in this group?

6)

The garbage truck comes on Thursdays.
I have an appointment on the 5th.
I arrived at the airport on time.

What does the word "on" mean in this group?

7)

Please turn the light on.
Keep (on) going straight until you see the stop sign. (to continue)
The building is on fire!

What does the word "on" mean in this group?

B) The Logic

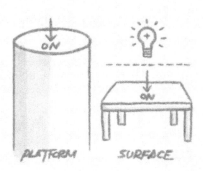

"on" is a one-way preposition

Explanation of the logic: The preposition "on" is a nice preposition that has a generally positive feel, and there's a good reason for this. The most basic idea is that something physically touches the surface of another thing, but as we'll see, the preposition "on" can be used for so much more than that. It's one of the most used prepositions in phrasal verbs, as well. "On" is always a "positive state/active state". Many times, the idea of a "positive state/active state" isn't necessary, but there are a few uses of "on" where the idea of a surface or platform doesn't apply. However, in 95 percent of cases, the word "on" is a surface or a platform. A platform is a more specific type of surface, but it's not always physical. For example, we use social media platforms like Facebook and Twitter. A platform simply has a purpose or allows you to do something special. For example, connect on the internet. In this case, it's like an abstract surface with a purpose. I use both words (surface and platform) because there are many cases where "surface" is a better word, and many cases where "platform" is a better word.

Please note that the logic of the preposition "on" doesn't have two parts. It's not like the preposition "of", which has two

45

clearly separate ideas. "On" is always a positive state/active state, even if it's also a surface or a platform because "surface" and "platform" are more specific versions of "positive state/active state". In fact, we find this hierarchy: positive state/active state → surface → platform. Normally, hierarchies happen between the logic and specific meanings that are "above the surface" (remember the farm analogy). In this case, we find a hierarchy inside the logic itself.

Etymology notes: There are no useful notes for this preposition.

Now, go back to the example sentences and try to apply the logic. Ask yourself: "How is 'on' a positive state/active state in this sentence? Is it also a surface or a platform?"

C) Detailed Explanations of the Example Sentences.

1) *Surface, usually physical*

The book is on the table. The table is a physical surface. The book is on top of the table, which means that the surface of the book is touching the surface of the table. Of course, this is also a positive state/active state, but it's very abstract. This is where "active" and "existence" are very close. The book is "active" or "existing" on the table specifically, meaning that it's not on something else. If I put the book on the floor, now the table is a "negative state/inactive state" for the book (table = false), and the floor is the "positive state/active state" (floor = true). It's one possible answer to the question "Where is the book?", which really means "Where is the book existing?" In this case, on the table. This is very abstract, so if it's confusing, just remember the first idea of a surface.

ALTERNATIVES: "The book's on top of the table." This is the same thing. In fact, "top of" is implied in the background of the original sentence, but we rarely say it. In group two, we'll see that sometimes "on top of" is necessary because just using "on" means something different.

There's a picture (that's hanging) on the wall. This one might seem a little different. Why do we say "on the wall"? Well, a wall is a surface. The only difference is that the surface is vertical (up and down) instead of horizontal (left to right, like a table). We can also say that this is a positive/active state because it's true that the pictures is on the wall. The picture is either "on" the wall (wall = true) or "off" of the wall (wall = false). Again, the idea of a "positive/active state" always applies, but it might be very abstract in certain sentences.

(Giving directions:) The library is on the right (side). This is another one that might seem strange. When we're talking about right and left sides, imagine a line that goes from the left to the

47

right in front of you, like looking at the horizon of the ocean. This line is an abstract surface (or platform) that things are then "placed" on. Now it's just like a table. You can put a book on the right side of the table, the left side of the table, or somewhere else. How is this a positive/active state? Well, if it's on the right side, it's not on the left side. But it's also on top of the imaginary surface, which means it's active/existing on that surface.

ALTERNATIVES: "The library is to the right". When we say this, we don't use the word "side". In this context, the prepositions "on" and "to" touch. The preposition "to" is an "end point", so if you go "to" the right, you are going to the place that is located "on" the right. We're still talking about the location of the library, but when we use the preposition "to", we're looking at it from the perspective of direction instead of location.

NOTE: We'll see the preposition "to" soon. However, it's very important to note that the preposition "to" does NOT mean "direction". You can use "to" with the surface meaning of "direction", but the logic of the preposition is specifically about the idea of an "end point" (like a destination), which sometimes includes the idea of "direction". This is an extremely important point because if we say that "to" is a "direction", it causes a lot of problems and confusion with a couple (of) other prepositions. We'll see more information about this later.

They live on Main Street. Obviously, this doesn't mean that they physically live on top of the street. The purpose of a street is to provide a path that you can use to go places, particularly with cars. What we're really saying when we say "on Main Street" is that if you travel on that path you will find the location of their house or apartment. So in reality, you are on the street. You use the street (in order) to reach the specific location where they live. Because the house or apartment is located next to that path, we simply say that they live on that path, even though we're not talking about being physically on top of the path itself.

48

It might help if we remember the special connection between the prepositions "at", "on", and "in". We saw a small example of that talking about time earlier in the book. But how does it work with space?   We can say, "They live at 123 Main Street". We use the preposition "at" in this case because it's a very specific location. Then we have, "They live on Main Street". In this special relationship, we use the preposition "on" when we're being less specific. If I just tell you the street, you don't know the exact house or apartment. Lastly, "They live in Los Angeles". This is even less specific and we can see that the area that we're talking about continues to become larger.

ALTERNATIVES: "They live at 123 Main Street." This sentence doesn't mean exactly the same thing, but it's close. In the example sentence, we're simply talking about the street that they live on. In this sentence, we're talking about the specific address that's on that street. There's actually a very interesting relationship between the prepositions "in", "on", and "at", but we'll see all (of) that later in the book.

2) *Surface related to body parts*

(playing ping-pong:) I missed and the ball hit me on my chest. Obviously the outside of your body is a surface. So, a ball hits me "on" my leg because the surface of the ball touches the surface of my chest. However, we can also use the preposition "in" if there's more force because the part of my body that's hit goes more inward with more force. When talking about the stomach, for example, we usually say "in" because there's usually more force (such as a punch or a kick). If you say, "The ball hit me on my stomach", it sounds like you weren't hit very hard.

You can use one or both prepositions depending on what you mean and depending on the verb. For example, if someone punches you in the face, we don't use the preposition "on" because a punch usually has more force. The verb "to hit" is very general and can be soft (less force) or hard (more force), so we

49

can use both prepositions, depending on how hard someone or something hits you. This is also a positive/active state. In this case, the ball didn't hit my foot, my face, etc... It hit my chest, so that's where the surface of the ball touched the surface of my body. Let's say we have a list of body parts. Which part of my body? My chest. We can put a check mark next to "chest".

ALTERNATIVES: "The ball hit my chest." This is a simpler way to say it. We only need the preposition when we include who the ball hit. The ball hit me. Where? On my chest. If we don't say who, then we can omit the preposition and just directly say what the ball hit. This is also true with other verbs like "to punch". "He punched me in the face" or "He punched my face".

You should put a coat on. When we talk about wearing clothes, the inside surface of the clothes touches the surface of your body. Anything that you wear – including shoes, rings, and hats – go on top of and around the surface of your body. Yes, shoes, too. You physically put your foot into a shoe, but when your foot is inside and you are now wearing it, the shoe is on your foot. It's not physically on top of your foot, but it's "on" your body. It's strange that in English, we use the preposition "on" in this context because you could say that your body is inside the clothes. However, this is how English looks at it. There are special cases where we use the preposition "in", which we'll see later.

This is also a positive/active state because the coat is either on your body or it's not.

ALTERNATIVES: "You should put on a coat." This is a phrasal verb. Sometimes phrasal verbs are separable (you can separate the verb and the preposition by putting something between them). Some phrasal verbs are inseparable (you can't separate the verb and preposition). Some phrasal verbs are both. In this case, you can say "put something on" or "put on something".

50

"You should wear a coat". This basically means the same thing, but we don't use it in all the exact same contexts. This is a little complicated, but it is an alternative.

That man doesn't have anything on! This sentence is the opposite idea of the previous one. Instead of wearing a coat, this man isn't wearing anything. Don't get confused here. "On" is a positive/active state, but this is a negative statement. However, it's only "negative" grammatically and there's no "good" or "bad". We're saying that there aren't any clothes on his body. A statement can be negative, but still use the idea of a positive/active state. Remember, "positive state" is a neutral description and it doesn't mean "good".

ALTERNATIVES: "That man is naked!" "That man isn't wearing any clothes!" "That man isn't wearing anything!" "That man has nothing on!"

3) *A platform, physical or not*

He loves being on stage. In this sentence, we can clearly see that a stage is a surface, and you can definitely think of it that way. But this sentence fits better in this group because a stage has a special purpose: so that people will watch and/or listen to you. So it's also a platform because a platform is like a surface with a special purpose. Remember, we have the hierarchy: positive/active state → surface → platform, so a platform is a specific type of surface. This means that when we talk about a platform, we're talking about a surface, but it's not always physical and sometimes it's very abstract.
This sentence is also a positive/active state because he's on the stage. Either he's on it or he's off (of) it.

ALTERNATIVES: "He loves being up on stage." You can add the preposition "up" because a platform is a raised surface. We still need the preposition "on" because "on stage" is one chunk/idea. We often use the preposition "up" when it's not necessary. This is possible because of the logic, which we'll talk about later. Don't worry, we'll see a lot of examples that use the preposition "up" when it's not necessary because it's so common.

He's on the 3rd floor. You might think that the 3rd floor is a surface, which it is. However, in this context we're not thinking about it as just a surface. We can't say, "He's on top of the third floor." So here, the 3rd floor is actually a platform. Each floor in a building is like its own platform that supports everything that's located on that floor. By stacking platforms in a vertical (up and down) way, the result is a tall building. The basic meaning of "floor" ("ground") is just a surface, but in the example sentence, the meaning changes a little and it means "a level in a building". Because "floor" in the context of "3rd floor" is a more specific word for "platform", we have this hierarchy: Positive/active state → surface → platform → floor (level of a building). Note that in the basic meaning of "floor" ("ground", which is a specific word for "surface"), we have this hierarchy: Positive/active state → surface → ground.

This is also a positive/active state because he's currently located on the third floor (platform). He's not on the second floor, the first floor, or any other floor. Imagine you have a piece of paper that lists all the floors with a little square next to each floor. Where is he? On the third floor. So you put a check mark in the square that's next to "third floor".

ALTERNATIVES: "He's up on the third floor." We saw in the previous example that we can add the preposition "up". We can do the same thing here and for the same reason.

"He's on the 3rd level of the building." Because the word "floor" in this context means "level" instead of "ground", we can also say "the 3rd level". However, the word "floor" is more common.

I'm working on a new book. This example is very abstract. If you're working on something, that thing is the focus or topic of your work. This is like an abstract platform that your attention or

52

consciousness is focused on. You apply your effort to that thing, and it's like your effort is put onto that platform (or surface). Imagine that you put your hands on a table and you push down on the table with all your strength. When we're talking about a topic, we have this hierarchy: Positive/active state → surface → platform → topic.

This is also a positive/active state because either you're working on the book or you're not. Are you applying effort to it? Yes. Writing a book is a process, and that process is active until you finish writing the book or you decide not to finish it. Also, if something is a topic, then you're thinking about that topic, talking about that topic, or focusing on that topic and not some other topic. So every other possible topic or focus is a negative/inactive state because you're attention isn't on it. It's like you turn a light on and it shines (positive/active state). When you turn it off, it doesn't shine (negative/inactive state).

NOTE: In that explanation, you probably noticed that I said "talk about" and "think about", but the I said "focus on". All (of) these ideas are very closely related. When we talk about a topic, the prepositions "about" and "on" overlap OR touch, depending on the context. However, we don't usually say "think on" and "talk on". Those exist (and the meanings are different), but the verbs "to think" and "to talk" usually use the preposition "about". They're collocations, like I described in the introduction. We'll learn more about the difference between the prepositions "about" and "on" as we go.

ALTERNATIVES: "I'm writing a new book./I'm creating a new book." The verb "to write" is more common, but you can also use the verb "to create". Notice that if we say "writing on a new book", it sounds like you are physically writing on a book that you recently bought (for example, if you write notes on the pages).

"I'm in the process of writing a new book." We can also use the preposition "in". As we'll see soon, a process is often a special

53

kind of container. This is one place where the prepositions "on" and "in" touch.

He's working on the roof. This sentence can have two meanings. The first meaning is that he's working and he's physically on top of the roof. This meaning is actually part of group one ("surface") and it isn't a platform because of the context. It's like the sentence, "He's on the roof", but he's also working at the same time. The thing that he's doing isn't about the roof, it's about something else. For example, he might be installing a satellite dish.

The second meaning is that he's working and the focus of his work is the roof. Maybe he's repairing the roof or he's building a completely new roof. This meaning is part of this group. It's like the sentence, "I'm working on a new book" because the roof is the focus. If someone is working on the roof (with the group three meaning), that person is probably also physically on top of the roof, so we can apply both meanings at the same time. The only way to know the difference between these two is from the context. This is a good example of how two different meanings can come from the same sentence. This is possible because of the logic of the prepositions.

ALTERNATIVES: "He's working up on the roof." Interesting. In this context, when we add the preposition "up", there's only one meaning. This sentence only means that he's working, and his physical location is on top of the roof. Why? Because when we add "up", we're emphasizing the fact that he's on a raised surface. In this specific context, it's not a platform, it's just in a higher position. So this version of the sentence is part of group one. In reality, the focus of his work can be the roof, but we don't know that from this sentence because this sentence is just about his physical location.

This book is on Gandhi. In this sentence, Gandhi is the topic of the book. We saw in the previous examples that a topic is like a special type of platform, and this topic is the current (active) topic that you're talking about, thinking about, focusing on,

54

etc..., so it's a positive/active state. You can think of it like the Gandhi "light" is on/active, but other topics are not the focus, so they are "off" (also, off (of) the platform) because other topics are not the focus of the book.

An interesting note here is that the idea of a positive/active state is used in many cases that involve the concept of "consciousness". In other words, something that you're focusing on or something that you're aware of. This is true in this example (the book focuses on Gandhi specifically and not someone or something else), but it's also true in the previous two examples (the book or roof that you're working on is your focus). It's like the "light" of your mind is shining on those things, which makes them active. We'll see later that the idea of consciousness/awareness (and the opposite) applies to a few prepositions because those prepositions are in some way attached to the idea of a positive/active state or existence (and the opposite).

ALTERNATIVES: "This book is about Gandhi." This is one context where the prepositions "on" and "about" overlap, so they're completely interchangeable. Remember that when there's a topic, these two prepositions touch OR overlap, depending on the specific context. It might help to know that the preposition "about" is the default option, but "on" also works. If you're not sure which one you should use, "about" is a better guess most of the time, but it also depends on the specific verb that's used. For example, "focus on" is a collocation, and we don't say "focus about".

4) _Platform related to communications systems_

She's talking on the phone. A phone is connected to various communications systems that provide cellphone signals, internet, TV, etc... This also includes the power grid (electricity). This system of communications – wires, electricity, etc... - is an abstract platform that gives you the ability to communicate over a long distance. Notice that one way to say that you're on the internet is to say, "I'm online". The preposition "on" + the word "line" (which is the physical cable that connects you to the internet) = on the internet. When we talk specifically about a phone, it means the person is using the phone, and we use the preposition "on" because she's using the communication systems platform (in order) to talk to someone who's far away.

This sentence is also a positive/active state because you're either actively on the phone or you're not. You can also look at it this way: the phone call is active.

ALTERNATIVES: "She's on the phone." In this case, "talking" is implied. There are two reasons: 1) that's what it meant before smart phones and the internet; 2) if someone is using the internet on their phone, we don't use this phrase. Instead, we say something like, "She's on the internet" or "She's using the internet on her phone".

He's always on his computer. A computer allows you to manage files, use applications, access the internet, and more, so it's like an abstract platform. You use this platform to do these things, so you are on that platform. Remember, a platform is like a surface with a purpose. The purpose of the computer is to be able to do these things. Notice that the main screen of your computer is called the "desktop", exactly like the surface of a physical desk. The only difference is that desktop of a computer is virtual and not physical. From the desktop, you can run programs. The program runs in a box that's called a "window". This window covers the desktop, meaning it is on top of the desktop. So, yes, it makes sense that your computer is a special platform. We're not talking about the physical computer itself. We're talking about the interface that allows you to do things.

ALTERNATIVES: "He's always using his computer." The basic meaning is the same, but we actually use this in a slightly different way. When we say, "He's always on his computer", this means that he's always using his computer. But if we actually say, "He's always using his computer", it sounds like I want to use it for some reason but I can't because he's always using it. "He's always on his computer" can mean this, too, but we usually say "using" when we specifically mean the second context. So this is an alternative, but it depends a little bit on the specific context.

You can find me on Facebook. Websites like Facebook and Twitter are social media platforms. (The phrase "social media platform (or site)" is what we call these websites. It's a normal part of English and not just me trying to say that they're platforms.) Why platforms? Because they allow you to do all (of) the things that you do on social media. They're platforms where you can make your voice/opinions heard, socialize, and share experiences. If you're on that platform, then you can interact with everyone else who's on that platform. If you're not, then you don't have access to those people in that way.

There's another reason why this is a platform. The basic concept of a social media website is that it's a social network. Notice that when we talk about networks, we can use the preposition "on", depending on the context. Why? Because we can also look at a network as a special platform. The purpose of this platform is to connect people and allow them to communicate. A network is also part of a "communication system" (either global or local, online or offline; it depends on the type of network that you're talking about).

NOTE: We don't say, "You can find me at Facebook". If you say that, it means the physical building where the company is located. We also don't say, "You can find me in Facebook" because it's not a container, it's a platform.

Is the file on your computer? In this case, we're not talking about someone using the computer. We're talking about data that's stored on the computer. Why don't we use the preposition "in"? Well, if something is "in" your computer, it means that there's something in the physical hardware. For example, an insect or dust can go inside your computer. We store data "on" the computer, because the storage device (the hard drive) is a special platform that allows us to access the data and interact with it. No computer = no platform to do these things on.

NOTE: This also works for data on phones, USB drives, and anything else that can store data.

NOTE: We can use the preposition "in" when talking about data, but it's not the same. For example, if there's a database, you search in(side) the database because a database is a container that has a lot of data, like a box that you can search inside of. Another example: we save files ON a computer, but you can open the file. When you open the file, now you are in(side) that file because a file is a container that we put the data inside of.

What's on TV tonight? Like the phone and the internet, a TV is part of our communications systems. Instead of accessing websites or talking to someone from a long distance, the TV allows you to watch programs from a long distance. Also like the other examples, if something is "in" your TV, it means something is physically inside it, so when we talk about the shows or movies that play on the TV, we use the preposition "on". This also is a positive/active state because if a certain show or movie is "on", it means that something else isn't "on". Of course, there are many different TV channels, but each channel can only show one thing at a time.

5) *Surface or platform related to transportation*

Note: the exceptions to this are cars and trucks. For those, we use the preposition "in" because they're more like boxes (containers) that are made for personal use.

It's easy to reach the beach on foot. "On" is very commonly used for modes of transportation. In this case, we're traveling "on foot". Why? Because the surface of your feet (or shoes) are touching the surface of the ground. Also, your body is on top of your feet, so you can look at it that way, too. Either way, you can't walk in the air, so if you're walking, you're on a (solid) surface.

ALTERNATIVES: "It's easy to get to the beach by foot." When talking about transportation, the prepositions "on" and "by" are mostly interchangeable. They overlap or touch, depending on the type of verb you're using. If you use a verb of motion (for example, "to go"), they overlap and you can use both of them. If you say, "I'm on foot", meaning "not using a vehicle" (this does NOT mean "standing"), you can't use the preposition "by". This is because the verb "to be" is not a verb of motion. When we're talking about transportation, the verb "by" needs a verb of motion. This is because of the logic of the preposition "by": a "path or way". You can often ask the question "How?" or "In what way?" The preposition "by" works because we can ask, "How are we getting to the beach?" or "In what way are we getting to the beach?"

I saw two people (who were) on horseback. This one is clearly a surface because you're physically on top of the horse's back.

ALTERNATIVES: "I saw two people (who were) riding horse-back." "I saw two people (who were) riding horses." "I saw two people (who were) riding on horses."

A note about "by horseback". Like the previous sentence, we're not using a verb of motion, so we can't use the preposition "by". If you say, "I saw two people (who were) traveling on horseback", then you can also use "by" because "to travel" is a verb of motion: "I saw two people (who were) traveling by horseback". Again, the preposition "by" works in this case because we can ask, "How are they traveling?" or "In what way are they traveling?"

She's on the bus. Why do we use the preposition "on" in this sentence? Why don't we use the preposition "in"? Well, you are physically inside the bus, but that's not how we think about buses. A bus is large and can transport many people, so it's more of a transportation platform than a surface. It has walls and a roof, but it has the special purpose of transporting many people. If you say, "She's in the bus", it sounds like she's inside the walls or maybe inside the engine, just like with computers and TVs. If you want to talk about being physically on top of the bus (meaning that she's on the roof), you have to specifically say that: "She's on top of the bus" or "She's on the roof of the bus". This is the same for planes, trains, and boats. Boats are a little different and it depends on what exactly you're talking about, but the basic and most common preposition that we use is the preposition "on".

A note about "by bus". All the same details about "by horseback" apply to "by bus". For example, "She's traveling on the bus" and "She's traveling by bus". There is one difference. When talk about buses, planes, trains, and boats, we have to use the word "the" if we use the preposition "on": "on the bus". However, when we use the preposition "by", we don't use the word "the": "by bus". This is because if we say "by the bus", it sounds like "next to the bus", which is a different surface meaning of the preposition "by".

6) *Time*

Time is interesting with prepositions. How can the logic of "positive/active state" or "surface/platform" apply to time? They're a little more abstract, but they work perfectly well.

The garbage truck comes on Thursdays. If we're talking about something that happens on Thursday, imagine that Thursday is elevated above the other days. This makes a platform. The garbage truck doesn't come on Mondays, not on Tuesdays, not on Wednesdays. It comes on Thursdays. Another way to think about this is as a surface. We physically write things ON a calendar, just like we write ON paper.

As for "positive/active state", we can ask, "In this sentence, which day of the week is active? Which day 'exists' or is actively expressed in this sentence?" In this case, Thursday is the active day. If today is Monday, Thursday is not active; it's not currently existing. So, the garbage truck doesn't come. The garbage truck only comes when Thursday is the active/currently existing day.

ALTERNATIVES: "The garbage truck comes Thursdays." It's possible to omit the preposition "on", but this is a more informal/casual way to say it that's not grammatically correct. The preposition "on" is implied.

I have an appointment on the 5th. This example works exactly like the previous one because we're still talking about a specific day. The only thing that changes is that we can use the name of the day of the week or the number of the day of the month. In fact we can combine these two: "I have an appointment on Monday, the 5th". We usually do this to make it clear which Monday we're talking about.

I arrived at the airport on time. What does the phrase "on time" mean? This is very confusing for many English learners because we also have the phrase "in time". "In time" can mean a couple of different things, which we'll see later. "On time", however, means that you're not late. You might be a little early, but not late. If you have a meeting at 5:00 PM (17:00) and you say, "I'll be there on time", you mean that you will arrive at or a little before 5.

Ok, so, how does the logic apply here? Well, normally we talk about a specific time using the preposition "at", but "at" is just a description of the time. It doesn't tell us anything about being late or not. So, when we use the phrase "on time", the specific time becomes an abstract platform. Then, just like a physical platform, you can arrive on it. Either you're on that platform (not late), or you're off that platform (late).

This is a positive state/active state because if "on time" = 5:00, and I arrive at 4:45, it's not 5:00 and I'm early. If I arrive at 5:05, it's after 5:00 and I'm late. Only 5:00 (or a few minutes before) is the active time. If you're not there at 5:00, then you're location is somewhere else at that time.

If you want to say exactly 5:00 and not one minute or second before or after, you can say: "I arrived at the airport at exactly 5:00", "I arrived at the airport exactly on time" or "I arrived at the airport at 5:00 on the dot". Notice that we say "on the dot". The "dot" is the specific point ("at") 5:00 and it works for all the same reasons that the phrase "on time" works. We'll see later that the preposition "at" is a specific point, but it's a little flexible and can include a little bit of the space or time around it (both before and after). So, if we want to be very specific and talk about the exact time – not more and not less – we have to add some words or change some words.

7) *Positive state/active state only (no surface/platform)*

In this last group, we find a few examples that are purely or almost purely "positive/active states". The idea of a surface or a platform doesn't really apply, although it is possible to get very creative and apply them in very abstract ways.

Please turn the light on. We've already talked about "light" as an example before. I include it here because it's a good example and it's the most basic idea of a "positive/active state".

Keep (on) going straight until you see the stop sign. This is a really great example sentence. You're going in a particular

62

direction. Let's say that you're walking along Main Street. You stop and ask for directions to a store. The person tells you, "Keep on going straight until you see the stop sign". So, you continue walking along Main Street. You see a stop sign, then you notice the store. The store can be across the street, next to you, etc… It doesn't matter exactly where it is because You've found the store). "Keep on" means "to continue". Why? Because if you "keep doing something", you don't stop doing that action. If you're walking along Main Street, don't stop, just continue walking along Main Street. So the action ("going"/"walking") is already a positive/active state and you want it to continue as a positive/active state. It's like keeping the light on.

As you can see, the preposition "on" is optional in this sentence. That's because it's not necessary. When we use the verb "to keep" with another verb (in the "-ing" form), the meaning of "to continue" is already there. But because of the logic of the preposition "on", we can add it. For some reason, in English, we like to add prepositions whenever we can. That's why phrasal verbs are so common. However, I do not define "keep on" as a phrasal verb because there's no change in meaning. Remember that I call this a "false" phrasal verb. Either way, it doesn't matter because the logic still works.

In this particular sentence, part of the idea is "move forward". The idea of "forward" is more part of the preposition "up", but there are times when "up" and "on" touch. This makes sense because of the logic of the preposition "up": part of that logic is a connection between the prepositions "on" and "off". We'll see this more clearly when we talk about the preposition "up" later.

ALTERNATIVES: "Continue going straight until you see the stop sign." There are many different possible alternatives. This is just one of them. Note that we don't say, "Continue on going straight...", but it is possible to say "Continue on until...". In that case, the preposition "on" replaces the words "going straight".

The building is on fire! Wait, what? How does this one make any sense? This must be an exception, right? It's not, but it is very abstract. Clearly, we're not saying that the building is physically on top of a fire. And fire usually isn't physically on top of a building. If there's a fire inside (of) the building, we still say that the building is "on fire", just like if my shirt or car is "on fire". The word order is "on", then "fire", but it's better to think about it the other way, like a light: "the light is on" → "the fire is on". Now, we don't say "the fire is on", but the fire exists. It has come into existence and is now burning the building. When fire burns something, it's not "on top" of that thing. Instead, it uses that thing as fuel, getting inside of it and turning it into more fire. So literally, if something is "on fire", parts of that thing are now fire. Let's say some wood is on fire. As the fire burns, the wood slowly goes out of existence (a negative/inactive state) and more fire slowly comes into existence (a positive/active state).

There's another way to look at this that might make a lot more sense. In English, we have a prefix "a-". A prefix is part of a word that is attached to the beginning. For example, the word "preposition" has the prefix "pre-" and the word "position". The prefix "pre-" means "before". So a preposition is a grammar word that is (usually) placed/positioned before the word that it influences. For example, "The keys are on the table". Where are the keys? <u>On the table</u>.

Ok, back to the prefix "a-". Remember that the word "etymology" means "the history and roots of words". According to the *Etymology Dictionary Online*, the prefix "a-" has many different meanings because it was a prefix in Old English, Greek, and Latin, and all of these languages have influenced Modern English. However, one of the meanings in Old English is "on". 3 That's right, the preposition "on". There's a word in Modern English that is less common and sounds more poetic these days: "aflame". Literally, "on flame", but the meaning is "on fire". So, in Modern English it's very common to say "on fire", but this was originally the word "flame" with the prefix "a-". That's why it seems so strange to say, "The building is <u>on fire</u>". We can say, "The building is aflame", but as I said, this makes it sound more

64

poetic. Whether you use "on fire" or "aflame", the logic of the preposition "on" is still there. The word order in this case is simply because of the history of the English language.

To make this really clear, similar words include "asleep", "aboard", and "awake". Notice that we do say "on board" (meaning on a plane or a train), but we don't say "on wake" or "on sleep". However, the logic of the preposition "on" still applies. If you're awake, your consciousness/awareness is "active". If you're asleep, your consciousness/awareness is "inactive", but the state of sleeping is "active".

ALTERNATIVES: "There's a fire in the building." The basic meaning here is the same, but we're specifically saying where the fire is (inside the building, not inside and/or outside (like the roof)). When we use "on", we're simply saying that a fire exists in relation to the building. In other words, the building is burning. Notice that if we're talking about a person, we won't use this alternative. We'll only say "He's on fire".

D) Some verbs that often use the preposition "on"

Focus on	Decide on	Depend on
Rely on	Spend (money/time) on	Agree on

E) **Phrasal Verbs.**

The preposition "on" is used in a lot of phrasal verbs. Remember, a phrasal verb is a preposition that's put into action by a verb. Like we saw with the preposition "of", there are times when the preposition "on" is just a connector between the phrasal verb and the object. Most resources call this a "two preposition phrasal verb" or a "two part phrasal verb" because it's: verb + preposition + preposition. For example, "cut back on". However, usually the preposition "on" is part of the phrasal verb (verb + on).

Let's move on to another topic. This is one of my favorite phrasal verbs. If you're talking about a topic and you want to change the topic to something else, you can "move on" to another topic. Remember that a topic is like a special platform. If you "move on" to another topic, you leave the first platform and go to the new platform, like you're physically moving from one place to another place. Now this new platform is the positive/active state and the old topic is a negative/inactive state. "Move on" has a few other meanings, but in this context, the meaning of the verb "to move" is putting the logic of the preposition "on" into action. This gives the feeling of moving forward to the next topic/discussion point. So, in a very literal way, you are "moving" the logic of the preposition "on" from one platform to the next platform.

I'm counting on you! To count on someone means to rely on someone/something or to depend on someone/something, except those two aren't phrasal verbs and we don't use all three of these in the same contexts. They both use the preposition "on" naturally, but the verb "to count" changes it's basic meaning when we add the preposition "on". The meaning of the verb "to count" isn't about numbers in this case. Instead, it means that I need something to happen or I need someone to do something for me. If it doesn't happen, then something bad will happen.

    With all three of these verbs, you're putting some kind of weight on someone/something. For example, "I'm counting on my check arriving before Monday so that I can pay the bills on time". The person or thing that you're counting on becomes an abstract surface or maybe an abstract platform that supports you. This is very clear with "depend on". For example, "He depends on his family". Clearly, his family is his support that helps him do what he needs to do and what he wants to do. So he places his "weight" on them. The example sentence "I'm counting on you" means that I'm putting my "weight" on you because I'm trusting that you will do something for me. If you don't, then it's like I "fall off the platform" (something bad happens) because you didn't support me by doing what I needed you to do.

Notice we have idioms and phrases that make this point even stronger: "Stand on your own two feet!" (meaning don't rely on anyone for help/support; we can express the same idea with the phrase "Don't lean on anyone!") Another example: "He carries the weight of the world on his shoulders" (He has many responsibilities and things to worry about, especially with his family, work, etc...). In this case, his shoulders have to hold/support the weight of "the world", which is very heavy! "The world" in this context is his responsibilities and worries. They're like a heavy weight that he has to carry around with him wherever he goes. In other words, if he ignores his responsibilities, things will start to fail because he isn't "holding them up". He's the "support" that holds these things up and keeps them working. Otherwise, everything will fall apart.

The example sentence "I'm counting on you" is also a positive/active state because I'm counting on you specifically, not someone else. You are the "light" that is turned on (activated).

ALTERNATIVES: For this particular context, we can also use "depend" and "rely": "I'm relying on you." "I'm depending on you." However, the phrasal verb "to count on" is probably the most common, and as I mentioned, it depends on the context (for example, we don't say, "It counts on the context"). The basic idea is the same with all three options, but the context matters. Also note that when we say, "I'm relying on you" or "I'm depending on you", it's more natural to add something after that. For example, "I'm depending on you helping me". You can also do this "to count on", but as long as the details are clear because of the context, we often just say, "I'm counting on you".

I have to cut back on (the) junk food. We saw before that the prepositions "on" and "about" either overlap or touch when we talk about a topic. Here, the topic is "junk food", which is food that is unhealthy and doesn't have a lot of nutrients. For example, potato chips and candy. In this sentence, the person is eating more junk food than they think is acceptable, so they want to (or have to) eat less of it.

But why do we say "cut back"? Imagine you have square-shaped a cake and you're going to cut the cake into piece from one end to the other end. When you cut it and take a big piece, meaning that the place you cut is farther forward (away from you) on the cake. Or you can cut it and take a small piece. If you take a small piece, the place where you cut is farther back (closer to you) than where you cut for a big piece. So, you're getting less cake.

Because I don't have to cut back on anything other than junk food in the example sentence, junk food is a positive/active state. Plus, junk food is the topic, so it's the thing that's "active" or that you're focusing on/talking about.

ALTERNATIVES: "I have to eat less junk food." "I have to stop eating so much junk food."

I saw him getting on the bus. As we know, a bus is a platform. The verb "to get" has a lot of different meanings. In this context, "to get on the bus" means "to board the bus". In other words, you're entering the vehicle. If we apply the logic of the preposition "on", we can see that he's getting onto the platform. This also means that he's moving from a negative/inactive state in relation to the bus ("off the bus") to a positive/active state ("on the bus"). It's like "I got an 'A' in math class" (a perfect or near-perfect grade). You acquired (got) the "A"; similarly, when he boards the bus, he acquires (gets) the status of being on the bus. So we have a positive/active state and a platform.

ALTERNATIVES: "I saw him boarding the bus." Note that the verb "to board" sounds very formal, so this alternative isn't used often.

Hang on while I grab my coat. This one's interesting and might seem strange. In this case, "hang on" means to wait for a moment. Let's say you're leaving the house, so you're in the process of an action (leaving). But your friend wants to grab his coat so he can wear it because it's cold outside. So, he asks you to wait for a moment (hang on). The action (leaving) is now in a negative state because you temporarily stopped leaving, and the new action (waiting) is in a positive/active state. So the action "to hang" is "on", exactly like the "light" is "on". More specifically, you can think of this as the "red light" is "on", making you stop and wait for other cars to pass. When your friend grabs his coat and joins you, you both leave. This means the action "to hang" is now "off" (a negative/inactive state) because you are stopped waiting, and the action "to leave" is "on" again (a positive/active state) because you started leaving again.

If it helps, you can think of this phrasal verb in its literal meaning: to hang onto something. Imagine your friend is hanging over a cliff. She's holding the edge of the cliff and trying not to fall. You run to where she is and try to pull her up. In this process, you might say, "Hang on!" This means "Don't let go!" This context is very different, but you can see that in the first example ("Hang on while I grab my coat"), the basic idea is similar. You want your friend to "hang" for a few seconds, which means to wait. Continuing the action (leaving) is like letting go of the edge of the cliff because in that example, your friend was falling, but she stopped falling when she grabbed the cliff. If this helps, great. If it's confusing, you can forget it. I just put it here because it might help you understand better.

ALTERNATIVES: "Wait while I grab my coat."/"Wait (for) a second while I grab my coat." We're not talking about a literal second of time. We use the word "second" like this (in order) to express that the action will be very quick.

"Hold on while I grab my coat."

"Hold up while I grab my coat." The phrasal verb "hold up" can mean the same thing. We'll see why when we talk about the preposition "up", but this is another example where "up" and "on" connect. In this case, they overlap. The only difference here is that "hold up" sounds even more informal than "hold on".

Hold on a second. "Hold on" has a few meanings, but when we use it with the meaning of "to wait", it's exactly the same as the previous example sentence. They are completely interchangeable in this context. So everything that was explained in the previous example is also true here. The reason that they're interchangeable is because the verb "to hold" and the verb "to hang" are similar. The meanings of these two verbs aren't the same, but they share the same basic idea.

I hate people who look down on others. If you think you're superior to someone, it means you think that that person is inferior and that you're better than them. This means that in your mind, you see yourself in a higher position. It's easy to imagine this higher position as a platform, like a stage. Interestingly, we have a phrase, "to put someone on a pedestal". A pedestal is like a small, special platform for displaying things. When we put someone on a pedestal, we're not literally putting them on a pedestal. It means that that person is so amazing, perfect, etc... that you raise them in your mind to a non-human level that's closer to the gods. It's like that person is so good and amazing that they can't do anything wrong. If you look down on other people, then it means that you kind of put *yourself* on a pedestal because you think that you're better than them. So, from your pedestal (a platform), you are in a higher position than other people (in your mind, not literally), so it's completely logical to say that you look "down" on them.

Now, this sentence feels pretty negative because we're using words like "hate" and "down". But remember, the logic of the preposition is inside the preposition itself and the general feel of the sentence doesn't matter. The preposition "on" is connecting the action "look down" with the object "others". So can "on" be a positive/active state in this case? Yes. It's similar to "count on" or "depend on" because you are putting your gaze (look) on that person and it has some "weight" (in this case, you're judging them). Notice that we have the phrase, "the weight of his gaze (on me)", which doesn't have to be about judgment, but there's always some kind of intention or emotion that feels heavy.

ALTERNATIVES: "I hate people who think (that) they're better than others." "I hate people who think (that) they're all high-and-mighty."

I'm going to try these jeans on, but I don't think (that) they'll fit. This is similar to the phrasal verb "put on" when talking about clothing. "Try on" is almost the same thing. The difference is that you put the clothes on (in order) to see if they fit and if you like the way that they look, so you are "trying" them. So, it's "put on" + the idea of "try". Everything about wearing clothes that we talked about earlier apply here.

Come on! We're going to be late for the movie! The logic of the phrasal verb "come on" is similar to the logic of "move on", but the surface meaning is very different. We use the verb "to come" when the speaker wants the listener to come closer to his/her location. If the speaker is already going somewhere, or wants to start going somewhere, but the listener isn't ready or is moving too slowly, then "come on" means that the speaker wants the listener to hurry (go faster). So the speaker is already on an abstract platform that we can call "ready" or a platform that we can call "moving faster than the listener", depending on the context. The listener is not on this platform yet, and the speaker wants him/her to move faster and join the speaker on the platform so they can get to their destination faster. It's almost like telling someone to get in your car so you can both get to the destination faster.

Of course, the positive/active state is if you're "on" or "off" (of) the platform. If you're ready (on the platform), that's a positive/active state and you can leave. If you're not ready (off the platform), that's a negative/inactive state and you can't leave yet (or you don't want to leave yet).

Another way to look at this is: if we're talking about moving too slowly (or not at all) instead of talking about getting ready, then the positive/active state and negative/inactive state is about the process of doing something (in this case, going to the movie theater). If the person is too slow, they're not going the same speed as you, which means that the speeds don't match, so you're on different "platforms". Let's say one platform is 5 MPH and the other is 8 MPH. They don't match, so there's a negative/inactive state between them. You want the other person to go the same speed as you (be on the same "speed platform"), so you say, "Come on!" so that they'll join you on the faster "speed platform".

An interesting side note: "come on" has other meanings that are different, but the logic still works. Knowing the logic can make it much easier to learn and remember ALL (of) the different meanings that a phrasal verb has. One of the other meanings of "come on", for example, is something like, "Oh my God!", when you're upset, frustrated, or you don't understand how someone can believe something that's really stupid. For example, your friend says, "I was abducted (taken) by aliens". To you, this is obviously nonsense because you don't believe that aliens exist and you don't understand how your friend could believe that, so you say, "Come on. Really?" How does the logic work in this case? Well, your friend has one belief or point of view and you have a different belief or point of view. You're standing on one platform (the point of view/belief) which is based on what you think is logically true about the world. In this case, you don't believe that aliens exist. When you use "come on", the meaning is that you don't believe your friend and you don't understand how he could believe that. However, what's really happening is that you're saying, "Join me. Come onto my platform and see the truth." It's interesting how the logic of one preposition can create such different meanings with the same verb, isn't it? This is why it can be so hard to learn phrasal verbs, but hopefully you can see how the logic is very useful and makes the process easier.

ALTERNATIVES: "Hurry up!" "Move faster!/Go faster!" "Let's go!"

F) Examples of idioms that use the preposition "on", with detailed explanations.

"I understand! It works this way." "Exactly! You hit the nail on the head!" If you hit the nail on the head, it means that you say something that is exactly correct. Imagine you have a picture that you want to hang on the wall. You need to use a hammer to hit the nail into the wall. The top of the nail (the flat part) is called the "head". If you hit the nail directly on the head, it's a good hit and the nail goes further into the wall. If you don't hit it directly on the head, the nail might bend. So, we use this idiom to describe saying something that's exactly correct. In this case, there is no real nail, but the idea is the same, and the same logic applies to both meanings of the sentence (the idiom and physically hitting a nail with a hammer). Notice that the head of the nail is a flat <u>surface</u>, and you hit it with a hammer, so the surface of the hammer hits the flat surface of the nail. If you hit the nail perfectly, it also has the added idea of a positive/active state: either you hit the nail directly and firmly on the head or you miss.

"What do you think about the president's new policy?" "I don't know. I'm on the fence about it." "To be on the fence" literally means that you are on top of a fence. As an idiom, it means that you're not sure which side of an issue that you agree with or support. You could be on one side and support the idea, or the other side and oppose the idea, or you could be "on the

73

fence", which is in the middle and between the two. If you don't care about either side, you're neutral, which is not the same as being on the fence.

How does the logic apply? We have a positive/active state because you're on BOTH platforms at the same time. Imagine you have two stages or some other kind of platform. You have one foot on one stage and the other foot on the other stage because you're between the two sides. It's like you have a light: one side of the light is green (support), but the other side is red (oppose). If you're neutral, you're not on any platform.

On the one hand, I think the new policy will increase security. On the other hand, it'll also decrease privacy. This is an idiom we use to make a comparison. Normally, we say something is "in" your hand if you're holding it. We can say "on" your hand if the surface of something is physically touching the surface of your hand (ink, dirt, an insect, etc...). This idiom is a little weird because you probably expect it to be "in the one hand". However, the preposition "in", as we'll see later, is a container, not a surface/platform. When you're comparing two things, you can think of those things as either 1) topics (similar to "This book is on Gandhi"), or 2) general things that you're focusing ON, as if you put them side by side on a table to analyze them and see the differences. So, in this case, it's like your hands are platforms that display the two things that you're comparing. This is even part of our body language. Most of the time, when we use this idiom, we raise one hand a little with the palm facing up (so that it looks like a platform that you put the idea on top of) and say "on the one hand"; when we say "on the other hand", we do the same thing with the other hand.

Are we still on for Sunday? This is a very common and extremely natural expression. You can use this with any day of the week, as well as the words "tomorrow", "next week", "this weekend", "the 5th", etc... We use this phrase when we have already made plans with someone (for example, to go to the beach with them on Sunday) and we want to confirm that the plans haven't changed. Why do we use the preposition "on"? Because the plans is in a positive state/active state.

TO

A) Example Sentences. Remember to follow the instructions in section A from previous prepositions.

1)

We all went to the beach.
He mailed a letter to me last week.
If he's mean, don't respond to him.
What's the answer to his question?
Tie him to the tree!
Does this make any sense to you?
$100 isn't much to a millionaire.
Canada is to the north of the US.

What does the word "to" mean in this group?

2)

The snow was piled to the roof.
The price could rise to $50.
(Giving directions:) Go to the corner and turn right.

What does the word "to" mean in this group?

3)

I work (from) Monday to Thursday.
Every year, we travel (from) June to August.
Call me at 5 to 11. (5 minutes before 11:00, which is 10:55)

What does the word "to" mean in this group?

4)

To be honest, I don't care.
To live is to love.

What does the word "to" mean in this group?

5)

I need to drink more water.
I was afraid to tell him about it.
If you continue to practice English, you will improve.
I stopped to tie my shoe.
"Are you going to the party?" "I want to, but I don't know if I can."
I have to cook dinner.

What does the word "to" mean in this group?

6)

I came (in order) to help.
Knives are used (in order) to cut food.

What does the word "to" mean in this group?

7)

I'm close to finishing the project.
I'm used to speaking English.

What does the word "to" mean in this group?

B) The Logic

: an end point

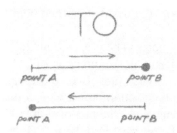

"to" is a one-way preposition

Explanation of the logic: The end point can be about time, space, an action (verb), or a person. For example, if you go to the store, that's your destination, which is a physical end point. If I give a gift to my friend, they are the recipient (the person who receives something), so the person is the end point.

Before we move forward, we need to talk about something that's extremely important: the difference between the prepositions "to" and "toward". They're slightly different and the dictionary definition will confuse you. "Toward" means "in the direction of an end point", not the end point itself. This can be confusing because the preposition "to" implies a direction, which means that it contains the idea of "toward", but it's not about the direction.

There's a detail here that can help make this clearer: the suffix "-ward", which we attach to the end of many (but not all) prepositions. This suffix has a couple (of) definitions, but it basically means "in a specific direction". So, "upward" means "in an 'up' direction", "downward" means "in a 'down' direction", "forward" means "in a 'fore' (front) direction", etc… This means that "toward" means "in a 'to' direction". To what? The place that you're going (the end point). In other words, "toward" means "in the direction of an end point", but not the end point itself. "I'm going toward the store" = "I'm going in the direction of where the store is located." If you're going to the store, the store is the

79

direction and the end point (destination), but we only care about the end point. This means that the preposition "to" includes the idea of "toward" because "to" implies a direction. But we use "toward" when we want to say that you're only going in that direction and it's not your destination (end point).

Etymology notes: The preposition "to" has survived since Old English and meant "in the direction of", "for the purpose of", and "furthermore". The first two meanings still exist (but remember that the preposition "toward" is a direction and "to" is an end point). When we use the preposition "to" with the meaning "for the purpose of", we say "in order to". However, 99 percent of the time, we omit the words "in order" because it's implied by the context. In this book, I write the words "in order" in parentheses before the preposition "to" when this is the case. For example, "(In order) to graduate from college, you have to study a lot." (Note: this is so common that I might miss it sometimes.) We'll see the most important parts of the etymology in groups four, five, and six. 4

Now, go back to the example sentences and try to apply the logic. Ask yourself: "How is 'to' an end point in these sentences?" Remember, the end point could be a place, a time, a person, an action, etc...

C) Detailed Explanations of the Example Sentences.

1) general end point (often physical)

The words "destination" and "recipient" are more specific words for "end point", so we get these hierarchies: 1) end point → destination; 2) end point → recipient

We all went to the beach. This is the simplest and easiest example. In this sentence, the beach is the destination. However, be careful. The dictionary says that this use of the preposition "to"

means "in the direction of" or "towards a destination". As native speakers, it's natural to try to define the preposition "to" this way, but it's not completely accurate. Remember what I said earlier: the preposition "toward" means "in the direction of an end point", but the preposition "to" means the specific end point itself. The preposition "to" implies a direction, but it's not about the direction. So, if you go "to" the beach, the beach is your destination (end point). If you go "toward" the beach, you are currently going in the direction of where the beach is, but it's probably not your destination. For example, maybe you're currently one mile (1.6 km) east of the beach and your destination is a coffee shop that's half of a mile (0.8 km) from the beach. So, (in order) to reach your destination, you have to go <u>toward</u> the beach.

He mailed a letter to me last week. You can easily see how the logic applies to this group. In this sentence, the letter was mailed to me. Because I'm the recipient (the person who is supposed to receive the letter), I am the end point.

ALTERNATIVES: "He mailed me a letter last week". Notice the words "mailed me" and not "mailed to me". These are details of English grammar, but it's very common in English that we can say either 1) verb + direct object + to + indirect object; or 2) verb + indirect object + direct object. This works with verbs like "to give", "to send", etc…, but it doesn't work with all verbs. So, we can say "mailed a letter to me" or "mailed me a letter".

If he's mean, don't respond to him. The preposition "to" is very often used after the verb "to respond". But why? The verb "to respond" means "to give/send a response". So, the response (noun) goes to the person and the person is the <u>recipient</u> of the response. It's like saying, "I gave a dollar to him" or "I sent a letter to him". The example sentence says "don't respond", so in this case you're not giving a response. Let's say the guy is mean and he yells at you. You don't like that, so later you tell your friend about it. You friend's advice is to not give a response if he's mean (only give a response if he's nice). In other words, if he's mean, ignore him.

ALTERNATIVES: If he's mean, ignore him.

What's the answer to his question? This group is more abstract. The answer to a question means the answer "goes to" the question. In other words, the answer "belongs to" the question. It's almost like the question and answer are puzzle pieces that have to fit together. Think of it like this: someone asks a question. That question is now floating in the air. Someone else answers the question. The answer is supposed to "solve" the question, so it goes into the air and meets the question. If the answer is correct, it "solves" or "erases" the question and the question disappears. So you "send" the answer to the question, just like you send a letter to someone or like you go to the beach. The question is the destination/end point of the answer. The only difference is that the end point isn't physical.

An important note: In this sentence, the preposition "to" is part of the words "his question": "the answer" + "to his question". So the words "to his question" is a chunk. Let's say I ask you a question and you don't answer. I want you to answer, so I might (rudely) say: "Answer me!" or "Answer my question!" If we use "answer" as a verb like this, you're not sending the answer to me or my question because "answer" is now a verb (action), NOT a noun. You can't send a verb, but you can send a noun. In the example sentence, we're asking, "What's THE answer", so answer is a noun. The verb "to answer" rarely uses the preposition "to" after it.

A note about "to" and "of": I mentioned above that the question and the answer are like puzzle pieces. The interesting thing is, the logic of the prepositions "to" and "of" touch in this context: "The last piece of the puzzle." "The last piece to the puzzle." If we talk about puzzles specifically, they can overlap and can be interchangeable, but if we just have the idea of puzzle pieces, then they usually just touch. So, we do <u>not</u> say "What's the answer of his question?" The logic definitely works, but unfortunately English doesn't allow the preposition "of" to be used here. In this case, we're not looking at the word "answer" as a "part" or "content". The answer is definitely not the content of the question, because the question has its own content. The answer isn't a part of the question. When we look at it like a part, you can see how it might work, but it doesn't. Why? The answer has its own content and the question has its own content. So, we're talking about one piece going to the other piece, not that they are pieces of each other. They're separate, individual pieces. So, just like I can go to the beach, the answer goes to the question.

Tie him to the tree! This sentence is a little different, but it fits best in this group. It means that I want you to grab him, take some rope or similar material, put him against the tree, wrap the rope around both him and the tree, and secure the rope (tie it with a knot). That way, he's tied to the tree and can't leave. The tree is the specific end point that you want to use (in order) to stop him from leaving. Tie him to what? A pole? A car? A building? No, a tree.

Does this make any sense to you? This type of sentence often causes problems for English learners who aren't sure if they should use the preposition "to" or the preposition "for". Depending on the context, both can be correct. Let's say I read an article in the newspaper, but the writer didn't write the article very well, so it doesn't make any sense. I ask you, "Does this make any sense to you?" We use the preposition "to" because the word "you" is the end point. It doesn't make sense to me, but it might make sense to you. The preposition "to" points to the specific person, so the "sense" goes "to" the person. So you read the article and you receive the information. In an abstract way, if the information in the article doesn't make sense to you, it's like you receive a letter in the mail but the letter isn't addressed to you.

FOR: The preposition "for" is used in a sentence like this when you're asking about if something is good, bad, or whatever for a particular person based on their circumstances. For example, Tom owns a car, but he takes the bus to work everyday. He can pay for gas, his insurance is active, etc… Let's say that there's absolutely no reason that he can't drive his car. But he still pays to ride the bus everyday for some unknown reason. So, does it make sense FOR Tom to ride the bus instead of driving his car to work? We're not asking if it makes any sense TO him because he's not the end point. In other words, he's not <u>receiving</u> the idea and trying to make sense of it. We're saying that, <u>based on</u> (basis/cause) his circumstances, does it make any sense that he chooses to take the bus? The idea of a basis/cause is a big part of the preposition "for", which we'll see later.

$100 isn't much to a millionaire. The end point is "a millionaire". If we change the end point to "a homeless person", for example, then $100 is a lot ("$100 is a lot to a homeless person"). We're making an indirect comparison by specifically pointing to a particular part of the comparison. So, we're comparing a millionaire and people who aren't millionaires (specifically homeless people in this case), but we're only choosing ONE of them as the end point in our sentence. If this is still confusing, you can think of it this way: if I send $100 to a millionaire, will it be a lot? No. If I send $100 to a homeless person, will it be a lot? Yes.

ALTERNATIVES: "$100 isn't much for a millionaire." We can also use the preposition "for" in this case. This is one of the rare times that the prepositions "for" and "to" are interchangeable, but the logic behind them is very different. If we use the preposition "for", we're talking about the millionaire as a basis. Based on the millionaire's situation (which is the fact that a millionaire has a lot of money), $100 isn't much. We'll see many more sentences like this when we talk about the preposition "for" later. It's almost like saying, "If we use $1,000,000 as the basis, is $100 a lot of money?" In other words, if we compare $100 to $1,000,000 we can see that $100 isn't a lot.

Canada is to the north of the US. Ok, so there's Canada and the US. The preposition "to" is about an end point. If we're in the US, which direction is do we have to go (in order) to get to Canada? North. But the question is this: if the preposition "to" is about an end point, what's the end point? Is it the word "Canada" or is it "the north"? Yes, the sentence itself is about Canada, but we're not focusing on that. If I say, "The keys are on the table", the sentence is about the keys, but the preposition "on" deals with "the table". Remember, this is a one-way preposition, so the logic flows with the sentence (left to right). So, the end point in this sentence is "the north". This is a sentence where the preposition "to" is strongly tied to the idea of "direction", and the surface meaning in this case is definitely a direction. However, remember that the logic of the preposition "to" is an end point, even if it has the surface meaning of "direction". Here's the key: notice that we have to say "the north" and not just "north". That's because "the north" is a location, and a location is an end point, NOT a direction.

ALTERNATIVES: "Canada is north of the US." What happened to the word "the" that was before the word "north"? Well, we're not using the preposition "to", so we don't need to say the word "the". Remember, "the north" is a location. However, the word "north" (without the word "the") is a direction. Any dictionary will tell you this. Test it and see: if I tell you, "Travel north", does that work? Yes. I'm telling you which direction that you have to travel in. Is it correct to say, "Travel to the north?" Yes. But this is like "Travel to the beach". And does it work if I say, "Travel the north"? Well, it can work, but it's not a direction. Now I'm telling you to travel inside the location/area that is "the north". For example, if we're in the US and I say, "Travel the north", you're going to travel around the northern states. In other words, the states that are in the north. Back to the alternative sentence, "Canada is north of the US". The specific meaning is slightly different, but this sentence and the example sentence are so close in meaning that it doesn't matter. They're interchangeable, at least in this case.

"Canada is above the US". This sentence is not grammatically correct. However, we can say this for a special reason. Imagine a map of North America (that's hanging on the wall). If you look at that map, can you say, "Canada is above the US (on the map)"? Yes. We'll talk a little bit about the preposition "above" when we talk about the preposition "over", but "above" is basically a static point that is higher than something else. For example, you might have a fan above your kitchen table. Or when you enter a building, the ceiling is above you. So if we look at a map that's on the wall, what's above the US? Canada. I tell you to imagine a map that's on the wall because it makes things simpler. It doesn't matter if the map is flat on a table, we can still use the preposition "above".

TOWARD: If we say, "toward the north of the US", it sounds like we're talking about something that's in the US or near the US. For example, "New York is located toward the north of the US". This simply means, "in the direction of the northern US". We can say "Canada is toward the north of the US", and it means that Canada is near the north of the US. Remember, "the north" is a location, so if you use the preposition "toward", it's similar to the sentence, "I'm walking toward the beach".

2) *limit-point (more specific word for "end point"), often in an upward direction*

This group is like a subgroup of group one. You can often apply the idea of a "limit-point" to the sentences in group one, but these sentences are specifically a "limit-point". We have this hierarchy: end point → limit-point.

The snow was piled to the roof. What does "pile" mean? Imagine you have dirty clothes and you throw them all into one place so that the height of the group of clothes gets higher, like a little hill. That's a "pile". The verb "to pile" is very similar. In this example, let's say you were shoveling snow and you shoveled it all into the same place, so it made a big pile. Many English learners see this example and think that the pile starts on the roof. That's not what this means. The pile starts on the ground and the height of it reaches the same height as the bottom of the roof. For example, if the roof is 10 feet above the ground, then the snow is piled 10 feet high. The exact height of the roof doesn't matter. When we say this, we're just using the roof as a general reference of measurement. We say "to" the roof because the snow starts "from" the ground and goes "to" the roof. The point where the

87

bottom of the roof starts is the "end point" of the measurement of the snow's height.

ALTERNATIVES: "The snow was piled up to the roof." When we talked about the preposition "on", we saw that sometimes we can add the preposition "up". The reason in those cases was because we were talking about a high surface or platform. When we use the preposition "to", if we're talking about something that goes upward and we want to talk about the end point, then we can say "up to".

"The snow was piled as high as the roof." Of course, we can use "as high as". This just means that the height of the snow and the height of the roof are the same.

"The snow was at the level of the roof." There's a close relationship between the prepositions "to" (end point) and "at" (specific point or bubble). It's a little complicated, and we'll see more details later, but let's look at this example sentence. We say, "The snow was piled to the roof" because we're using the verb "to pile". However, we can also say, "The snow was at the level of the roof". This means the same thing, but we're using the preposition "at". Why? Well, for now, just know that both the prepositions "to" and "at" have the surface meaning of a "limit-point". It's where the logic of these two almost overlaps. I say 'almost' because they both use the idea of a "limit-point" in a very similar way, but they're not exactly the same. The simplest explanation here is that "to" has the added feeling of a direction, but "at" is a description of a static point without direction. Many of these details will become clearer when we talk about the preposition "at" later in the book.

The price could rise to $50. This sentence is a little easier. Let's say the price of something is $20. But it's an item that is becoming more and more popular. As demand rises, the price rises. The person who says, "The price could rise to $50" believes that it's possible for the price of the product to reach $50. Maybe it will go

88

higher than $50, but the person who says this thinks that $50 is the end point for how high the price might go. Because that person think that $50 is the highest price, that's the limit-point in this case.

ALTERNATIVES: "The price could rise as high as $50." Same reason as the previous example. In this case, we're not talking about a physical height, but a high price.

"The price could rise up to $50." Same reason as the previous example. Again, in this case, we're not talking about a physical height, but a high price.

NOTE: Like the previous example sentence, we can use the preposition "at" here, too. However, in this case, it's not an alternative. I just want to show you another example of how the prepositions "to" and "at" are related. Let's say the price has risen to $50. That means that the price is currently at $50. We don't always use "at" with a price, and it's more common just to say "The price is $50" because the price is what it is. However, this context is about a price that changes. For example, maybe we're talking about the price of gold or the price of a stock. In this context, we do use the preposition "at" because we're saying specifically what the price is at right now. It could change tomorrow. You can think of this in a similar way to group one: I'm at home right now, but I could go to the beach tomorrow and then I'll be at the beach. So, the price could go/rise to $75 tomorrow, and then it'll be at $75. But remember, this is a limit-point.

(Giving directions:) Go to the corner and turn right. This sentence might seem like it belongs to group one. As I said, this group is like a subgroup of group one. The main point of this sentence isn't a "destination". We're still talking about an end point, but it's specifically a limit-point. Why? Because you don't want to go to the corner and then stop. You want to go somewhere else, but (in order) to get there, first you have to go to the corner. Don't go past the corner, just <u>to</u> the corner, and then turn right and continue going to your destination. So you're walking forward and the corner <u>limits</u> you because you can't go forward anymore if you want to reach your destination. Instead, you have to turn.

ALTERNATIVES: "Go up to the corner and turn right." "Go down to the corner and turn right." In both of these sentences, we're not talking about an upward direction or a downward direction, so why do we use the prepositions "up" and "down"? This particular point is very complicated and we'll discuss it when we talk about the preposition "down" near the end of the book.

"Go straight until you reach the corner and turn right." The difference between the prepositions "to" and "until" is confusing to many English learners. The preposition "until" is simpler and doesn't have as many uses.

NOTE: In this case, we don't say, "Go as far as the corner". The construction "as ___ as something" is one way to talk about a limit-point, just like the preposition "to". However, in the context of giving directions, we usually don't say that. The reason is because "as far as" sounds like you don't have to go that far, but you can. Just don't go past that point. This might be something that a parent tells their child when the child is playing in front of the house: "You can go as far as the corner, but don't go any farther." This creates an area that the child can safely play in.

3) *end point in time*

I work (from) Monday to Thursday. These examples are very easy and you probably already know them. "From" is very commonly used as the opposite of "to" in both time and space, but we don't always have to use it. In fact, when talking about time, if you have a sentence with both "to" and "from", you can usually omit the preposition "from". Either way, when we use these two prepositions together, we're talking about a duration, which is a length of time. Other prepositions are also used to talk about a duration, but "to" and "from" are used together (in order) to emphasize the start point and the end point, not the time in between. I start work on Monday and I end work on Thursday.

ALTERNATIVES: "I work from Monday until Thursday." The preposition "until" can be used with days of the week, but we don't normally use it in this specific context (talking about the days of the week that I work). It's more common to use it as a deadline: "You have until Monday to finish the project". However, you can use it as an alternative in this context. If you do, it might sound more like you're specifically talking about THIS week and not every week. So here, I recommend just using the preposition "to", but you should know that it is possible to use "until".

Every year, we travel (from) June to August. In this sentence, "August" is the end point. It's the month when our traveling stops. It stops when the month starts or sometime during the month.

91

ALTERNATIVES: "Every year, we travel (from) June until August." Here we see the preposition "until" again, but now we're talking about time.

"Every year, we travel between June and August." This alternative sentence isn't 100% the same, but it can be. When we say "between June and August", it means any time that is between those two months. Let's say that every year, you have the time and money to travel between June and August. That doesn't mean that you will travel, it just means that you can travel. If you do travel, you might only travel from June to July, for example. However, you can also travel the whole time, so this can be an alternative to the example sentence, but the meaning of this sentence isn't exactly the same. This is because the prepositions "from" and "to" are about the start point and the end point, so we're talking about the whole time. This creates two lines on a timeline and we can look at this as a time-frame which is one whole thing. But the preposition "between" is about any time that is between the start point and the end point. In other words, "between" is more about any point or points that are inside the time-frame and not the whole time-frame itself.

Call me at 5 to 11. (5 minutes before 11:00, which is 10:55)
When telling time, we can use the preposition "to" with the meaning of "before" and we can use the preposition "past" with the meaning of "after". But why do we use "to" in this case? We're talking about the specific time 10:55. If you add five minutes, it will be 11:00. In other words, there are five minutes remaining until 11:00. As we go forward in time, we're going "to" 11:00. That's the specific end point.

ALTERNATIVES: "Call me 5 minutes before 11." If we say it this way, we don't use the preposition "at". Instead, we add the word "minutes". The reason is because when we use the preposition "before" in this context, we have to specify the unit of measurement (minutes). Think about the question: "How many

92

minutes before 11 do you want me to call you?" Instead of looking at it as, "Call me at 10:55", we're looking at it as, "Call me at 5 minutes before 11". Obviously the time that you call me is the same. These are just two different ways of looking at the same thing, but using the preposition "before" means that we have to change the exact time ("at 10:55") to a measurement ("5 minutes").

"Call me at 5 'til." The word " 'til " is a short version of the word "until". In this case, 11:00 (or whatever specific hour) is implied by details that were mentioned earlier in the conversation. This is an expression that we use only when talking about time. Please note: we <u>cannot</u> say, "Call me at 5 until". This is just a special case. Also note that we <u>cannot</u> say "Call me at 5 until 11". In this context, "at 5" sounds like I want you to call me at 5:00 and "until 11" sounds like we're going to talk until 11:00. Of course, that's possible, but if you want to say that, you have to say something like, "Call me at 5 <u>and we'll talk until</u> 11".

4) *Infinitives*

In order to completely understand this group, we need to look at the etymology. Verbs in Old English were inflected, which means that the conjugation of the verb itself showed who was doing the action. Many modern languages still work this way. In Spanish, for example, the infinitive (not conjugated) form of the verb "to eat" is "comer". If you want to say "I eat", you say "(yo) como". The "-o" ending means "I", so the word "I" ("yo" in Spanish) isn't necessary. We know that in Modern English we can't do this. We have to say "I eat", "you eat", etc… or we won't know who's doing the action.

Let's look at an example of the infinitive form between Old English and Modern English: the verb "to see" in Modern English was "seon" in Old English. In Middle English, speakers started to use the preposition "to" for the infinitive form, and this changed the way that we use and conjugate verbs in English. This use of the preposition "to" as part of the infinitive was

93

based on the Old English use of the preposition "to" with the dative case ("dative case" = indirect objects; example: "I give it to him"). According to the *Online Etymology Dictionary* (and probably every English teacher and English learning resource), this use of the preposition "to" has no meaning and it's just part of English grammar. However, you and I know that that's not true because languages are logical, and there's usually a logical reason why something changes in a language.

But why did Middle English speakers specifically use the word "to" when this change happened? We know that this was based on how Old English used the preposition "to" with the dative case, but how is it that the logic of the preposition "to" started applying to the infinitive form of verbs?

The answer is in the etymology, of course. First, don't forget that one of the meanings of the Old English preposition "to" was "in the direction of". Also remember that the Modern English preposition "to" includes the idea of "in the direction of", but the preposition "to" is about the end point, not the direction. Now to answer the question: Middle English speakers started thinking about verbs as end points. For example, in the dictionary, you'll find the verb "to see". What's happening here is that we have the word "to" pointing to the action of seeing. More specifically, the word "to" is pointing in the direction of the action of seeing. But this is exactly the same as saying, "I go to the store". I have to go in the direction of the store ("toward"), but we're talking about my destination (end point) and not the direction. It's the same with verbs. When we say "to see", we're using the word "to" so that we can make the action "see" the end point.

Because there's no other verb placed before "to see" (for example, "want to see"), it means that there's nothing particular pointing to the action of seeing. (We'll learn more about using two verbs in the next group). And because there's no other information after the verb (for example, "to see the sky"), the infinitive form is simply about seeing. This works because "to see" actually isn't the verb. The verb itself is "see". We point to the verb "see" as an end point with the word "to", just like I can point to "the store" as an end point when I say "I go to the store". When we conjugate the verb, we omit the word "to" and say "I see", "you saw", "he is seeing". The reason that we omit the word "to" is because "see" isn't an end point anymore, so we don't need to point to it. If I'm doing the action, then I simply say, "I see". But in the verb's most basic state (the infinitive), Middle English speakers started pointing to the action/verb as an end point using the word "to". That's how and why the Old English verb "seon" became "to see".

This is something that Modern English speakers are completely unaware of because it's subconscious (like most of the logic). Maybe it was a subconscious change for Middle English speakers, or maybe they started speaking this way intentionally. Either way, the Modern English language looks at the infinitive form of verbs as end points. In fact, it's even possible to use the infinitive by itself in a sentence, though it won't work all the time. That's what this group is about.

To be honest, I don't care. Here, we're starting the sentence with the infinitive of the verb. Why can't we just say, "Be honest, I don't care"? If we say that, "Be" is a command (the imperative), meaning that I'm telling you to be honest and then I'm saying that I don't care. It doesn't make sense. We need the word "to" here because we're pointing to the action/verb as an end point.

In this example, I'm only telling you that I don't care because I want to tell you the truth (which means that I have to be honest). We use the word "to" so that we can make "be honest" an end point. It's similar to saying "for the purpose of being honest".

ALTERNATIVES: Here are two possible alternatives: "If I'm being honest, I don't care." "Honestly, I don't care."

To live is to love. Here we're saying that one action/verb means another action/verb. In other words, if you want to truly live, you have to love. Without love, life is nothing. So, we're pointing to the action of living and then pointing to the action of loving. We put the word "is" between them (in order) to say that the action of living is the same as the action of loving. We can actually look at this sentence as a short version of "In order to (truly) live, you have to love."

5) *Two verbs (second verb = end point of first verb)*

When you start learning English grammar, it's useful to think of this structure as conjugated verb + infinitive of the verb → She agreed + to help; I want + to leave; He needs + to relax. However, when thinking about the logic, it's better to think of the word "to" as a special preposition or <u>linking word that helps the first verb point to the second verb</u>, which is the end point.

This means that it works the same way as "He sent an email to me". "Me" is the end point that the email goes to (email → me = email + to + me). "I need to drink more water" → the verb "to drink" is the end point that *my need* goes to (need → drink (verb) = need + to + drink). We can see that the logic of the preposition "to" works like it normally does. The only difference is that instead of using two nouns ("a letter to me") or a verb and a noun ("respond to him"), we're using two verbs ("need to drink"). The first action (verb) goes to the end point, which is the second action (verb). In other words, when we want to use an action/verb as the end point of another action/verb, we connect them with the word "to". This will become very clear after you look at the examples below.

Notice that I said "my need" (noun) goes to the verb "to drink". Don't be confused by this. This is the only way to explain what's happening, but the structure itself is verb to verb, not noun to verb. In fact, what's really happening in the background is that these types of verbs (need, want, agree, be afraid, etc...) are just making a noun concept into a verb form. A need (noun) becomes an action through the verb "to need"; a desire (noun) becomes an action through the verb "to want"; an agreement (noun) becomes an action through the verb "to agree"; a fear (noun) becomes an action through the verb phrase "to be afraid"; etc...

96

I need to drink more water. I have a need and that need points to the action/verb "drink". Need → drink (verb) = need + to + drink. My need goes to the act of drinking. Notice that if we use the word "drink" as a noun, we say, "I need a drink" and we don't have to use the preposition "to". Remember, this is a special use of the word "to" that links two verbs/actions, so when we have a verb and a noun, we don't use the word "to".

I was afraid to tell him about it. This is exactly like the previous one. I have a fear. What's my fear? It's not a noun. If it were a noun, I could say, "I'm afraid of spiders", for example. No, I'm afraid to do something. I'm afraid to tell someone about something. So, the action "tell" is the end point of the verb phrase "to be afraid". My fear goes to the act of telling him. Be afraid → tell = be afraid + to + tell.

If you continue to practice English, you will improve. This example works the same as the previous examples, but there's also something a little different. Some verbs can use the infinitive form ("to do") or the continuous form ("doing") of the second verb. The verb "to continue" can use both forms. For example, "continue to practice" or "continue practicing". Both of these mean the same thing. If we use the infinitive form ("to practice"), then the logic works the same as in the previous examples. You are already practicing English (not right now, but as a general process over time). So we have "continue" + "to" + "practice".

The biggest difference between this example and the other examples is that you are just continuing the second action/verb. If we use "continue practicing", then the logic of the preposition "to" doesn't apply, but we don't need it. This is just another way to say the same thing. The reason the continuous form ("practicing") works in this case is because you are already doing it, so you can simply continue that process. Notice that we call it the "continuous" form (some teachers, particularly British teachers, call it the "progressive" form, but the idea is the same: you are progressing forward or making progress with that action.

I stopped to tie my shoe. This is an example where there's a different meaning if we use either the infinitive form or the continuous form. "I stopped to tie my shoe" means that I was doing something else, but I noticed that my shoe wasn't tied, so I stopped what I was doing (in order) to tie my shoe. Notice "in order to". We'll talk more about that use of the preposition "to" after we see the next group, but when we say "I stopped to do something", it's actually the short version of "I stopped in order to tie my shoe". We usually omit the words "in order" because they're implied by the context, or by the specific verb. Because of this, when we use the verb "to stop" with the preposition "to", the preposition "to" can only mean that I stopped what I was doing so that I could do something else. So, we have "stop" (+ "in order") + "to" + "tie".

But what if we say, "I stopped tying my shoe"? That means that I was tying my shoe and then I stopped tying my shoe. Notice that because we're specifically using the continuous form of the verb "to tie", it means that we're stopping the process of that action ("tying").

Notice that when we say "continue to practice", the meaning is the same as "continue practicing" because "continue to practice" is <u>not</u> the short version of "continue in order to practice". As we'll see soon, "in order to" is about a purpose + the ability to fulfill that purpose. When we say "continue to practice", we're not talking about a purpose or an ability. We can if we say something like: "I speak with natives (in order) to continue practicing / (in order) to continue to practice."

As a final note here, we now know that "stop to do" and "stop doing" have different meanings. Is it the same with the verb "to start", which is the opposite? No. "I started learning English when I was ten." This sentence means that you started the process of learning. "I started to learn English when I was ten." The meaning of this sentence is the same. Why? Because we're not saying that I started in order to learn English, we're simply saying "start" + "to" + learn". The idea of "starting" is pointing to the action/verb "learn". If we want to talk about doing something in order to learn English, we can say, "I started taking classes in order to learn English" or "I started to take classes in order to learn English". But notice that the "in order to" is not connected to the verb "to start". You started doing something else so that you could learn English.

"Are you going to the party?" "I want to, but I don't know if I can." This example is a little different than the others. I included this example because it proves that the preposition "to" shows the end point from one verb to another verb. "Are you going to the party?" → "I want to (go), but I don't know if I can (go)." We omit the verb "go" because it has already been mentioned in the previous sentence. You can see that when we say "can", we don't add the word "to" because we don't use the preposition "to" with modal verbs. However, the verb "to want" is not a modal verb. "To want" means that you have a desire. For example, "I want to go to the beach". What is the end point of your desire? In other words, what does your desire point to? It points to the action of going to the beach.

In cases where the main verb has already been mentioned ("Are you going?"), we simply drop the verb ("go"), but we usually keep the word "to". Why? Because if your answer is "I want", the other person will say "You want what?" The word "to" in the phrase "I want to" points to the action/verb already mentioned ("go"). We can clearly see that the word "to" is the connection between the two verbs, and in this specific case, it points to the end point of my desire.

As a final note for this example, let's quickly talk about why we don't use the word "to" with modal verbs. The modal verbs are: can, could, should, would, will, must, might, and may. We don't use the preposition "to" because these verbs change the "mode" of the main verb. I can go, I would go, I will go, I might go, etc... All (of) these "modes" give the verb a new form of expression. Instead of "I go", which is just a statement of what I do, the word "can" allows us to talk about the ability to go. In other words, what I'm able to do. "Might" allows us to talk about the possibility of going; and so on.

Another very important point here is that a modal verb works exactly like a conjugation (past, present, future). Notice that we say, "I go", "You go", "He goes". But when we use a modal verb such as "can", we say, "I can go", "You can go", "He can go". The reason that we don't say, "He can goes" is because the modal verb "can" is like a conjugation. The verb "to go" has already been changed ("he can go"), so we don't change it again. And that's the other reason that we don't use the preposition "to" with modal verbs: the main verb has already been changed and there is no "to" that we can use. In other words, a modal verb can't "point to" another verb because it's modifying the basic meaning/expression of that verb.

I have to cook dinner. This example is extra special. We've seen that you can use the preposition "to" with the verbs "want/need/etc..." when you want to connect two verbs in this special way. But notice something interesting: "I want a car" → "I want to cook". The meaning of the verb "to want" doesn't change. Either you want something (car) or you want to do something (cook). In both cases, you have a desire, but one desire is for a noun and the other desire is for an action (verb). The verb "to have" works the same way: "I have a car" → "I have to cook". In the first sentence, I have something (a car). In this case, the verb "to have" means "to own" or "to possess" something (which is a noun). In the second sentence, I have an obligation to do something (cook). In other words, it's the same as the modal verb "must". This use of the verb "to have" started in the 1500's. 5

It makes perfect sense. "Have to" and "must" have almost exactly the same meaning. In fact, in American English, we almost always use "have to" instead of "must" (though there are certain contexts where "must" is common). There's a logical reason why they basically mean the same thing (which is "an obligation" or "a duty"). The idea is that you can use the verb "to have" (which means "to own" or "to possess") and add a verb after it. If you "have" a verb/action, then it means that you own/possess the

100

obligation/duty to do that action. In other words, you have an obligation/duty and that obligation/duty points to a specific action, which is the end point. This is exactly the same as "want to" and "need to", for example, except that "want to" is a desire that points to a specific action and "need to" is a need/necessity that points to a specific action. Just remember that modal verbs work differently than normal verbs. "Must" does not use the word "to", but the verb "to have" is a normal verb, so we need the word "to" (in order) to point to the second action/verb.

6) *in order + to (which means "ability" + "purpose")*

This group isn't very difficult, but there is one difficult part. This meaning of the preposition "to" is where its logic touches the preposition "for". The preposition "for" is complicated, which we'll see later, but a big part of the preposition "for" is the idea of a purpose. Because these two only touch and don't overlap, you usually can't use one in place of the other. This particular issue is one of those small details that you just have to get used to. However, I've done my best to explain the differences using the specific example sentences. Lastly, this group actually works in a very similar way to the previous two groups, as we'll see in the examples.

I came (in order) to help. The phrase "in order to" describes the purpose of something. That purpose specifically points to an action. As I said before, we usually don't say the words "in order" and instead we just say "to" because the words "in order" are implied by the context of the sentence. There are times when the context isn't clear enough, or when it's just naturally said, but we usually omit it. So, we usually just say, "I'm here to help".

But why do we use the specific words "in", "order", and "to"? And how does the logic of the preposition "to" work in this group? The phrase "in order to" is a chunk (and a collocation). When you combine these words in this way, it creates its own meaning, as if it were a single word. But we can look at the pieces and see why it means "an ability" + "a purpose". We

101

know that the preposition "to" is always about an end point, but in this group we're talking about a purpose. Well, a purpose can be a special kind of end point. As we'll see later, the idea of a purpose is usually part of the preposition "for". However, when we combine "in order" with the preposition "to", this combination makes the end point into a purpose. Don't forget that one of the meanings of the Old English preposition "to" was "for the purpose of". Here's the trick: when we use the preposition "for" as a purpose, we can put a noun or a verb after it, but when we use the preposition "to" as a purpose, we can only use a verb. So the preposition "to" in Old English with the meaning of "for the purpose of" has become "for the purpose of doing something" in Modern English, and this only happens when we use "in order to".

The preposition "in" is about a container. The word "order" is the container. When we use the words "in" and "order" together in this context, we create the idea of "organized in a way that X is possible" or "aligned in a way that X is possible". (Note that in other contexts, "in" + "order" doesn't mean this. It's only when we use "in" + "order" + "to" that this special meaning is created.)

So what we're doing with "in" + "order" is that we're aligning the first action ("I'm here") with the second action ("to help") in a way that makes the second action possible. In other words, if I'm not here, I can't help. And if I can't help, then the purpose doesn't matter. When we add the word "to", we're also saying that the second action is the purpose of the first action. In other words, "I'm here for the purpose of being able to help", or more simply, "I'm here so that I can help". (Notice that we have "purpose" + "of" + "being able to help": "being able to help", or more specifically "helping", is the content of the purpose (A ← B).)

Notice that this actually works in a very similar way to "want to", "need to", etc… The difference is that we're saying "in-order" + "to" + "help". "In order" gives us the idea of an ability instead of a desire, a need, etc…, so we're talking about the ability to help. If we break the whole sentence into pieces, we

102

have: "I came" (action 1) + "in order" (ability) + "to" (points to action 2 and makes it a purpose) + "help" (action 2).

It's important to note that just like we can say "in order to", we can also say "in order for". For example, "In order for a computer to work, you have to turn it on." In other words, a computer <u>can</u> only work if it's turned on. The preposition "for" is often about a purpose, but the logic has two parts: "purpose" and "basis". We'll talk more about that later in the book when we see the preposition "for", but the "for" that's in the phrase "in order for" is <u>not</u> a purpose. It's a basis. This is because we're saying, "<u>Based</u> on computers, ..." In other words, if computers are what we're talking about, then based on that that topic, X is true (X = "you have to turn it on"). However, we can also say, "In order to work, a computer must be turned on." As I said earlier, we use the preposition "to" when we're directly connecting to a verb (to + work), and that's true even when we add "in order". But we use "in order for" when we're <u>not</u> directly connecting to a verb ("for a computer" + "to work"). So, in this case, these are two ways to say the same thing, but it depends on the context and what it is that you specifically want to say.

Notice that because the idea of a purpose is normally part of the logic of the preposition "for" and not the preposition "to", when we use "in order to", the preposition "to" is taking one of the applications of the logic of the preposition "for". So, when we say "in order for", we can only use it as a basis because the preposition "to" stole that part of the logic from the preposition "for".

ALTERNATIVES: "I'm here so (that) I can help." When we use the phrase "so that", we often omit the word "that". In fact, we almost always omit the word "that" when it joins two parts of a sentence, unless the context isn't clear or it happens to be said naturally (Note: the word "that" as in "this and that" is different).

FOR: Can we say, "I'm here for helping"? (Remember, we have to use the "-ing" form of the verb after any preposition except the preposition "to".) Unfortunately, this sentence doesn't make any sense. If we use the preposition "for" here, we're talking about a basis. Why? We know that we often omit "in order" and just say "to". Remember that in this context, we're not just talking about a purpose or a basis, we're also talking about the ability to help, which means that we're doing the same thing that we do with "(in order) to" → "(in order) for helping". But we can't use a verb after "in order for", so it doesn't work. Note that "in order for" isn't the only way that the preposition "for" becomes a basis. As I said, we'll see more about that later.

Knives are used (in order) to cut food. This is exactly like the previous one, but in this case we're talking about a tool (and we're using passive voice). In fact, we can expand the sentence and say, "Knives are tools that are used in order to cut food". So, we have the idea of using knives (action 1) + "in order" (purpose) + "to" (points to action 2) + "cut food" (action 2).

FOR: Can we say, "Knives are used for cutting food"? Yes, in this case, it works. In this case, the preposition "for" is a purpose. We're not saying "in order for" because when we use the preposition "for" in this context, we're not talking about the ability to cut food, we're only talking about the purpose of the knives. If we use the preposition "to", it only works if we're using the preposition "to" as a linking word between the ability and the action so that we can show that the purpose of the ability is to be able to do that action. But when we use the preposition "for", we don't need the idea of an ability in this context and we can just directly talk about the purpose.

Generally, the preposition "for" can be a purpose or a basis depending on the context and we don't need extra words to create one meaning or the other. In the context of this example ("for cutting food"), it's clear that the preposition "for" is about a purpose and not a basis. Why? Well, what is the use of a knife? In other words, what is the purpose of using a knife? Because we're talking about what something is used for, it means that we're talking about the purpose of something. Just don't forget that the preposition "for" can be about a basis without the words "in

104

order", but if we do use the words "in order" (meaning the idea of an ability), then the preposition "for" can only be a basis.

7) "to" + -ing form of verbs

I'm close to finishing the project. We know that if we use a verb after the preposition "to", the verb is normally not conjugated. We've seen many different examples of this: "want to go", "in order to cut", etc... However, there are rare cases in which we don't use the basic form of the verb. Instead, we use the "-ing" form (the continuous or progressive form). This is one point that confuses and annoys many English learners, but there's a very simple and logical reason why this happens.

First, remember that earlier I told you that the verb itself is actually just the word without the preposition "to". In other words, the verb isn't "to see", it's "see". We use the preposition "to" so that we can point to the verb, and these two words together are what we call the infinitive/basic form of the verb. We also know that we have to use the "-ing" form of a verb after a preposition, except when we use the word "to" before the verb. Lastly, remember that we have the idea of "chunks", which are words that go together like one big word or idea (not collocations, which are chunks of words that we often use together). Let's put all (of) these ideas together.

In the example sentence, "I'm close to finishing the project", is the word "to" attached to the verb or is it attached to the word "close"? "Close to" is usually a chunk. Also notice the verb "to be" ("I'm") before the word "close". If we remove the words "close to", we get: "I'm finishing the project". But if we only remove the word "close", we get: "I'm to finishing the project". It doesn't make sense and there's no reason to use the word "to" here. So we know that "close to" is a chunk. If "close to" is a chunk, that means that the word "to" is not attached to the verb, so we have to use the "-ing" form of the verb, which is what we always do after a preposition (in this case, "to" actually is a preposition and not a special linking word). So, we have "close to" + "finishing".

105

But notice that we can also say, "I'm too close to see", for example. You might say this if you need glasses (in order) to see things that are really close to you, but you can easily see things that are farther away. In this sentence, we have the words "close", "to", and "see". The question is: is the word "to" attached to the word "close" or is it attached to the verb "to see"? Obviously, it's attached to the verb or we would use the "-ing" form of the verb ("seeing"). But why? Simple. Remember that native speakers usually just say "to" instead of "in order to". And that's exactly what's happening in this case. The full sentence is: "I'm too close in order to see". In this specific case, I don't think a native speaker would ever say the words "in order" because it sounds a little weird, but the meaning of "in order" is still there in the background. Notice that at the beginning of this paragraph, I said, "… you need glasses (in order) to see".

In this sentence, the preposition "to" does point to the verb, but in a different way. For example, if you say, "I'm close to the store", it means that your current location is near the location of the store. When we say, "I'm close to finishing the project", it works exactly the same way, except that now we're talking about 1) time and 2) a verb. That's why the verb "to be" that's before the word "close" is so important. When I say this sentence, I'm saying it in the present moment (now). There's only a short amount of time between now and the point in time when the project will be finished. In other words, just like the preposition "to" can point to a specific hour (9:00), it can also point to the specific time/moment when an action will be completed. So the preposition "to" in this case isn't pointing to the verb as the end point, it's pointing to that moment in time, but we use a verb because something will happen at that moment. This also proves the idea that the word "to" usually makes the verb itself into an end point ("to do", "to finish", "to see"), and that's the reason why we make the infinitive with the word "to".

I'm used to speaking English. This example sentence is almost the same as the previous one. The big difference here is that we're saying "used to" instead of "close to". In this case, "used to" means "accustomed to". In other words, it's something that's normal for you. For example, if you study English everyday, then you're used to/accustomed to studying English.

Again, notice that in the example sentence we have the verb "to be" ("I'm") before the word "used". If we remove the words "used to", we get: "I'm speaking English". In the previous example, the preposition "to" was pointing to a moment in the near future. In this example, the preposition "to" is pointing to the current, normal state of things. In other words, it's pointing to the things that are normal for you now.

Like the previous example sentence, we can use the infinitive form: "I used to speak English". This sentence means that in the past, I regularly spoke English. This is similar to the past continuous ("I was speaking"), but we're not talking about just one time. Notice that we're not using the verb "to be". This means that the word "used" is the first verb just like in "want to do", "need to do", etc... The word "used" in this case is actually the past tense form of the verb "to use", but we're using it in a special way. In the previous example sentence, we saw that the words "in order" were in the background. In this case, they're not. That would be something like, "I used my phone (in order) to speak English", which is the normal way that we use the verb "to use" in the past tense. Remember, when we say, "I'm used to speaking English", the verb "to use" works the same way as "want to", "need to", etc...

Also notice that the word "used" in the sentence, "I'm used to speaking English" is the past participle of the verb "to use" and not the past tense → "use" (present), "used" (past), "used" (past participle); for example, "I have already used all of the paper (so there's none left)". This is another reason why "used to do" and "to be used to doing" are different and use different forms of the verb after the word "to".

D) Some verbs that often use the preposition "to"

Respond to	Reply to	Go to
Give to	Agree to	Say (something) to (someone)
Need to	Have to	Want to

E) **Phrasal Verbs.** Look up each phrasal verb and try to understand how the logic of the word "to" applies. Remember, a phrasal verb is basically a preposition put into action by a verb.

Note: The preposition "to" is not often used directly in phrasal verbs. Remember, the preposition "to" simply points to an end point. Usually, you'll see it used as a "connector" between some phrasal verbs and their object, or as compounds with the prepositions "on" (onto) and "in" (into).

Your total comes out to *$150*. The phrasal verb "come out" has different meanings depending on the context. In this case, it means the total cost. You can simply say, "Your total is $150". Because we're using the verb "to come", we have an abstract form of movement, so we add the preposition "to". You can also say, "Your total comes to $150" because we like to add some prepositions even when we don't need them, particularly the prepositions "up" and "out". We can use "come out" in this case because we're in the process of adding all the items and the result (what comes out of that process) is a cost of $150.

For example, let's say that we have three items. The first costs $70, the second costs $50, and the third costs $30. First, we add the first item. The total (which is the end point) is currently $70. Then, we add the second item and add $50 TO the $70, which makes the current total $120 (which is the new end point). Then we add the third item which costs $30. This $30 is added to the $120, which makes a total of $150. After we add each item, the total (end point) changes to a new total (a new end point).

This is exactly like saying, "I went to the beach, then I went to the park, and then I went to the store", except that we're talking about money in this case, so each end point is added together. When all the items are added, we get a final total (in this case, $150). So, when we say that the total comes out to $150, "$150" is the official end point.

I'm looking forward to *my vacation*. Literally, "look forward" means that you are looking directly in front of you. In this case, we aren't using it literally. We're talking about a point in time when something will happen and it's something that I want. Let's say that I'll go on vacation in the summer and it's currently April. So, I "look forward" to the point in time when I'll be going on vacation. It's like saying, "I want to go on vacation", but the vacation is already planned and I'm anticipating it. In the example sentence, "vacation" is the end point of my desire, which will happen at a point in the future.

My younger brother looks up to *me*. You can literally "look up" at someone (not a phrasal verb) if they're a lot taller than you or you're physically in a lower position, but again, that's not what we mean here. The phrasal verb gives us a new meaning, which is "to see someone as a role model". The word "me" is the end point because I'm the role model. But why do we use the preposition "up"? We've seen this before when we talked about the phrasal verb "to look down on". Remember that it's possible to "put someone on a pedestal" in your mind, which means that you see that person as perfect or a lot better than other people. Well, a role model is someone that who is kind of on a pedestal, but it's a little different here. Specifically, "role model" means a person you can try to be so that you can learn and become better at something. In this case, I'm the role model and my younger brother looks to me for guidance about how he should handle life. So because I'm older, I'm kind of at a "higher point" that my younger brother wants to reach. You can also add more of the platform idea: the role model is on a kind of abstract platform and the other person wants to be like the role model, so they

109

want to get on that platform. As I said before, the prepositions "to", "on", and "up" have a special connection.

After a long break, I finally got back into *learning English.* This sentence means that I started studying English again after not studying for a long time. The preposition "in" is a container. The process ("-ing") of an action (verb) can be a type of abstract container. This sentence is one of the few cases where we need to use the preposition "into" (usually, we can reduce "into" to just "in" and the preposition "to" is implied by the context). The point here is that "in" + "to" shows movement from being outside of something and moving to the inside of something, like a box ("Put the book in(to) the box."). This example is a little special because we have to combine the logic of the prepositions "in" and "to". Why? Because the full preposition is "into", so the logic of both are added together. "Learning English" is the process, which means that it's the container. For example, "In learning a language, you have to practice a lot". "In learning" is actually short for "in the process of learning", so a process can be a container.

And the preposition "to"? Well, you were learning English, so you were inside that container. Then you stopped, so you got out of the container (stopped the process). Then you returned and started again, which means that you "got back into" the container (got into the container again → started the process of learning again). The process of learning English is the end point. This is just like when we say, "Put the book in(to) the box". The word "box" is the end point. Just remember that when we say "into", we're saying "in" + "to", which means "container" + "end point", so the container and the end point are the same.

110

F) Examples of idioms that use the preposition "to", with detailed explanations.

We're in debt up to our eyeballs. This idiom means that you have a LOT of debt. The preposition "to" in this sentence works the same as in the sentence, "The snow was piled to the roof". The words "our eyeballs" is the end point.

There's a method to my madness. If there's a method, it means that there's a structure. "Madness" in this sentence means that I seem to be doing something in a random, unstructured, and/or illogical way. So, there's a structure, but you don't see it yet. The preposition "to" in this sentence is used the same as in the phrase "the answer to his question".

My brother and I don't see eye to eye. When two people disagree on one or more things, you can say that they don't see eye to eye. "Eye" to "eye" implies being at the same level or height, but we don't mean this literally. It means how you look at things (your perspective and beliefs), so we're not talking about literal eyes. If my "eye" doesn't match his "eye" (in other words, if my perspective/belief doesn't match his perspective/belief), then we disagree. In the example sentence, the end point is the word "eye". However, because we're not talking about a literal eye, the end point is actually my perspective/belief. Because we're talking about two perspectives, we're saying that they don't match, so this is similar to "the answer to his question" if we say, "That's not the answer to his question".

You have to stick to what you believe is right. This sentence means, "You have to do what you believe is morally correct", but there's a little extra meaning here. The verb "to stick" is hard to define in a simple way. The most basic idea of the verb "to stick" is like tape that you use to seal a box. In the context of the example sentence, you stay on something or with something and don't move from that spot or away from that thing. Let's say that I believe that it's "right" (morally correct) to hold the door open for

111

other people. But my friend thinks that that idea is stupid and that I shouldn't do it. The example sentence comes from a third person saying that I shouldn't change my behavior just because my friend thinks that it's stupid. I have to "stick" to my belief and not change. So even if my friend thinks that holding the door open for other people is stupid, I do it anyway because I believe that it's right. The end point is the phrase "what you believe is right", which is a chunk, so it's like one whole unit. You are sticking yourself (noun 1) to your belief (noun 2). This is like saying, "Stick the tape to the box." OR you can look at it as sticking your actions (verbs) to your belief (noun).

IN

A) Example Sentences. Remember to follow the instructions in section A from previous prepositions.

1)

My birthday is in May.
My family goes on vacation in the summer.
I was born in 1990.
I don't like to get up early in the morning.
"Do you know this man?" (shows a picture) "I've never seen him in my life."
I'll be home in two days.
In time, you will understand.
I arrived at the airport in time.

What does the word "in" mean in this group?

2)

Put it in the box.
I live in New York.
I'm sitting in my car.
There's a sign (that's hanging) in the window.
Who's the old man (that's) in that picture?
Tom punched Alex in the face.

What does the word "in" mean in this group?

3)

Does this bike come in green?
Please sit in a circle. (does NOT mean "inside")
We waited in line for the store to open.
This shirt comes in small, medium, and large.
They didn't have the pants in my size.

What does the word "in" mean in this group?

4)

In learning a language, it's important to study.
You have to plan carefully in creating a business.
I ran too fast. In doing so, I tripped.
We might see him there, in which case he can join us.

What does the word "in" mean in this group?

5)

Do you believe in fairies?
I'm not interested in sports.

What does the word "in" mean in this group?

6) Miscellaneous

Can we speak in private?
I'm in love!
Why is he in a bad mood?
I work in marketing.
Can we speak in English, please?
The chance of seeing him here is one in a million.
Fast food isn't rich in nutrients.

B) The Logic

Key Idea(s): a container

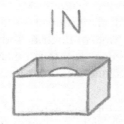

"in" is a one-way preposition

Explanation of the logic: The preposition "in" is generally very simple: it describes a container of some kind. However, the container is often abstract. It can be time ("in May"), space ("in New York"), an action (process) that might "contain" another action ("In learning English, ..."), or a concept, a person, or even an emotion ("I'm not interested in sports."/"I believe in you."/"He's in a bad mood."). Lastly, "color/shape/size" is a special group of "containers".We'll see many different, specific examples that show how the preposition "in" is about a "container".

Note that if the context is clear, you can usually use the preposition "in" instead of the prepositions "into" or "inside". For example, "The dog jumped into the lake." If we say, "The dog jumped in the lake", that actually means "The dog jumped while it was in the water". In other words, the dog is in the water and then jumps, which is impossible. Because it's impossible, you can simply use the preposition "in" and the context makes it clear that you mean "into".

Etymology notes: The preposition "in" has a very long history. Old English had two different prepositions: 1) "in", which meant what we now use as "in", "into", "upon", "on", "at",

115

"among", "about", and "during", depending on the context; 2) "inne", which meant "within" and "inside". What makes things worse is that in Middle English, "in" and "inne" were combined into one word: the preposition that we know now as "in". Over time, many of the meanings of the Old English "in" were separated into different prepositions. All (of) this information is important because of all the different surface meanings that the preposition "in" has in Modern English. Today, we can clearly say that "in" is "in", but it does still touch many other prepositions, depending on the context and the surface meaning. 6

Now, go back to the example sentences and try to apply the logic. Ask yourself: "How is 'in' talking about a container?"

C) Detailed Explanations of the Example Sentences.

1) *a period ("container") of time*

My birthday is in May. As we know, when talking about time and space, it's very common to use the preposition "at" for something specific (at 9:00), the preposition "on" for something a little less specific/bigger (on Monday), and the preposition "in" for anything bigger/less specific than that. Here, we use "in May" because a month is such a large amount of time that it "contains" everything that's inside (of) it.

ALTERNATIVES: "My birthday is May 5th." If you say the month AND the day, we don't use any prepositions. Why? Because we normally use the preposition "in" with months, but the preposition "on" with days. Here we have both. It's not necessary to say, "My birthday is in May on the 5th." That's too long and we don't like it. However, because the day is more specific, it is possible to say, "My birthday is on May 5th" or "My birthday is on the 5th of May".

116

My family goes on vacation in the summer. A season is an even larger container than a month, so we still use the preposition "in".

ALTERNATIVES: "My family goes on vacation every summer." The preposition "in" doesn't mean "every". However, in this specific context, "every" is the intended surface meaning. We don't say "in the summers", so the other way to say this is "every summer". If we want to talk about one specific vacation that will happen this summer, we say, "My family is going on vacation in the summer" or "My family is going on vacation this summer". So, in this context, the exact meaning of the preposition "in" depends on other parts of the sentence.

I was born in 1990. A year is an even larger container than a season, so we still use the preposition "in".

ALTERNATIVES: Just like with the words "May 5th", we can get more specific: "I was born May 5th, 1990." The preposition is not needed. However, it is possible to say, "I was born on May 5th, 1990" or "I was born on the 5th of May, 1990". Notice that we use a comma before the year instead of the preposition "in". That's simply the structure we use.

I don't like to get up early in the morning. And this one? Earlier, I said that we use "on Monday", but the morning is a shorter period of time than a day. So why do we use the preposition "in"? Simple. A day only has 24 hours, but the

117

morning is a large piece of those 24 hours, so it's like a special container. Remember, prepositions are relative to/dependent on a specific context. A day has three containers: the morning, the afternoon, and the evening. However, we usually say "at night". There's a good reason for this, which we'll discuss in the The Logic of the Preposition "at".

ALTERNATIVES: You can simply say, "I don't like to get up early". Most people get up in the morning, so it's implied.

"Do you know this man?" (shows a picture) "I've never seen him in my life." When you've never experienced something and say "in my life", you're talking about your entire life. The amount of time that you've lived is the "container" of all (of) your experiences.

ALTERNATIVES: "I've never seen him before." We can use the preposition "before" because we're saying "before now". You see a picture of the man, so now you've seen him, but not in real life.

I'll be home in two days. This sentence is slightly different than the others. It might seem very confusing on the surface because the meaning is: "I'll be home the day after tomorrow". When we talk about "tomorrow", that's one day, so "the day after tomorrow" is two days from today. I'll arrive on that day. This does <u>not</u> mean that I will arrive sometime inside that period of time. If you want to talk about something happening inside that period of time, we say "within two days", which means you might be home sooner (maybe tomorrow), but not later than the day after tomorrow). Why do we use the preposition "in" if it happens "on" that day? Good question. It's because we're thinking of it as a period of time, which is a container, not a surface/platform. This makes more sense if we increase the amount of time: "I'll be home in a week." → we can assume this means "in 7 days", but it might be a little more or less; "I'll be home in a month." → here, we have no idea exactly when I'll arrive, but it's some time around 30 days.

118

As you can see, it makes more sense to think of this as a period of time (container) than a surface/platform.

ALTERNATIVES: "I'll be home the day after tomorrow." You might notice that we don't use the preposition "on" here. This is a little detail that often confuses English learners. Most of the time, we use the preposition "on" with days of the week and days of the month (though it's possible to omit it sometimes). However, there's a special thing that happens when we use specifying words like "this", "that", "next", "last", etc... We don't say "I saw him on last Monday". We say, "I saw him last Monday". For some reason, these words usually replace the preposition. This is a special grammar rule.

"I'll be home in a couple (of) days". Because the word "couple" means "two", we can say it this way, too.

In time, you will understand. When we say "in time", we mean that the thing that we're talking about will happen at some unknown point in the future, or that it will progress over time. In this case, you don't understand something now, but in the future, you will. The phrases "in time" and "in the future" aren't exactly the same, but in this context they're close enough.

ALTERNATIVES: "In the future, you'll understand." We can also say it this way. The biggest difference here is that "in the future" doesn't include the idea of "progress over time".

"Eventually, you'll understand."

"At some point, you'll understand". In this context, the phrase "at some point" implies "in the future".

I arrived at the airport in time. Earlier, we saw the sentence, "I arrived at the airport on time", and we know that it means "not late". So what does the phrase "in time" mean? It means "not too late". There's something that's going to happen, and if I don't arrive "in time", then that thing will happen and there will be a negative result. Let's say that the plane is supposed to leave at 5:00 PM (17:00). If it leaves at that time, then it leaves "on time". If there's some problem that causes it not to leave at 5, then it doesn't leave "on time". Also, if the plane leaves on time, I have to be there on time so that I can get on the plane ("on time" for me would probably be 4:30 or sometime earlier because I need enough time to do everything that I need to do before getting on the plane). That's the phrase "on time".

Now let's say that the plane is leaving at 5 and right now it's 4:50, but I'm not at the airport yet. So I have to rush and do everything as fast as possible (in order) to get on the plane before it leaves. If I do everything I need to do and get on the plane, then I arrived "in time". Remember, "in time" means "not too late". In other words, I didn't arrive too late because I was able to get on the plane before it left. I arrived later than I wanted to (which was 4:30), but I still had enough time to get on the plane.

Another example: Let's say that your girlfriend or boyfriend recently broke up with you so that they can move to Germany for work. You refused to tell them goodbye because you think that they're making a stupid decision that you don't support and you're mad at them. But 30 minutes before the plane leaves, you feel that you have to stop them and tell them that they should stay with you and not move to Germany. You try to call them, but their phone is dead. So you rush to the airport and try to find them. If you go to where their plane is and the plane is already gone, you're too late, so you didn't arrive in time. If you go to where their plane is and they haven't gotten on the plane yet, then you're not too late, meaning that you arrived in time.

Ok, but how exactly does the logic of the preposition "in" work here? Why do we use that preposition and not some other preposition? We know that the preposition "in" is about a container and the phrase "in time" means "not too late". So, there's a period of time (which is a container) before something happens. In this case, it's an airplane leaving. If you arrive in the period of time before the plane leaves, then you are "in time", meaning that you are inside the period of time when it's not yet too late.

2) *"containers" of space (sometimes very abstract)*

Put it in the box. This is the easiest example and you probably already know it. Obviously, a box is a literal container.

ALTERNATIVES: "Put it into the box."

I live in New York. This is another one that's very easy, but why do we use the preposition "in"? Remember that we have a special connection here: very specific ("at 123 Main Street"), less specific/bigger ("on Main Street"), and even less specific/bigger ("in New York"). A city is so large that you are inside (of) it, so it's a large and abstract "container".

I'm sitting in my car. I mentioned before that for most forms of transportation, we use the preposition "on". This is because you are either physically on top of something (a horse, a bike, etc…), or you're on a platform that has the purpose of transporting many people (bus, boat, train, plane). But when we talk about cars and trucks, these are more like boxes or containers for personal use and they only transport a small number of people. Compared to a horse or a bike, a car has walls and you're surrounded by the walls, so it makes sense to use "in". Compared to buses and trains, which also have walls like a container, a car or truck isn't designed to be a large platform that

121

can carry many people. They're smaller, personal vehicles, so we think of them as containers.

Why do we use the preposition "on" for one and the preposition "in" for the other? The function. Buses are <u>designed</u> to transport many people, so a bus is a platform with the specific purpose of transporting many people. Although a bus has walls and we can logically look at it as a large "container", we use the preposition "on" because of its function (platform). This is a perfect example of something that's generally logical, but English applies the logic in a certain way, so we use the preposition "on" instead of the preposition "in".

To further prove this point, let's look at a strange example. Some people have started buying small buses (in order) to convert them into personal living spaces. If you're inside one of these buses, we don't usually say that you're on the bus, we say that you're in the bus. Why? The function. The purpose of the bus isn't to transport many people anymore. It's now your personal vehicle, just like a car, and since you're living in it, it's also your "house".

Note: If you say "I'm sitting on my car", it means that you're physically on top of the car.

There's a sign (that's hanging) in the window. This one is a little strange. You might think that we would use the preposition "on". If something is on a window (which is a surface), then you can use "on". For example, let's say that I'm painting the walls and some drops of paint land on the window. Now there's paint <u>on</u> the window. But remember, we want to think of the context and the function of the words. So when and why do we say "in the window"? If you put something in the window, the purpose is to display it. It's something that you want people to see. For example, maybe a business is looking for a new employee, so they put a "Help Wanted" sign in the window. That way, anyone looking for a job will see it and apply for the job. Now, the idea of a "display" can use both the prepositions "on" and "in", depending on what you want to say. If there are items in the window so that they will attract customers, or if there's a precious diamond or painting in a museum, we say that these things are "on display". We use "on" here because a display is like a special platform that has the purpose of making something visible so that people will see it. However, you can also put something "in the display (case)". This is the physical container that holds the items. So, when you hang something in the window, the window is the "display" that "contains" the sign. It's a little abstract in this context. It might help to look at it this way: You put a picture in(to) a picture frame. The purpose of a picture frame is to display the picture. After you put it in the frame, you can then put the picture frame on a table, for example, so that people will see it. Now the picture is "on display", but it's also in the frame. Even if the idea of a platform doesn't seem to work, we can definitely see that this is a "positive state/active state".

ALTERNATIVES: "There's a sign (that's hanging) up in that window." This is another context in which we can add the preposition "up". Why? In most cases, a sign is physically hanging above the window sill (the inside edge at the bottom of the window). However, sometimes a sign is just placed on the window sill and it's not physically hanging. The preposition "up" works in both cases. In the first case, obviously it's hanging, which means that it's in a higher position than the bottom of the window, so it's "up". In the second case, the sign is still above the floor, so we can say that it's "up". In both cases, we have a connection with the idea of "positive/active state". Again, we'll talk about the preposition "up" later, but part of the logic is the connection from a "negative/inactive state" to a "positive/active state". Remember, the sign is "on display", so even if we're using the preposition "in" in this particular sentence, the idea of "on display" is still active in the background.

Who's the old man (that's) in that picture? In this sentence, the logic of the preposition "in" touches the logic of the preposition "of". Do you remember the sentence, "This is a picture of a dog"? We know that the dog is the content of the

123

picture. Another way to say that is: "A dog is in this picture". This is a point where these two prepositions only touch, not overlap. Note that we do not say, "Who's the old man of that picture?" It seems ok, it doesn't sound too bad, and the logic works (more or less), but it's not what we say. This is why the prepositions "in" and "of" only touch in this case and do not overlap. Also, notice that we say, "The table is made of wood", but we don't say, "There's wood in the table" because tables and pictures are different things, the context is different, and the functions of the words around them are different. If something is "in" a table, it usually means that there's a drawer that's part of the table and you put that thing in(to) the drawer. But here we're talking about a picture, and a picture is a container that holds images. In fact, a picture is just a frozen moment of time and space that has been captured. If something is "captured" it's in some kind of container. A table is not a container that holds wood; it's made of wood. So a picture is less like a table and more like a box: "What are the contents of the box?" → "What's in(side) the box?" Notice that when we say, "the contents of the box", we mean, "the things that are inside the box", not "what the box is made of". These are two slightly different meanings of the word "content(s)".

An important thing to notice is that a picture is kind of like a window in a way. Something can be in a window and something can be in a picture. However, these aren't exactly the same. For example, you look in(to) or through a window, but you look at a picture. The reason the window idea is important is because many English learners try to say, "Who's the old man (that's) on that picture?" If we use the preposition "on" when talking about pictures, it means that something is physically on top of the surface of the picture. For example, if I accidentally spill some paint and it lands on the picture, then there's paint on the picture. The paint isn't in the picture, it's physically on the surface.

Tom punched Alex in the face. Lastly, we also use the preposition "in" with body parts. We saw before that you can use the preposition "on" to describe being hit by something: "The ball hit me on my chest". When there's more force, we use "in": "The ball hit me in the chest". If we want to use the preposition "in" with this sentence, we'll have to change the type of ball. A ping-pong ball is so small and light that it can't hit someone with a lot of force. But let's say we have a soccer ball. Someone throws the soccer ball really hard and it hits you in the chest.

There are certain verbs that imply force, like the verb "to punch". So, you can be hit ON the chest (less force), you can be hit IN the chest (more force), or you can be punched IN the chest ("punch" is just a more specific word for "hit"). But you cannot be punched ON the chest because the verb "to punch" implies more force. The reason that we use the preposition "in" (in order) to show more force is because the thing that gets hit goes farther inward. For example, if I hit you in the arm, your arm will be pushed inward toward your body, but if I hit you on the arm, your arm doesn't do much because the hit is softer (less force). This is especially true when we talk about the stomach and the eyes, which can go be pushed inward more easily. It's particularly common to use the preposition "in" with: stomach, face, nose, ears, eyes, mouth, lip, head. In other words, the stomach and any part of the head.

Just remember: it depends on how much force there is, and some verbs will more often or always use "in" because they're naturally more forceful ("to punch" and "to kick", for example), while other verbs can use either more force or less force (hit).

3) *properties of a container (color/shape/size)*

This group is special and abstract, but we can still clearly see the idea of a container. The difference with this group is that instead of talking about the container itself, we're talking about the color, shape, and/or size of the container. This can sometimes make things a little weird. Remember when I said that the preposition "in" likes to get into trouble and go places that it probably doesn't belong? Some of the sentences that are in this group are part of the reason.

Does this bike come in green? This sentence means: "Is this bike available in green?" In other words, there's a specific bike that I want, but I don't like the color of it, so I want to know if the store has the same bike, but one that's green. Green is the color of the container, not the container itself. The container is the paint. It might seem weird to think of paint as a container, but when you paint a bike, the paint completely covers most of the bike, so it's like you're wrapping it in some material. It's like saying, "Does this bike come in green paint?", but we omit the word "paint" because it's implied.

A very similar example is: "She's dressed in green". When we say this, we're talking about what color her clothes are, just like the color of the paint. Green is the color of the container (the clothes). So, you can also say, "She's dressed in green clothes", for example.

We don't usually think of clothes as "containers". Usually, we say that clothes are "on" your body because we think of your body as a surface that your clothes go on top of, but clothes do go around the parts of your body, so you're also wrapped "in" the clothes after you put them on. So you can look at clothes in two ways: as containers that go around your body, or as things that you put on the surface of your body. In English, both of these perspectives work, but it depends on the specific

126

context. Also, the preposition "on" is much more common. A couple (of) more examples: "The woman in the red dress is pretty" and "I don't like the man in the black suit".

Actually, after you put a piece of clothing on, the clothing is on the surface of your body and you're inside (of) the clothing at the same time. Let's look at this example: "You look good in that hat!" This sentence doesn't use a color, but we can still use the "in" idea in this case because we can look at it both ways. So we're looking at the hat like a container for your head because it's covering your head.

An interesting note: When we talk about the paint on the bike, we use the preposition "on": "The paint (that's) on this bike is green". This is because we put the paint on the surface of the bike. After the paint is on, we say that the bike is "in" green. So this works exactly like clothing and we can look at it both ways.

ALTERNATIVES: "Is this bike available in green?"

"Do you have this bike in green?"

Please sit in a circle. (does NOT mean "inside") As it says, this sentence does not mean "inside" a circle. Let's say there's a classroom of ten kids. The teacher tells the kids, "Please sit in a circle". The teacher wants the kids to sit next to each other in a way that makes the shape of a circle (see the picture that's below). If you want to talk about sitting inside of a circle that is drawn on the floor, for example, we say, "Please sit inside (of) the circle" (or "a circle" if there's more than one circle). Notice that when we use the preposition "inside", we also use the word "of", but we can omit it (it's still there in the background). We're talking about the inside part of the circle (remember, "of" = part or content), but if we use the preposition "in", we never say, "Please sit in of a circle" because it doesn't make any sense. So, the sentence, "Please sit in a circle" means: sit in a way that makes the shape of a circle. The sentence, "Please sit inside (of) a circle" means: there's a circle and I want you to sit inside of it. However, as I mentioned earlier, if the context is very clear, such

127

as if you can see that there are circles drawn on the floor, you can say, "Please sit in a circle" and it means "inside" because when the context is very clear, we usually reduce the prepositions "inside" and "into" to the preposition "in" because it's shorter and easier.

But how does the logic of the preposition "in" work in the example sentence? We have a phrase: "in the shape of something" or "in the form of something". So, we're actually talking about the shape of the container, not the container itself. For example, a box is usually square. So, a box is a container that's in the shape of a square. A balloon is a container that you put air into, but balloons are usually round. So, a balloon is a container that's in the shape of a circle. When we say "sit in a circle", we're just omitting the words "the shape of", so the complete phrase is: "sit in the shape of a circle".

So, when the people sit in a way that creates the shape of a circle, they're bodies create the circle, which means they create the "container", which contains the space inside (of) the circle. In other words, the people are creating the shape of the container. If they sit in a way that makes the shape of a square, then they're creating a square-shaped container.

ALTERNATIVES: "Please sit in the shape of a circle." It's possible to say the complete phrase, but we usually don't.

"Please form a circle." "Please make a circle." Both of these are possible because of the context. If the context is different, then the

128

meaning changes a little. For example, if you have a pen and a piece of paper and I tell you, "Please make a circle", I want to you to draw a circle on the paper.

We waited in line for the store to open. The phrase "in line" means that there are some people and they all stand behind each other one person at a time. So I stand behind Tom, Tom stands behind Alex, Alex stand behind Lena, etc... This creates a line, like if you draw a straight line on a piece of paper, but the line is made of people who are standing. If you're "in line", or in some cases "in a line", the outline of the line is the shape of the container. This is strange because a line isn't a shape, but it is a basic part of creating shapes, so we extend the idea to lines.

This shirt comes in small, medium, and large. Now it's time for sizes. Just like colors and shapes, we're not talking about the container itself (the shirt). We're talking about the size of the container (the size of the shirt). To make this easier, imagine two brown boxes. You have a small, square, brown box and a large, square, brown box. Remember, a box is a container. The **color** of both containers is brown. The **shape** of both containers is square. The **size** of one container is small and the **size** of the other container is large. If you could magically make the small box larger, you would be changing the size of the container. So, instead of changing the color (brown → green, for example) or the shape (square → circle, for example), you're changing the size (small → large). These are all properties of the container.

Earlier, we saw the sentence, "Does this shirt come in green?" When we say that a shirt comes in a certain size, we're simply talking about the size of the container instead of the color of the container itself. The full sentence is: "This shirt comes in sizes small, medium, and large". In other words, it comes in a small size, a medium size, and a large size. We simply omit the word "size" (and because the noun ("size") is gone, we also omit the article "a").

ALTERNATIVES: "This shirt's available in small, medium, and large."

"We have this shirt in small, medium, and large."

They didn't have the pants in my size. I included this sentence to give you another example of how the logic is applied. There's a pair of pants that's available in different sizes. Let's say "my size" is 30. This sentence is saying that the pair of pants wasn't available in size 30, but there were other sizes, maybe 28, 32, etc... "Pants" is the container. The size of the container (the size of the pants) in this context = whatever "my size" is (30).

ALTERNATIVES: "My size wasn't available."

4) *actions/verbs as containers (processes)*

Many times, this happens with two actions. The process of one action is the container for the other action. Or one action could be the basis for the other action.

In learning a language, it's important to study. Here we have two actions/verbs: 1) to learn, and 2) to study. So, first, we have "learning a language". That's a process, which is why we use the continuous/progressive form (the "-ing" ending of the verb). What we're really saying here is "In **the process of** learning a language, ..." You can say it that way, but, like many other times when we use the preposition "in", we can drop the phrase "the process of". Next, we have the verb/action "to study". Specifically: "it is important to study". So, when is it important to study? While you're in the process learning a language. Let's say you're driving a car. Would you say, "In driving a car, it's important to study"? Of course not. You only study if we're talking about the process of learning something. So the second action/verb happens during the process of the first action/verb.

Note that this isn't the same as talking about two actions that happen at the same time. I can say, "I read a book while my brother watches TV". Or, if we're talking about the actions happening, "I'm reading a book while/and my brother's watching TV." We can also mix them: "I read a book while/when my brother's watching TV". What's the difference between these sentences and the example sentence? In these sentences, the actions happen at the same time, but they're not connected. In the example sentence, the second action (study) happens INSIDE the process of the first action (learning). This means that the preposition "in" is talking about a container, which is "(the process of) learning a language".

ALTERNATIVES: "When (you're) learning a language, it's important to study." We can use the word "when" instead of the preposition "in". Because we're talking about a process, the preposition "in" has the surface meaning of "during". Note that we don't use the preposition "during" in this case because these two prepositions usually only touch. In this context, we can also use the word "when". If we do, then "you are" (general "you" = "one") is implied. You can say it if you want, but it's not necessary. Notice that we don't say "you are" with the preposition "in" in this context.

"If you want to learn a language, it's important to study."/"If you want to learn a language, you have to study." These two are just more ways to say the same thing with a slightly different structure.

"You can't learn a language if you don't study."/"You can't learn a language unless you study." At least in this context, these

131

sentences mean the same thing, but the structure is very different then the other alternatives. As you can see, there are many possible ways to express this idea.

You have to plan carefully in creating a business. Notice in the previous sentence that there was a comma (,). This is because the standard word order was broken (which is a very common use of the comma). It's still grammatically correct and natural, just in a different order. This new sentence uses the standard word order, so we don't use a comma. However, the logic is still the same. The container is "creating a business". In the process of creating a business, what happens? You have to plan carefully. So, "to plan carefully" happens inside the process of the "creating a business".

ALTERNATIVES: "You have to plan carefully when creating a business."

"You have to plan carefully if you want to create a business."

"Unless you plan carefully, you can't create a successful business."/"If you don't plan carefully, you can't create a successful business." In this case, you can still create a business even if you don't plan carefully, so I added the word "successful".

I ran too fast. In doing so, I tripped. In this sentence, we're doing something a little different. It's ok to say, "In running too fast, I tripped". We're more likely to say, "Because I was running too fast, I tripped" or something similar, where we use running as a reason instead of a container. In the example sentence, the phrase "in doing so" refers back to the phrase "in running too fast" and replaces it. This is exactly like when we say "I like the red car, but I also like the blue one", where the word "one" replaces the word "car". It's very easy to see how the second action (tripping) happens in the process of the first action (running).

ALTERNATIVES: "I was running too fast and tripped." "Because I was running too fast, I tripped."

132

We might see him there, in which case he can join us. This sentence is different than the others. In the previous examples, the process of one action was the container for another action. In this example, The first action is the basis of the other action. We use the phrase "in which case" to point back to the previous action and replace it so that we don't have to say it again. So, this is the same as saying, "If we see him there, he can join us". The word "if" means a hypothetical situation. Obviously, if we don't see him there, he can't join us. But if we <u>do</u> see him, then the verb "to see" is the basis which contains the action "join".

ALTERNATIVES: "If we see him there, he can join us." "We might see him there. If we do, he can join us."

5) *Concepts/ideas/people as containers (for beliefs, interests, and opinions)*

Do you believe in fairies? This sentence means: "Do you believe that fairies exist?" We often use the preposition "in" when talking about beliefs because the thing that you believe in is like an abstract container. It's the same with the word "trust". Just think of whatever you believe or trust as a container. You put your belief or trust into that container. Some other examples: I believe in you, I believe in God, I don't believe in his abilities (since it's negative, you DON'T put your belief into that container), I trust in his abilities, I trust in mathematics, etc… Note, however, that there are cases where we can omit the preposition "in" or we don't use it at all. Sometimes we do this because it makes a slight difference in meaning, but sometimes it's because we can't omit it. Unfortunately, this is just something you have to get used to. Generally, using "in" will be fine, though it is more commonly used with the words "believe" and "belief" than the word "trust".

There's another way to look at this sentence. The preposition "in" is a one-way preposition, but there are a few rare cases where it goes the other direction. For this entire group, you can think of it two ways: 1) You put your belief, interest, or opinion

133

(including "trust") into something and that thing is the container, or 2) You put the thing into the container of "belief", "interest", or "opinion". In that case, instead of "belief" → "fairies", we have ""belief" ← "fairies". Imagine you have three boxes. One is labeled "beliefs". Do you believe that fairies exist? If you do, then you put the idea that fairies exist into the box labeled "beliefs". If you don't believe that fairies exist, then you don't put it into that box.

ALTERNATIVES: "Do you believe that fairies exist?"

I'm not interested in sports. This is another example of a concept or idea as a container. If you have an interest, you put your interest into that thing, or you put that thing into the box labeled "interests".

ALTERNATIVES: "I have no interest in sports." Notice that an interest is something that you can "have", like a box.

"I don't like sports." This sentence doesn't mean exactly the same thing, but if you don't like sports, then you're not interested in sports, so this sentence works as an alternative.

6) *Miscellaneous*

Unfortunately, we have a miscellaneous group because the preposition "in" has so many uses and some of them don't fit into clear groups.

Can we speak in private? You can do something "in private" or "in public". These are two opposite containers. If you talk "in private", it means that you are alone with one or more people that you want to talk to and you don't want anyone else to hear. So, if your friend is talking to someone and you want to talk to your friend without that other person hearing what you say, you ask your friend, "Can we talk in private?" "In public" means a place where people can hear and see you. An example of "in public"

134

would be: "You're not allowed to be naked (when you're) in public."

ALTERNATIVES: "Can we speak privately?" We can also use the adverb "privately" to express the same idea.

"Can we speak alone?" This one is less common, but it works.

I'm in love! Why do we say "in love"? Well, we often use the preposition "in" when we talk about emotions as nouns. However, this doesn't always work. For example, we don't say, "I'm in anger"; we simply say, "I'm angry", using the adjective instead of the noun. However, you can say something like, "I did in anger", though in this case it's more common to say, "I did it out of anger". You might be confused by that, but it makes perfect sense. If you're "in anger" and you do something because you're angry, then the action comes out of that container called "anger".

Ok, so why do we say "in love"? You can't be "in" an adjective (though there might be a couple of exceptions). However, you *can* be inside a noun. "I'm in the building", "I'm in Paris", "It's in the box", etc… So, you can be "in love", meaning that you're deeply and romantically attached to someone, so this container is very abstract. If you add the person who you're talking about, we use the preposition "with": "I'm in love with Tom". So, it's like you and Tom are together in the same container (love). Tom might not feel the same, but you want him to be in the same container with you. If you're both in the container, then we say, "We're in love (with each other)".

Also note that we have a very common phrase: "to fall in love (with someone)". We don't say "into love", but it's implied. The only way that you can "fall" in(to) love is if "love" is a container. This doesn't work for all emotions, but it's more evidence that the preposition "in" is about a container in this case.

Why is he in a bad mood? The word "mood" refers to how someone is generally feeling emotionally. Instead of a specific emotion, it's how you feel in general over a period of time. There

135

are different moods that you can have, but usually we use either "good mood" or "bad mood". A good mood means you generally feel happy, positive, confident, etc... A bad mood generally means the opposite: angry, negative, agitated, etc... Often, a "bad mood" means angry. Either way, you (or your mind) are "inside" that mood. Think of it like a cloud around your body or your mind that creates an abstract container.

I work in marketing. Marketing is a profession. A profession is also called a "field of work" or a "line of work". It's not surprising that the preposition that we usually use with the words "field" and "line" is the preposition "in". "The farmers work in the field(s) all day." "I hate waiting in line at the store." (Remember, when talking about the internet, we say "online", not "in line" because the internet is a communications platform.)

So, when talking about your profession, you can say you are "in" a certain profession: "I work in marketing", "I work in finance", "I work in medicine", etc... When you work, you're work is happening inside that field/container. However, this doesn't work with everything. The other option is to simply use the noun: "I'm a marketer", "I'm a banker/broker/etc", "I'm a doctor/nurse". This is what we do for some professions and it's also the more common way to talk about your profession. For example, instead of saying, "I'm in teaching", it's more natural to say "I'm a teacher".

ALTERNATIVES: "I'm a marketer". We usually specify the type of marketing. For example, "telemarketer", which is someone who makes calls to people (in order) to try to sell a product on the phone.

Can we speak in English, please? A language is a container. You can think of it like "can we speak in a certain way", where the word "way" = "English" (or whatever language). However, also notice that we say, "I don't know how to put my feelings into words. (I don't know how to express my feelings/emotions.)" When we talk or write, we are putting our thoughts, emotions, etc... into words. Those words are like containers that carry meaning into the world. It's like you put a letter into an envelope and mail it to friend. Your friend receives the envelope, takes the letter out, and reads it. When you speak, you put meaning into spoken words (sounds). So, if we talk about putting meaning into words and we're talking about the words of a specific language, then in makes sense that you can express meaning in English, in Russian, in Japanese, etc... This is because a language is a certain set of sounds and/or written characters/letters) that meaning is put into so that it can be conveyed to someone else.

An important note: We don't always use the preposition "in" when talking about languages. For example, you can say, "I speak English". This is an ability that you have, just like if you say, "I play the piano". We usually say "in English" when we're talking about two different languages and you want to speak in English, not the other language. In other words, you want to change the container.

The chance of seeing him here is one in a million. When we talk about statistics or chance, we use the preposition "in". For example, we can say, "Three in ten people have blue eyes". This means that if there's a group of ten people, three of them probably have blue eyes. So, the total number (ten) is the container. Inside that container is the number of something that we want to talk about (the number of people with blue eyes, which is three). When we say that the chance of something happening is "one in a million", it means that thing is possible, but very unlikely to happen. Let's say that you have a million beans in a big pile and only one bean is painted red. If you put your hand into the pile and grab one random bean, you probably won't grab the red one.

ALTERNATIVES: "It's highly/very/extremely unlikely that we'll see him here."

"The odds of seeing him here are slim to none." This is an idiom that means exactly the same thing. The word "slim" means "skinny", like a person who doesn't weigh a lot. In this context, the word "slim" means "very small". The word "odds" in this context is another word for "chance(s)".

Fast food isn't rich in nutrients. This one's very abstract. The nutrients are actually "in" the food, meaning that "food" is the container. So why do we say "in nutrients"? When we say "rich", which is an adjective, we're implying "richness", which is a noun. A noun can usually be put into another noun. So, the richness is inside the nutrients (meaning that there are a lot of nutrients), and the nutrients are in the food. Since fast food isn't rich in nutrients, it means there is no "richness" in the nutrients. In other words, there aren't a lot of nutrients in fast food. If you have a lot of money, you're rich (in money). Interestingly, if someone inherits a lot of money from a family member or they win the lottery, we say that that person "has come into a lot of money". If you make a cake that has a lot of sugar, then the cake is rich in sugar (it has a lot of sugar/there's a lot of sugar in it). So, the nutrients are in the food, but we're really talking about the "richness" of the nutrients, or how many nutrients there are.

ALTERNATIVES: "There aren't a lot of nutrients in fast food." "Fast food doesn't have a lot of nutrients."

D) Some verbs that often use the preposition "in"

Bring in	Come in	Put in(to)
Go in(to)	Make into	Look into

138

Jump in	Fall in	

E) **Phrasal Verbs.** Look up each phrasal verb and try to understand how the logic of the word "in" applies. Remember, a phrasal verb is basically a preposition put into action by a verb.

Someone broke in(to my house) and stole my computer last night. We use the verb "to break" because someone who breaks in is not allowed to enter. There's usually a lock, which can be broken, picked, etc…, or someone can come in through a window, for example. Often, there's some sort of "breaking" (lock, window) that happens, but you don't have to literally break something for this phrasal verb to work. It simply means you entered without permission, often with force. You can break into someone's house, office, a cash register, or some other secure location, but notice that if you enter someone's room without permission, for example, you can only use "break in(to)" if the door was locked. Otherwise, we use "to go into" or "to enter". Of course, in a sentence like this, your house, office, or whatever is the container. It's like there's a lock on a box (container) and you break the lock so you can open the box and access what's inside.

These shoes are new. I'm still breaking them in. This is another meaning of "break in". In this case, you're wearing new shoes. The shoes might feel a little uncomfortable. They fit, but they aren't shaped exactly to your feet. Over time, your feet start to make a little indent or impression on the inside of the shoe (especially the bottom) and then they feel comfortable. At this point, the shoes are "broken in" because you "broke" the basic, factory-designed shape (of the container) a little. "To break" might seem like a weird verb to use in this context, but that's what we use. We don't break in clothes, but you can break in anything that you wear which has to fit the shape of your body, or anything which is very new and stiff – for example, a baseball mitt (glove), or the seat in a new car. Basically, the original shape of the "container" is being "broken" or adjusted to your use of that thing.

139

"I'm at the hotel." "Have you checked in yet?" When you stay at a hotel, you have to "check in", which means you go to the front desk. Whether you have a reservation or not doesn't matter. Either way, you get your room key and whatever else you might need. When you check in, you're temporarily putting yourself into a container (the hotel generally; a room specifically) that you can live in. The verb "to check" in this context is because you have to tell the hotel staff that you're there and get the key. It's like you're name is on a list and they put a check mark next to it because you're there.

If we all chip in, we can buy it. "To chip in" means to put some money toward a purchase with other people. For example, you want to buy a really expensive gift for your friend's birthday, but you can't afford it by yourself. So you ask some mutual friends (friends that you and your friend are both friends with) if they want to "chip in" so you can buy the gift. This is different than borrowing money. When you borrow, you have to pay the money back later and the gift is from you. When people chip in, you are all paying for it and the gift comes from everyone, not just you. We use the verb "to chip" because a "chip" is a very small piece of something. Let's say the gift costs $300. You chip in $100, another person chips in $25, another 50$, etc..., until you have a total of $300. The total amount is the "container".

Sorry to drop in so late, but I have to talk to you. "To drop in" is another way to say "to drop by", which we'll see later. Like we saw before, "to drop in" means to visit, usually for a short time. You're coming into someone's house or where they work and you're not planning to stay for very long (this is an abstract meaning of the verb "to drop"). Think of it this way: you drop some money. You wouldn't leave it on the ground. Instead, you would immediately pick it up, which means it only stayed on the ground for a short time. This is why we can use the verb "to drop" in the context of visiting someone for a short time because you're in and out quickly. The length of your visit might last longer than

140

you expect (for example, you might be there for thirty minutes, an hour, or more), but what matters is that you only planned to stay for a short time.

For each question, please fill in the blanks. There are blank spaces (_____ _____) on some kind of form. It could be a test, or maybe a healthcare document, for example. If there are blank spaces, whatever you write is going into the empty space because you are filling it in with information, such as your name, email address, etc... The blank space is like a container, even though it's just a line, because it "holds" the relevant information.

Tom's sick today, so I'm filling in for him. The phrasal verb "to fill in" has another meaning, which is to temporarily take someone's place. This usually happens at work when someone gets sick or has an emergency situation, but it could be for anything. If you're an actor in a play, for example, and you get sick, someone will have to fill in for you so that the show isn't canceled. When we use "to fill in" this way, the sick or absent person's role/job/etc.. is the container and someone else has to get into that container temporarily to perform the actions that are necessary.

The cake looked so good that I couldn't resist. I gave in and ate a piece. "To give in" is almost the same as "to give up", but they're used in slightly different contexts. "Give in" is often short for "give in to temptation", but you can also give in to a person who is trying to get something from you. For example, your brother is begging you for money but he's irresponsible and you know that he won't pay you back. If you give him the money, you "give in" to what he wants instead of standing firm. It's like a cave that collapses. In the example sentence, we're talking about temptation, which is the container. You can also look at yourself as the container because the temptation is inside of you. You're trying to lose weight, but the cake looks so delicious. You can hold onto your strength and not eat the cake (notice that "to hold" is one of the opposites of "to give"), or you can let the strength go

141

and give yourself to the temptation. This phrasal verb is very abstract and the connection to the logic is very weak, so some people might say that it's an exception. It could be, but I don't think so. If it is an exception, it's one of the very few that exist.

F) Examples of idioms that use the preposition "in", with detailed explanations.

He looked me (directly) in the eye. This one seems very strange, but it's not difficult. We use this idiom in very serious situations. When you look someone in the eye, it means that the focus of your vision and the focus of that person's vision meet. So I'm looking at your eyes and you're looking at my eyes. But not just any point of the eye. We're both looking into the iris, which is the black part that's in the center. You can say, "Look at my eye", but the meaning is a little different. The preposition "at" is about a specific point or "target". If I look at your eye, it's an object. I might be looking at the color, the white part, etc… But if I look in your eye, it's like I'm looking at your "soul". We have a phrase in English: "The eyes are the windows to the soul". So, just like you look into/through a window (in order) to see what's inside (of) a building, it's like you're looking into my eyes to see my soul/essence, which means the "inside" of me rather than the outside of me (my eye or my arm, for example). So, the eyes are like the opening of a container, just like a box has a part that you can open (in order) to see what's inside.

As a final note, we say "eye", not "eyes". It would make sense to say "eyes", but one eye or two eyes isn't the important part. It's the meaning of the idiom as a whole that's important; we're talking about directly looking at who the person is, not their body parts. In other words, it's not about the eyes, it's about the soul/essence of that person. This is also why we commonly add the word "directly".

142

FOR

A) Example Sentences. Remember to follow the instructions in section A from previous prepositions.

1)

You can use a computer for many things.
Did Tom leave a box here for me?
I like many things. For example, languages.
What's for dinner?
I made dinner for our anniversary.
I'm studying hard for my English exam.
He won an award for best actor.
I work for my family. (1)

What does the word "for" mean in this group?

2)

Thanks for all (of) your help.
"I got a new job!" "That's great! I'm really happy for you."
Tom's feelings for Jane are obvious.
I love her for so many reasons.
It's not for me to tell you what to do.
It's been cold for July.
For someone who likes languages, you don't talk much.
I think these pants are too small for me.
I work for my family. (2)

What does the word "for" mean in this group?

3)

Can you open the door for me?
I'll sell you my phone for $20.
What's another word for "smart"?

What does the word "for" mean in this group?

4)

We talked for three hours.
Madonna has been famous for many years.
We walked for ten miles!

What does the word "for" mean in this group?

B) The Logic

Key Idea(s): 1) purpose; 2) basis/cause; 3) SPECIAL (1+2): distance/duration

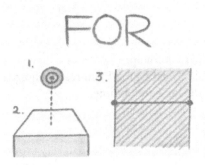

"for" is a two-way preposition

Explanation of the logic: As you can see, this preposition is a little complicated. It's important to note that some two-way prepositions mean that one way flows with the sentence and the other way flows against the sentence. We saw this with the preposition "of". The preposition "for" is one preposition that's a little different. Instead of one way flowing with the sentence and one way flowing against he sentence, we have two different directions that the logic itself flows. In other words, the logic is

144

split in half. In the picture, we see a target and a platform. The target is a "purpose". The platform is a "basis" or a "cause". In English, we use this one preposition for both of these ideas, so it's like the logic is split in half. There are some sentences in which you can apply both ideas at the same time, depending on the specific context and how you look at it. In most sentences, however, there's a clear difference between both ideas. Let's look at each part of the logic in detail:

The first part of the logic ("purpose") is simple. Remember that we can also use "(in order) to" when we want to talk about the purpose of something. This is where the prepositions "for" and "to" touch. However, "to" is an end point. A purpose is a special type of end point, so it makes sense that we can use the preposition "to". The preposition "for", however, is the main preposition that we use when we want to talk about a purpose. And remember, "for" and "(in order) to" are usually <u>not</u> interchangeable. The logic touches, but that doesn't mean that they're both used in all (of) the same contexts and ways. Another important thing to note about the idea of a purpose is that it's pretty common that if you can rephrase the sentence using "so that...", we're probably talking about a purpose and not a basis/cause.

The second part of the logic is the idea of a "basis", which includes a "cause". A cause is a specific type of basis, so we have this hierarchy: "basis" → "cause". The reason we see both of them together (basis/cause) is because sometimes the word "basis" is too general or abstract. Please notice something that's very important: the words "cause" and "reason" are very similar. A cause can be a reason, and a <u>purpose</u> can also be a reason. So it's important that you don't think about either part of the logic as a "reason". There are many times when the preposition "for" expresses a reason, but it's not always a reason. Sometimes, we use the preposition "for" when talking about an exchange, which is simply changing one basis for another equivalent basis. For example, $10,000 for a new car.

The preposition "for" has a third use that's special: distance (space) and duration (time). When we use it (in order) to

145

talk about time, it usually touches the prepositions "during" and "in", but these words aren't always interchangeable. This third part of the logic is special because it's actually based on the first two parts. There are two ways that you can look at it: 1) The unit of measurement is the basis, meaning that if you look at it this way, it's just a more specific kind of "basis" (hierarchy = "basis" → "distance" or "duration"). For example, "We walked for five miles" or "We walked for five hours". If we're talking about miles, that's the unit of measurement, which is the basis for how far you walked (miles vs feet or kilometers vs meters, for example). If we're talking about hours, then that's the basis (hours vs minutes vs days, for example); 2) The "basis" part becomes a regular start point in space or time and the "purpose" part becomes a regular end point in space or time. Usually, the preposition "from" is a start point, which is a specific type of "origin point" (which is the logic of "from"). We know that the preposition "to" is an end point. So, we can say, "I walked from the store to my house". In this case, we're focusing on the start point ("store") and the end point ("house"). But when we say, "I walked for five miles", the start point and the end point aren't the focus and they don't matter as much. Instead, we're focusing on the distance. In other words, we're focusing on what's <u>between</u> the start point and the end point because we're talking about <u>how far</u> you walked. Time works the same way. The only difference with time is that we're not talking about distance ("how far"), we're talking about duration ("<u>how long</u> (in time)").

Etymology notes: The word "for" was also a preposition in Old English. It had many possible meanings: "before/in the presence of" (another meaning of "before" in Modern English), "before" (time), "during", "on account of", "for the sake of", "instead of". In late Old English, it also developed the meaning of "because", "since", "for the reason that", and "in order that". (Note: The words "for" and "fore" (front) used to be just "for", but this changed in Middle English. So, the word "forward" is actually a combination of "fore" (front) and "-ward" (direction),

146

so the word "forward" isn't directly connected to the preposition "for".) 7

Now, go back to the example sentences and try to apply the logic. Ask yourself: "How is 'for' a 'purpose', a 'basis', or a 'distance'/'duration'?"

C) Detailed Explanations of the Example Sentences.

1) Purpose

You can use a computer for many things. What's the purpose or use of a computer? "Many things". For example, you can write a book, send an email, watch a video, etc...

ALTERNATIVES: "A computer is useful for many things." This isn't exactly the same, but it's very close. In the example sentence, we're not exactly talking about the "usefulness" of the computer, just the "use" of it. However, many of those things (writing a book, for example) are things that are useful, so this alternative is basically saying the same thing.

Did Tom leave a box here for me? Why would Tom leave a box? So that I can receive it. It's not intended for someone else to receive. Also, I'm not the cause, so this sentence isn't about a "cause". He left it so that I could receive it, so this sentence is about a purpose.

I like many things. For example, languages. I'm sure that you know the phrase "for example". This phrase fits the logic perfectly. I'm giving you an example of something that I like, which in this case is "languages". The purpose of giving you that example is so that you know one of the many things that I like.

What's for dinner? This questions asks what food is being prepared or will be prepared for the purpose of eating in the evening.

I made dinner for our anniversary. There are some sentences in which you can look at the preposition "for" as both a "purpose" and a "basis" (cause). The preposition "for" in this sentence is more of a purpose, because we're talking about the end point (the purpose) of the dinner: it's a special dinner that we're going to eat on the day of our anniversary. It's also true that I made dinner because ("cause") it's our anniversary, but the emphasis here is on the purpose, not the cause. However, it's possible to think of this as a "cause", also.

ALTERNATIVES: "I made dinner because it's our anniversary." In this case, the emphasis is the "cause" and not the "purpose", but the surface meaning is the same. The difference between the words "because" and "for" is something that can be really confusing because these two words often complement each other. It's very common to change the wording of the sentence and use the word "because" instead of the preposition "for". It's not always possible, but when it is possible, you're simply looking at the same sentence/idea from a different perspective ("cause" instead of "purpose").

I'm studying hard for my English exam. Why am I studying? Because I have an English exam ("cause"). But why study for it? In other words, what's the purpose of studying? Well, I want to pass the exam, so what we're really saying here is that I'm studying so that I can pass (which is the "purpose").

ALTERNATIVES: "I'm studying hard because I want to pass my English exam." Again, now the emphasis is the "cause" instead of the "purpose", but the surface meaning is the same.

He won an award for best actor. The purpose of the award is to give recognition to the actor with the best acting skills.

148

ALTERNATIVES: "He won an award for being the best actor."/"He won an award because he was the best actor." We usually just say "for best actor", but these two are also possible. All (of) these sentences mean the same thing, but if we use these two alternatives, the focus is the "cause".

I work for my family. (1) Notice the "(1)" next to this sentence. The same sentence is also in the next group because this sentence has two meanings. It has two meanings because we can use the preposition "for" both ways ("basis/cause" and "purpose") in this context.

The meaning in this group is that I work (in order) to provide what my family needs (food, housing, clothes, etc...). My family is the purpose of my work. My family might not be the only purpose, but in this sentence that's what we're talking about.

ALTERNATIVES: "I work because of my family." "I work because my family needs food, housing, clothes, etc..."

2) *Basis (including "cause")*

Thanks for all (of) your help. If someone helps you, you thank them. The help is the reason why you're thanking them, which is the basis or the cause of your thanks.

"I got a new job!" "That's great! I'm really happy for you." In this sentence, "happy for you" doesn't mean that you're happy because of them. They aren't causing your happiness. We are talking about a cause, but that's not the cause. We say this when something good happens to someone else. That good thing makes you feel happy. So, what we're really saying is, "I'm happy because something good happened to you". The good thing is the cause/basis, not the person.

Tom's feelings for Jane are obvious. There's an implied meaning in this sentence. We're not just talking about any feel-

149

ings. We're talking specifically about romantic feelings. If you "have feelings for someone", it's always romantic. Here, Jane is the cause/basis of Tom's romantic feelings. If you want to talk about how you feel (and there's an object), but it's not romantic, we use the preposition "about". For example, "I don't know how I feel about your brother living with us." This makes perfect sense because you can think about something and you can also feel a certain way about something. Of course if there is no object and you're just talking about how you generally feel right now, we just use the adjective: "I feel happy".

ALTERNATIVES: "It's obvious that Tom likes Jane."

I love her for so many reasons. Remember that a "cause" and a "purpose" are both types of reasons. In this case, "so many reasons" aren't the purpose of your love. The reasons are the cause/basis of your love.

ALTERNATIVES: "There are so many reasons why I love her."

It's not for me to tell you what to do. This means that I have no right to tell you what to do and that you have to decide for yourself. Notice the words "for yourself", which is the same idea as in the example sentence. If it's not for me to tell you what to do, then I'm not the basis; you are. You're decisions come from you, meaning based on what you decide. Note that this sentence is a good example of something that's just a "basis", but not a "cause". Remember that the idea of a "basis" is the bigger, more general idea and that "cause" is just a more specific version.

ALTERNATIVES: "You have to make your own decisions." "You have to decide for yourself." "It's your decision, not mine."

It's been cold for July. You can look at this sentence with the "cause" idea, but it's better to look at it as a simple "basis". This sentence is said by a person living in the northern hemisphere of the planet. So what does this sentence mean? July is normally a warm or hot month. We're not saying that it's cold, we're saying that it's cold compared to the normal temperature. Let's say that the average temperature in July is 90° F (32° C). But this year, the average temperature in July has been 75° F (24° C). That's not "cold", but it's a lot colder than the normal temperature. So, "the average temperature in July" is the "basis". <u>Based on</u> the average that we expect, this year's July has been colder.

ALTERNATIVES: "This July has been cold compared to the average / compared to what it normally is."

For someone who likes languages, you don't talk much. You would expect that someone who likes languages would also likes to speak a lot because language is about communication. However, this isn't always true. For example, I don't talk much compared to other people, but I love languages. In this sentence, the basis is "someone who likes languages", including all the qualities you expect to go with that type of person. Looking at that basis and looking at me, we see a difference. Just like the sentence about July, we're using the basis (in order) to compare.

ALTERNATIVES: "Are you sure (that) you like languages? You don't talk much."

I think these pants are too small for me. My pants size is the basis (we use the word "me", but in this context it's referring to "the pants size that fits my body"). If I wear a size 10 and the pants I want to buy are size 8, then they won't fit. Based on my size, these pants are too small. Again, we have a comparison. If the context is clear, you can omit the words "for me".

ALTERNATIVES: "I don't think these pants fit/will fit."

I work for my family. (2) We saw this sentence in group one. This time, we're using the second meaning, which is a basis/cause. In this case, it means that I'm an employee in my family's

151

business. My family is the source of my employment, which is an abstract kind of "basis".

ALTERNATIVES: "I work because of my family." Again, we can use this alternative. However, in this context, "because of my family" means "because my family gave me a job". So my family is the cause of my job, not the purpose.

3) *Exchanging one basis for another basis*

This group includes the ideas of "instead of" and "in exchange for".

Can you open the door for me? You can look at this sentence two ways: 1) open the door so that I (or someone else) can enter/exit ("purpose"); 2) open the door because I can't or don't want to (exchanging one basis for another basis). In this sentence, both of these are true at the same time, but they're two ways that you can think about the meaning. When we talk about "exchanging", we're changing the basis from one thing to another thing. In this sentence, we're exchanging one person for another person. Instead of you opening the door, you want me to open it, so I do the action instead of you. In other words, I'm the basis of the action instead of you because the action comes from me and not you.

Notice the phrase "instead of". The word "instead" is a combination of the words "in" and "stead". "Stead" is an older word that we don't use very much these days, but it's still very common as part of the word "instead". A synonym is "place" or "position". So, we can say either "instead of" or "in place of", but "instead of" is more common. Why is this important? Because it fits the logic of the preposition "for". If I open the door for you, then I'm doing it "in place of you"/"instead of you". I'm in the "place" that you would be (opening the door), meaning that I'm "standing" on that place in a very abstract way. So we have a "basis", but we're exchanging your position for

152

mine. Here we see touching points between the prepositions "on", "in", and "for", depending on how we talk about it.

I'll sell you my phone for $20. I have a phone (basis 1), you have $20 (basis 2). I give you the phone, you give me the $20. We're exchanging/trading one thing (basis) for another thing (basis). Now what used to my phone is $20 and what used to be your $20 is a phone.

What's another word for "smart"? We're trying to find <u>another word</u> (basis 2) that has the same meaning as <u>the word "smart"</u> (basis 1). If I give you the word "intelligent", you can now choose to use that word instead of the word "smart".

ALTERNATIVES: "What's a word other than 'smart'?"

4) *distance/duration*

We talked for three hours. "Hours" is the unit of time that we're using to measure, meaning that it's the basis for describing the duration. In other words, "How long?" Remember that we're talking about the amount of time between two points, not the start and end. For example, let's say that we started walking at 9:00 and we walk for 3 hours, which means that we stopped walking at 12:00. We're not talking about starting at 9 and ending at 12. We're talking about the amount of time between 9 and 12, which is 3 hours.

Madonna has been famous for many years. This is the same as the last example, but "years" is the basis for describing the duration, again meaning "How long?" The start year and end year don't matter.

We walked for ten miles! Finally, we have an example that deals with distance (space) instead of duration (time). It's the same as the previous two examples. "Miles" is the basis for distance, meaning "How far?" Let's say we start at the park. My car was

153

stolen, so we had to walk home and I live ten miles from the park. Point A (the park) and point B (my house) don't matter. We're talking about the number of miles between those two points.

D) Some verbs that often use the preposition "for"

Pay for	Look for	Wait for
Call for (someone)	Leave for (a place)	Ask for
Send for	Pray for	Send for

E) **Phrasal Verbs.**

The preposition "for" is not often used in phrasal verbs, but we sometimes need it as a connector.

I could really go for a hamburger! (phrasal verb) When we use the phrasal verb "go for" in a sentence like this, it means that you want something. The verb "to go" does not mean what it normally means (moving from one place to another place). In this sentence, you can look at the preposition "for" as either a "purpose" or as a "basis" because we're talking about something that you want. Based on your desire = "basis". For the purpose of something (in this case, "eating") = "purpose".

Look out for that car! (connector) Someone is crossing the street and they don't see that a car is about to hit them. "Look out" is the phrasal verb. In fact, you can simply say, "Look out!" However, if you specify the object (in this case, "car"), you need the preposition "for". The logic is about a "basis" if we think of it like this: getting hit by a car will cause you harm, so you have to see it and avoid it. In other words, "Look out because that car is going to hit you!" It can also be a purpose (meaning: look and

154

move so that you don't get hit), but in this sentence it's more of a basis.

Keep a look out for any suspicious activity. (connector) The meaning of this sentence is very similar to the previous one, but here we're definitely talking about a "purpose". In this sentence, the reason (purpose) that we're looking out is so that we can find anyone acting suspicious.

I'm just here for my stuff. (connector) Let's say that an ex-boyfriend recently moved out after breaking up with his girlfriend and he came to her house (in order) to get whatever he left there. So he came for a specific reason, which is a "purpose" in this case.

F) Examples of idioms that use the preposition "for", with detailed explanations.

A penny for your thoughts? This is a strange idiom. It means that I'm curious about what you're thinking right now. The preposition "for" is clearly about an exchange in this case. Just like I'll sell you my phone for $20, I'll give you a penny (in order) to know your thoughts. Of course, we don't actually give people pennies; it's just an expression.

This calls for a celebration! When something "calls for" something else, we're saying that some situation or event deserves a particular result (which is a "purpose" in this case). For example, I got a new job which is going to pay me a lot of money. I go home and tell my family. My wife says, "This calls for a celebration!" and she opens a bottle of wine (in order) to celebrate.

155

AT

A) Example Sentences. Remember to follow the instructions in section A from previous prepositions.

1)

I live at 123 Main Street.
I'm at work right now.
I'll meet you at the beach.
Because he's a sailor, he spends a lot of time at sea.

What does the word "at" mean in this group?

2)

The meeting is at 11.
He wasn't able to go with us because he was out of the country <u>at the time</u>. (<u>then</u>)
Mr. Jones is in a meeting <u>at the moment</u>. (<u>now</u>)

What does the word "at" mean in this group?

3)

He smiled at hearing her voice.
She was sad at the thought of her ex-husband.

What does the word "at" mean in this group?

4)

Aim at the target.
He threw the ball at me.
When I fell, he laughed at me!
Someone was waving at me.
You can email me at example123@youmail.com.

What does the word "at" mean in this group?

5)

We were driving at 110 miles per hour!
There was a giant hurricane in this city. The repairs are estimated at $100,000.
Water freezes at 32 degrees Fahrenheit (0 degrees Celsius).
I don't like him at all.

What does the word "at" mean in this group?

6)

During the Spanish-American war, Spain was at war with the United States.
It's hard to feel at ease in a graveyard.
(street sign:) Caution! Children at play.
I'm good at English/speaking English.
I'm at your service.

What does the word "at" mean in this group?

B) The Logic

Key Idea(s): a specific point or "bubble"

"at" is a one-way preposition

158

Explanation of the logic: This preposition can be used in very abstract ways, and it connects in some way with many other prepositions, which makes it a kind of prepositions intersection. In fact, the preposition "at" is the central preposition around which almost all other prepositions revolve (see appendix B for more info). This preposition is one of the most important prepositions in this book. If you can master all (of) the ways that we use it, you're English skills will improve a lot.

The idea of a "specific point" can be about time, space ("location"), a target, or even a cause.

The preposition "at" can also be an abstract "bubble". For example, if you're at the beach, we don't know exactly where you are. The idea of "beach" as a location includes being in the ocean, on the sand, on the pier, and any area directly connected with it, such as any shops that might be across the street. So there's a kind of "bubble" of space. Think of this on a big scale. If you look at a map, the a specific location is just a dot on the map (a specific point). But if you physically go that location, you can go "inside" the specific point. That's part of the "bubble" idea, but the "bubble" also includes any nearby areas that are part of it. We saw the beach example, but another example to make this clearer: If you're in the parking lot of a store, you can still say that you're "at the store" because the parking lot is attached to the store and it's inside the bubble of the specific point. We'll see a lot of specific examples later.

Lastly, "target" can be a very abstract idea. This idea isn't always needed, but it's useful for understanding some groups and individual example sentences (especially group six, where we target/aim at a state or a process). A target is some specific point (usually in space) that you focus on. The reason we use the preposition "at" and not "on" in these cases is because we're limiting the focus to a specific point (or bubble). We saw earlier that the preposition "to" can be about a "limit-point" as a special type of "end point", and we know that the prepositions "to" and "at" share a very close connection, but they're clearly separate. The preposition "at" isn't about a "limit-point" specifically, but it

159

does use a little bit of the "limit" idea. This is because when you're trying to hit a target, there's a limited area that you're trying to hit.

Etymology notes: Old English came from a language called "Proto-Germanic", which came from a language called "Proto-Indo-European". The preposition "at" originally came from Proto-Indo-European and it meant what is now "at", "to", or "near" in Modern English. This is unfortunate because it makes the preposition "at" a little complicated (in fact, both the prepositions "to" and "near" touch the preposition "at", especially the preposition "to"). However, it also makes a lot of sense and helps explain a lot of the details and different uses that we'll see in the example sentences. 8

Now, go back to the example sentences and try to apply the logic. Ask yourself: "How is 'at' a specific point/bubble in these sentences? Is it also a target?"

C) Detailed Explanations of the Example Sentences.

1) a specific location (specific point and/or bubble in space)

I live at 123 Main Street. This is the easiest and most basic example. When we talk about a specific point in space, we use the preposition "at". But it's also a kind of "bubble". For example, if you're "at home", you might be inside the house, in the yard, upstairs, downstairs, on the roof, etc... It doesn't matter if you're inside or outside (of) the house. It's all part of one specific location and that specific location is inside the "bubble" of the preposition "at". If you go to the neighbor's house next door, or you go across the street, you're not "at home" anymore. But when you are "at home/at your house", you can go inside the preposition "at" in this context when you go into the house.

This just shows that the prepositions are closely related. In fact, as you can see on "The Full Cone of Existence" map

(Appendix B), most prepositions revolve around the preposition "at". In other words, the preposition "at" is like the core preposition and most other prepositions are defined in relation to it. This is partially because wherever something is located is the center of that things existence. You can read more about this idea in Appendix B.

I'm at work right now. This is another very basic example. Where am I? What's the specific location or point that I am at? Work. More specifically, the building (or other place) where I work. If we compare where I work to a larger area (like a map of the city), we see that it's a specific point. But if we talk about the location as a place of work, it's more like a bubble. You might go outside so that you can get some fresh air, for example, but you're still "at work" even though you're not working right now.

I'll meet you at the beach. Again, the beach is a specific location, especially compared to other locations (the store, home, the movie theater, etc...). However, the beach also covers a certain area. There's the physical sand and the ocean, but there's also the area just outside the beach itself that we consider part of being "at" the beach. In this way, it's also a specific bubble. If you call me on the phone and tell me that you're at the beach, I don't know exactly where you are. All I know is that you're somewhere inside that bubble.

For some English learners, there's some confusion between "at the beach", "on the beach", and sometimes "in the beach". "On the beach" talks about being physically on top of the sand and not just in the general area of the bubble. "In the beach" doesn't work. If you put your toes inside or under the sand, for example, we actually say "in the sand" or "under the sand" (they're interchangeable). So you'll never use "in the beach", only "at the beach" and "on the beach".

Because he's a sailor, he spends a lot of time at sea. You might wonder why we use the preposition "at" in this sentence. The sea

161

is definitely not a specific point, and if it's a bubble, it's a very big bubble. It's useful to know that there's a difference between the word "sea" and the word "ocean". A sea is smaller. However, when we say "at sea", we mean that the person is on a boat or a ship that's somewhere in either the sea OR the ocean.

Ok, so, if we say "in the sea", that means inside the water: "I like to swim in the sea". It's much more common to say "in the ocean", but it depends on where you live. "In the sea/ocean" is much more common, but it doesn't mean what we want to say in the example sentence. Can we say "on the sea"? Yes, but again, the meaning is different. In that case, we're talking about the boat or ship that's floating on the surface of the sea. So if we want to talk about the location of <u>someone</u> who's on a ship that's sailing in the ocean, we say that the person is "at sea". Why?

In this context, we look at the word "sea" (in this case meaning both "sea" and "ocean") like one big location. It's like "at the beach", but much larger. This probably seems weird because the preposition "at" is supposed to be a specific point or bubble, but an ocean or a sea is a very large area that doesn't seem specific at all. Here's the trick: we don't know his specific location. All we know is that he's somewhere that's not on land. Because we don't know his specific location, we look at the entire sea/ocean as one, big, specific point (location). It's specific because it's not "on land" (it's "away from land"), meaning that we have two choices: either he's on land or he's at sea. (Note: the reason we say "on land" and not "at land" is because 1) there are specific points (locations) on land where he can be, but the ocean is mostly just one big body water without many distinct locations, and 2) "on land" is actually the opposite of "on a ship" in this context.)

ALTERNATIVES: "Because he's a sailor, he spends a lot of time out at sea." We can add the preposition "out" because in this context it means "away from land". He's simply somewhere "out there".

"Because he's a sailor, he spends a lot of time out to sea." In this case, we can't just use the preposition "to"; we need both the preposition "out" and the preposition "to". This sentence is almost exactly like the previous alternative. There's a very close and sometimes confusing relationship between the prepositions "to" and "at". As we know, the preposition "to" is an "end point". The preposition "at" is a "specific point". Well, an "end point" is a "specific point", so that's why there are many confusing cases. We'll look at the difference between them as we see more example sentences and groups that use the preposition "at". In this particular alternative sentence, the reason that we can say "out to sea" is because we can look at it as an "outward" direction (again, "away from land"). The surface meaning is the same as "at sea" and "out at sea" because if you're "at sea", it means that you're away from land.

2) *a specific point in time or a bubble of time*

The meeting is at 11. This is another very easy and simple example. We use "at" when talking about a specific point in time, particularly a specific time on the clock. This is exactly like talking about a specific location, but the "location" is a point in time, not space.

He wasn't able to go with us because he was out of the country <u>at the time</u>. (<u>then</u>) This sentence is a little more difficult. We use the phrase "at the time" to refer to a specific point or bubble in time that was already mentioned earlier in the conversation. We went somewhere. Let's say that it was last summer and we went to see a new movie that was just released in theaters. That's the moment in time that we're talking about. But he was out of the country when we went to see the movie. So we're talking about two things that are happening at the same time. In other words, we have a specific point in time, but we're talking about two different locations. We're simply using the specific point in time (the time when we went to the movie theater) and using that specific point to say where he was at that same point in time. So we say "at the time". It's exactly like saying, "I arrived at 12:00" and someone asks, "Where was your

163

son at the time?" At the time = 12:00, which is the time that I arrived.

ALTERNATIVES: "He wasn't able to go with us because he was out of the country (when we went)."

Mr. Jones is in a meeting at the moment. (now) This is similar to the previous sentence. In the previous sentence, we were talking about two things that happened at a specific point in time in the past. In this sentence, we're only talking about one thing and that thing is happening now. Right now (the present moment) is the point in time. We can also extend that point to a bubble that includes the whole time of the meeting because it's a process that's still happening.

ALTERNATIVES: "Mr. Jones is in a meeting (right) now."

3) a cause (source)

Notice that we say "at the source". For example: "Two competing ideas are at the source of the political battle." The idea of a "source" is related to the idea of a "cause". In this group, one action is the cause/source for the other action.

He smiled at hearing her voice. What this sentence means is: She says something and it causes him to smile. So here we see that the preposition "at" is overlapping with the logic of a couple (of) other prepositions ("by" and "for"; we'll compare these later in the book). Usually, the preposition "at" isn't used with this meaning, but it does exist. It's a small application of the logic, but "at" isn't often about a "cause".

Specifically, we can say that when he hears her voice, he smiles, but the two things don't just happen at the same time. They happen at the same time, but there's the added meaning that one thing causes a second thing to happen. She says something, and at the same time, her voice causes him to smile. So we can see that this sentence deals with time, but because it's specifically a

164

"cause", it fits better in a separate group than "time". Okay, so how does the logic of "at" work here? We have two actions and one specific point in time. This is like one of the previous examples, except we have the added meaning that one causes the other. This is just implied by the context.

ALTERNATIVES: "He smiled when he heard her voice." This is the closest alternative. Notice that we say "at hearing", but "when he heard". Remember that 99 percent of the time, we have to use the "-ing" form of a verb that's placed after a preposition. So the structure changes a little, but the meaning is the same.

"Hearing her voice made him smile."

"He smiled upon hearing her voice." I include this alternative only because you might hear someone use the preposition "upon" and because many English learners have questions about it. The exact way that the logic of the preposition "upon" works is a little tricky because it's a combination of "up" and "on". We won't be looking at the logic of "upon", but you'll be able to understand it when you fully understand the prepositions "up" and "on". "Upon" is an old word that we rarely use. In this context, it means the same as the preposition "at" (at the same time + cause). These days, depending on the exact context and surface meaning, it has been replaced by the prepositions "on" and "at". The most common place that you'll hear the preposition "upon" is at the beginning of old stories and fairy tales: "Once upon a time…"

"He smiled because he heard her voice." This alternative isn't exactly the same, but because of the specific details of the context, the practical meaning is the same in this case. The word "because" is a cause, but it doesn't imply that two things happen at the same time. For example, the Grand Canyon was created over many, many, many years. The river flowed, and flowed, and flowed, until today. Over all that time, the water slowly created the canyon because it eroded the rock. So, the Grand Canyon exists because of all that water flowing for so many years.

Note that it's possible to say, "The Grand Canyon was created at the flowing of the river". It sounds a little weird because of what it means, so we would never say it, but it is grammatically correct. If you say this, it means that the river started flowing and at the same time the Grand Canyon was immediately created because of it. So, depending on the specific details of the context, the practical meaning can be the same, but you can't always use "because" instead of "at" because the word "because" doesn't mean "at the same time".

A note about the preposition "for": Think about the sentence, "He smiled for hearing her voice". We've already seen the preposition "for", but this is a good example of the old use of "for" that we don't really use anymore. This is obviously a basis/cause, but if you use the preposition "for" in this case, it sounds very poetic.

She was sad at the thought of her ex-husband. This is the same as the last one and it's just so you have another example. She thinks about her ex-husband (or someone mentions him) and at the same time she feels sad because of that thought.

ALTERNATIVES: "The thought of her ex-husband made her sad."

"She was sad because of the thought of her ex-husband." Same explanation as last time. However, because the word "because" doesn't mean "at the same time", it sounds a little strange in this context.

Note: "upon" and "for" are the same as in the previous sentence's alternatives.

4) *a target*

Aim at the target. This sentence is the model for this group because it's the most basic. Usually, aiming at a target refers to using a gun, a bow and arrow, a rock, or other things that you can throw or shoot with. When we say this sentence, we're telling someone to focus on a very specific point and to try to hit whatever that point is. Another example: "Look at me". This means that I want you to direct your vision to the point/bubble in space that I'm occupying. This idea is very abstract, but there's a strong feeling behind it for native speakers. The idea of a "target" is very useful here. Notice that you aren't trying to hit something around the target. The word "target" limits your focus and then you try to hit inside the boundaries of that focus.

This also brings us to another point: the difference between "at" and "to", as well as the difference between "at" and "toward". Let's look at an easy example. If I shoot a bullet at a target, the bullet might hit the target, but it might not. Let's say it does hit. This means that it goes "to" the target. In other words, the target is the destination (end point) that you want to hit. The bullet definitely goes "toward" the target, but if it doesn't hit the target, it didn't go "to" the target. Remember, "to" and "toward" are prepositions of direction. "To" implies a direction, but it's always about the end point/destination. "Toward" is just a direction.

However, when you're aiming, we're not talking about the actual movement to or toward the target. The verb "to aim" is like the verb "to point" + the purpose of hitting something. It's not the actual movement of the bullet/arrow/etc... Yes, when you shoot, the bullet goes toward (meaning "in the direction of") the target, and if you're aim is good (meaning that you don't miss the target), the bullet travels to the target. But when we use the preposition "at", we're talking about where you want the bullet to hit or what you want the bullet to hit.

The prepositions "at" and "to" are two different prepositions with completely different meanings, but the application of the logic can be very close. Sometimes it just depends on how you're talking about something. The reason this is so confusing is because a target is a specific point, but that specific point is also an end point.

Another example to help make this clear: we can say, "Look at the sky" and "Look to the sky". However, there's a big difference here! This won't work in every context, but when I say,

167

"Look at the sky", I want you to focus on the sky itself, so the sky is the specific end point <u>and</u> the focus. But when I say, "Look to the sky", either 1) I want you to look upwards and there's no specific focus, or 2) the sky is the end point, but it's <u>not</u> the focus. Instead, there's something in the sky (a plane, a bird, a cloud, etc…) that I want you to focus on. As I said, it won't work that way in every context, but in a way, you can think of this group as a combination between the prepositions "to" and "on".

He threw the ball at me. This sentence will help to make the previous explanation a little clearer. When you throw a ball at someone, you're trying to hit them, which means that person is the target. If I say, "He threw the ball <u>to</u> me", then I'm the intended receiver, not the target. In that case, he wants me to catch the ball.

ALTERNATIVES: "He hit me/tried to hit me with the ball."

When I fell, he laughed at me! Why do we use the preposition "at" in this case? For the same reason as the last sentence. You're trying to "hit" the person with your laughter. This might seem strange, but you're laughing because what someone did or said was funny or stupid. However, the person didn't want it to be funny or stupid, so it "hits" them and hurts emotionally. You can think of "me" as the target of "laughter".

Someone was waving at me. This is another very similar example. If someone is waving at you, you are the focus of their waving. It's directed toward you and intended to "hit" you, not someone else. In this case, "hit" isn't the best word because waving isn't negative. But you're the target/limit-point because the person isn't waving at someone else.

ALTERNATIVES: "Someone was waving to me." In this sentence, the logic of "to" and the logic of "at" overlap and are 100% interchangeable. This doesn't happen very often, but it's possible. In this case, it's because of the verb "to wave", which can use both "at" and "to" without a change in meaning. The logic

168

is different, but the surface meaning is the same in this particular case.

You can email me at example123@youmail.com An email address is like an abstract/non-physical location. If you <u>send</u> an email, we use the preposition "to": "Please send an email to example123@youmail.com". This is because we're using the verb "to send" and talking about the address as a destination, which is an end point. This is exactly the same if we're talking about a physical address where someone lives: "Please send the letter to 123 Main Street."

However, it depends on the structure of the sentence. For example, "Please <u>send   me</u> an email <u>at</u> example123@youmail.com". "Send me" implies the preposition "to" because the word "me" is the indirect object, so when we say "an email", we use the preposition "at". This is just like if we say, "Please send me a letter at 123 Main Street." If we use email as a verb, we use the preposition "at" for the same reasons that we've seen in other examples from this group. It's like you're aiming the email at that address because it's an end point with a purpose, not just an end point. What's the difference? It's two different ways of looking at the same thing. We use the preposition "to" if the sentence structure emphasizes the end point (destination) itself, or we use the preposition "at" if the sentence structure emphasizes aiming at the end point as a target. In other words, because you want me to receive the email, in an abstract way you're targeting my email address or trying to "hit" my email address so that I receive it.

5) *a specific point in a measurement*

We were driving at 110 miles per hour! In this sentence, it's easy to imagine that the needle on the speedometer is at whatever specific point that tells you the speed of the car. (A speedometer is the thing in the car that tells you how fast you're driving). If the current speed is 110 miles per hour, that's the specific speed (point) that the needle is at. A speed is a type of measurement.

169

You're not driving at 120 miles per hour or some other speed, just like if I say "at 11:30", I don't mean "at 12:00".

ALTERNATIVES: "We were driving 110 miles per hour!" "We were traveling (at) 110 miles per hour!"

Note that some verbs don't use the preposition "at" when talking about speed. For example, "We were going 110 miles per hour!"

There was a giant hurricane in this city. The repairs are estimated at $100,000. This is the same as the previous sentence, but now we're talking about the amount of money that will be needed (in order) to repair the city. An amount of money is a type of measurement.

ALTERNATIVES: "The repairs are estimated to be $100,000."

"The repairs will cost about $100,000." In this sentence, the preposition "about" means "approximately". This only works here because of the word "estimated" in the example sentence. There's a very interesting connection between the prepositions "about", "around", and "at" that we'll talk more about later.

"The repairs will cost around $100,000." When the preposition "about" means "approximately", it's 100% interchangeable with the preposition "around", which also means "approximately". (There are rare exceptions.)

Water freezes at 32 degrees Fahrenheit (0 degrees Celsius). This is very similar to the previous examples, but now we're talking about degrees, which is another type of measurement.

I don't like him at all. This sentence is a little more abstract. We use "at all" in negative sentences and questions. In a negative sentence, it means "not in any way" or "not in any amount". This sentence is a little strange because when we use the word "all" negatively like this, it basically means "nothing". In other words,

170

there is nothing (no point) about him that I like. We can think of all the things that exist about him: his personality, his smell, his eyes, his clothes, etc... At each of those points, I don't like him. So, how much do I like him? A lot? No. Some? No. A little? No. I don't like him at all. We can make a scale. On a scale of 0 to 10, how much I like him = 0, which is a specific point of measurement.

ALTERNATIVES: "I don't like him one bit". This alternative and the example sentence are the most common options.

"I don't like anything about him." This sentence means that I don't like any<u>thing</u> related to him as a person (hair, eyes, personality, etc...). The prepositions "about" and "around" are very similar, and they share a common idea in some contexts: a circle that's surrounds a specific point. We'll talk more about these two later, but for now think about this: "I don't like him at all" means the same thing as "I don't like anything about him". If he's the center point of a circle, which is a specific point, then all the things "about" him are around him in an abstract way. In other words, they're abstractly "around" him like a circle. We can imagine that I "go" to his personality, and at that point I don't like him. I "go" to his eyes, and at that point I don't like him. Etc...

6) a targeted state/process (usually in pairs)

This group is very special. We've seen the preposition "on" and we know that it's always about a positive state/active state and it's also usually about a surface/platform. We've also seen the preposition "in" and we know that it's always about a container, which can include processes. Lastly, we know that the preposition "at" is closely related to the idea of a "target". This group is the intersection of these three ideas. In other words, it's a special combination of the prepositions "at", "on", and "in".

You might have noticed that we say "in a state".This might be a little confusing because the idea of a "state" is usually related to the preposition "on", but we're saying "in a state".

That's because if we talk about a state directly, the state is a container. Remember that the idea of a "positive state/active state" is a very abstract idea that just describes the logic of the preposition "on", but when we talk about the state itself, it's a container. In other words, we say "in a state" because a state is a container, but we apply the logic of the preposition "on" to the container (in order) to talk about the state being positive/active. We say "in a process" because a process is also a container, but notice that a process can be active or inactive, as well. So we can see that the prepositions "in" and "on" are very closely connected, which gives us strange things like this.

We'll see that the preposition "at" is also very closely connected to the prepositions "on" and "in". In fact, these three prepositions are probably the most basic and most important prepositions in the English language. The logic of these three almost always touch (but not overlap) in some way, though it depends on the specific context. See the explanation of "The Basic Cone" in Appendix B for more information.

The verb "to target" is very similar to the verb "to aim", but the verb "to target" fits better here. It just means that we're making something into a target, which we then aim at, so the basic idea is the same. What we're doing in this group is targeting/aiming at ("at") a particular state ("on") or process ("in"). In most of these examples, the word that's after the preposition "at" can be both a state and a process, depending on how you look at it. Also, in many cases, there's an opposite state/process. For example, "at war" vs "at peace". This group might seem like it doesn't fit the logic because in many cases, we don't think of "targeting/aiming at a state" or "targeting/aiming at a process", but that's exactly how the logic is working under the surface. I've done my best to make the explanations as clear as possible and to show the connections between all three prepositions, but some things will naturally seem very abstract. The good news is that this group is special because we only use it in certain contexts. That also means that you can't just apply it to any context.

During the Spanish-American war, Spain was at war with the United States. First, let's see how we can look at this as a state. For example, "The United States and Spain were in a state of war". What's really happening here is that the war is "on", meaning that it's <u>active</u>, just like a light can be "on". This also means that the opposite, ("peace") is "off", meaning that it's <u>inactive</u>. If we say "Spain and the United States are at peace" or "Spain and the United States are in a state peace", then "peace" is active ("on"), which means that "war" is inactive ("off"). So we can see that this works exactly like a light, but we have two lights. When you turn one light on, the other immediately turns off. When you turn the other light on, the first one immediately turns off. We can also look at this from another angle: if Spain and the United States are at war, and no other countries are part of that war, then Spain and the United States are the only two "active" countries in the war. All other countries are "inactive". This can also give us a special abstract platform that only Spain and the United States are on.

To make this clearer, let's see how we can look at this example sentence as a process. Another way to say the same thing is "Spain and the United States were engaged in war". Note that the word "war" here is a noun. That noun is the container. The verb "to engage" has a lot of definitions, but the general idea is that you are participating in a process or an action. So, it makes sense that we use the preposition "in" with the verb "to engage". The two countries are engaging in war, or engaging in the act of war.

Ok, so how exactly does the preposition "at" work in this case? If we look at "war" as a state, then the preposition "at" is targeting that state. Imagine that I have two targets. One target is labeled "war", the other target is labeled "peace". I'm only shooting at one of the targets. One target ("war") is currently "active" because I'm only trying to hit that target. In other words, it's the target that I'm actively trying to hit. This is "war" as a state, meaning that the state of war is the target. In other words,

173

it's like the preposition "at" is targeting/aiming at the preposition "on".

If we look at "war" as a process (which is a container), then the preposition "at" is targeting that process/container. This suggestion is very abstract, but if it helps, think of the bullets going into the target. Just like we can look at the state of war as a target, we can look at the process of war (container) as a target. In other words, it's like the preposition "at" is targeting/aiming at the preposition "in".

It's hard to feel at ease in a graveyard. When you feel "at ease", it means that you feel comfortable. Emotionally, you are "in a state of comfort". In other words, we're talking about an emotional <u>state</u>. We know that there are many different emotions, so this is like the previous example in which there were many different countries, but only two countries were at war. However, we also have an emotional state that is specifically the opposite of "at ease": "ill-at-ease". If "ease" (comfort) is active, then you don't feel "ill-at-ease", meaning that it's inactive.

You can also think of an emotional state as a process, although we usually don't. For example, if I feel happy, then that's a state. But as I continue to feel happy, it's like I'm experiencing "the process of being happy". So that process is also active.

Note that for most emotions, we don't use the preposition "at". However, there's a very good reason that we use the preposition "at" with the word "ease", and it proves that the logic works perfectly. If we look at the etymology of the word "ease", it originally came from the Old French word "aise", which came from the Latin word "adiacere". 9 "Adiacere" meant "to lie at", "to border upon", or "to lie near". In Modern English, we definitely don't think of "ease" as a location. <u>However, the literal meaning of "adiacere" was "to throw"</u>. If you throw something, you might not be trying to hit something else, but we can see a connection between the idea of "to throw" and "to target"/"to aim at" because when we throw something with the intention of hitting something else, we say "throw at": "He threw the ball at me."

174

(street sign:) Caution! Children at play. If children are at play, in means that they're playing (a process, which is a container). Another way to this that sounds more formal is: "the children are in a state of play". The preposition "at" works the same way in this example as it does in the previous examples. It's useful to note that "at play" has an opposite: "at work". This isn't the same as "I'm at work". If I say that, I'm talking about my physical location. This use of "at work" is a little different. For example, you might see a sign at a construction site that says "Men at work". This means that people are working. More specifically, they're building (houses, for example). Again, we have a process and a state.

I'm good at English/speaking English. This one is a little different, but the logic works the same. We're talking about "English" (the topic) as a skill or a subject that someone can learn. We can look at this in two ways: 1) the state of my English skills is good; or 2) if we're on the topic of English, I can tell you that my skill is good. Both the ideas of a "state" and a "topic" are related to the preposition "on". Notice that we can also say "I'm good at speaking English." This makes sense because "speaking" is a process. So, this example is just like saying "I'm good at hitting the target", except the target is "English" as either a state or a process. Of course, in this case, we also have an opposite: "I'm bad at English/speaking English".

I'm at your service. This sentence means: "Tell me what you want me to do, and I'll do it". In other words, I'm available to serve/help you (as long as it's a normal part of my job). This is something that a butler or a waiter might say, or it might be something that a private detective would say to a client. The idea of a "process" (container) is very weak here, so we won't talk about that. However, we can say that if we're talking about my availability to serve you or help you, my "status" (state) is "available". For example, a detective who has many clients is very busy, so he's not available to help. But if he's not busy, then he has the ability to offer you help. So in this case, we're not targeting the

175

word "service", we're targeting the availability. But there's another part here. The person also has to be willing to help (unless they're forced), meaning that they want to offer the help. So we're really saying that the person is "able and willing" to serve/help you, and that's what we're the preposition "at" is targeting.

D) Some verbs that often use the preposition "at"

Stare at	Look at	Stay at
Aim at	Meet at	Wave at

E) **Phrasal Verbs.** Look up each phrasal verb and try to understand how the logic of the word "at" applies. Remember, a phrasal verb is basically a preposition put into action by a verb.

Note: The preposition "at" is not used very often to make phrasal verbs. Just like the prepositions "of" and "to", it's usually just a connector.

"You wanna fight? Come at me!" This phrasal verb is more informal. The combination of the verb "come" and the preposition "at" in this context is only possible because of the logic of the preposition "at". If I say "Come at me!", I'm telling you to hit me. Of course, this means that I'm making myself into a target. Here, we're using the preposition "at" like we use it in group four ("a target"). However, we can also look at it as part of group six because if you hit me, the fight starts, meaning that the fight becomes active.

ALTERNATIVES: "You wanna fight? Bring it on!" This sentence means exactly the same thing. Again, we can see a close connection between the prepositions "on" and "at". Remember that "come at me" means that I'm telling you to hit me, which

176

starts the fight. So the fight becomes active. This is exactly like talking about a light and saying "Turn it on".

We also have the idea of a "weight" because a fight is a struggle and it's something more "negative" feeling, so it's like I'm telling you to put that weight on me and we'll see if you can win. Of course, I'm confident that I'll win, so I'm implying that I can hold the weight. Notice if a heavy weight is put on top of something that can't hold the weight, we can say that the thing gets "crushed". This word is closely related to the idea of winning a fight if you do extremely well and your opponent doesn't.

My friends and I like to hang out at my house. In this case, at is simply a connector and is being used in a very basic way. It's like "I'll see you at the beach." We're just talking about a location/specific point in space (my house).

"Why did you hit me?" "(In order) to get back at you for calling me stupid." The preposition "at" in this case simply connects the phrasal verb "get back" (meaning "to get revenge") with the object of the sentence, which is the word "you". We can rephrase the sentence so that it says, "To get you back for calling me stupid". The preposition "at" isn't needed in that case. And the logic? Here, again, we see that the preposition "at" is about a "target".

F) Examples of idioms that use the preposition "at", with detailed explanations.

If you need help, call me. I'll be there at the drop of a hat. This idiom isn't very common. The phrase "at the drop of a hat" means "immediately" or "instantly". Why? Because if you drop a hat, it will hit the ground very quickly. But why the preposition "at"? Drop a hat and <u>at that moment</u> I'll be there. In other words, you're saying that you will be there very quickly.

177

UP

A) Example Sentences. Remember to follow the instructions in section A from previous prepositions.

Note: we like to add the preposition "up" in many cases where it's not needed. This usually gives it a little extra feeling or emphasis. However, the logic always applies.

1)

Throw the ball straight up.
What goes up must come down.
I'm traveling (up) to Canada next month. (I live south of Canada. This can be the US, Mexico, Australia, etc...)
We're going (up) (in)to the mountains this weekend.
The divers came (up) to the surface of the water.
The price of gas is going up every week.
My phone is face-up on the table.

What does the word "up" mean in this group?

2)

He sleeps standing up.
The price of gas is up.
I live (up) on the tenth floor.
Don't put your feet (up) on the table.
Hang your clothes (up) in the closet.
I think she looks better with her hair up.
There's a "help wanted" sign (up) in the window of that restaurant.

What does the word "up" mean in this group?

179

3)

I have to open (up) Firefox. (Firefox is an internet browser.)
The servers are currently down. Do you know when they will be
(back) up?

What does the word "up" mean in this group?

4)

Finish (up) your dinner before it gets cold.
Can you fill this cup (up) with water?

What does the word "up" mean in this group?

5)

What's up? (What's wrong/happening?; also a common casual
greeting)
Hold up. I need to grab something before we leave.

What does the word "up" mean in this group?

6)

(Standing in line:) Move up, please. The line is moving.
(In the back of a store:) I'll meet you up front.
They live up the road from here.
The bathroom is just up this hall.

What does the word "up" mean in this group?

B) The Logic

Key Idea(s): 1) an upward or northward direction; or an upward/upright position;
2) a forward/closer to direction;
3) moving to a positive/active state or onto a platform OR moving to a negative/inactive state or off of a platform

"up" is a two-way preposition

Explanation of the logic: The most basic meaning of the preposition "up" is a direction upward or northward, or sometimes forward/closer to (we'll see what this means in the examples). It could also mean an "upward" or "upright" position. An "upward position" is a static (not moving) point that is higher than some other point, which is similar to the preposition "above". This could be a sign that's up in a window, for example. An "upright position" is like sitting instead of laying down, for example. Part 1 and part 3 of the logic are the more literal meanings.

In all other cases (part 3), we see the ideas of "completion" and "creation". More specifically, many of the uses of the preposition "up" are about either the completion of something or the creation of something, especially in phrasal verbs. The basic idea here is that the preposition "up" is often a bridge or connection between the prepositions "on" and "off" when we're talking about a positive state/active state ("on") and a

181

negative state/inactive state ("off"). (You can see this more clearly if you look at the map.)

When we go from positive/active to negative/inactive, we get the idea of "completion". For example, "Let's wrap up our conversation". This means that I want to finish (complete) our conversation. When we go from negative/inactive to positive/active, we get the idea of "creation". For example, "I'm glad that you brought up that topic". One of the meanings of the phrasal verb "bring up" is "to mention", which means that you introduce a topic into a conversation so that you can start (creation) talking about it, which also makes it the active topic. We'll see a lot more examples soon. It's not as difficult as it might seem. This idea of either "completion" or "creation" is why the preposition "up" is a two-way preposition. Like the preposition "for", we're not using "two-way" like we do with the preposition "of". You can see in the picture above (number 3) how the two directions work. Lastly, sometimes sentences that use part 3 of the logic also use part 1 or part 2.

Etymology notes: There's nothing useful in the etymology.

Now, go back to the example sentences and try to apply the logic. Ask yourself: "How does any part of the logic apply to this sentence?"

C) Detailed Explanations of the Example Sentences.

1) Upward or northward direction (the most basic meaning)

Note: I've given many examples to show you a lot of different contexts where we use the preposition "up". We often like to use it when it's not necessary because it gives a little extra feeling or possibly emphasis to the sentence. The preposition "up" is probably used this way more than any other preposition, and as I said before, it's important to get a feel for it because it will really help you sound like a native speaker.

Throw the ball straight up. This is an easy example. Throw the ball upward.

What goes up must come down. This one's very similar to the previous one. If something goes up, gravity will pull it back down, so we're talking about an upward (and then downward) direction.

I'm traveling (up) to Canada next month. (I live south of Canada. This can be the US, Mexico, Australia, etc...) This is an example of using the preposition "up" to mean "a northward direction". It's depends on where you are or the place that you're thinking about. If that location is south of the destination, you can use the preposition "up", but it's not necessary. You can do the same thing with the preposition "down" if you want to talk about "a southward direction".

We're going (up) (in)to the mountains this weekend. When you go (in)to the mountains, you're traveling to a place that is at a higher elevation, which is an upward direction. We don't need to use the preposition "up" because it's implied, but because we like to use the preposition "up" when it's not necessary, we often add it.

Also notice that in the word "into", we can omit the word "in" and keep the word "to". Normally, we omit the word "to" and keep the word "in", but this is a good example of when we don't. We keep the word "to" because it's the important part of the idea (the destination). If I say, "Put the book into the box", the important part of the idea is "in", so we can say, "Put the book in the box" and not "Put the book to the box". If we only use the preposition "to", it doesn't make sense and you might ask, "Onto or into?"

One last detail. If we say "go up to", that actually means something different. It means that you get very close to

183

something or someone. We'll see an example like that soon. However, it depends on the context. In the context of the example sentence, if you say "We're going up to the mountains", that can mean two different things. 1) You are going to the base of the mountain (where the mountain starts) and that's your destination. This is the most accurate and literal meaning because we're saying "up to". 2) When someone says that they're going up to the mountains, most people don't just stop at the base of the mountain. They mean that they are going to go upward and into the mountains because that's the most common meaning and we usually have enough information from the context.

The divers came (up) to the surface of the water. Here we have a similar sentence, but now we're talking about being under water and then coming to the surface, which is an upward direction.

The price of gas is going up every week. If the price or amount of something "goes up", it means that it increases. In other words, we have an upward direction of the price.

My phone is face-up on the table. What this sentence means is that the back of my phone is touching the table and the front of my phone, which is the screen, is on the opposite side. It's possible to use the word "face" instead of "front" when we talk about certain objects (this sometimes depends on the context). So the "face" (front) of the phone is up and the back is down. The phone is facing an upward direction. In other words, the front (face) of the phone is pointing upward. If you put the front of the phone on the table and the back of the phone is pointing upward, then we say that the phone is "face-down". You can probably also say that this example fits in group two, but the logic still works, so it doesn't matter.

2) *An upward/upright position*

He sleeps standing up. Normally, people sleep lying down on a bed or some other surface. Here, we're talking about a man who sleeps while he's standing. The preposition "up" isn't always needed when using the verb "to stand", but in this case it sounds better to use it because we're emphasizing the fact that he sleeps very differently than most people. So, his position is upright, which means "not lying down" or in a position that is down. (Please note that "downright" is not the opposite of "upright").

The price of gas is up. This is an example where "up" is not a preposition. In this case, the price of gas has increased. Let's say that the price of gas was $2. If the price is "up", now it might be worth $3, for example. So in this example, we're not talking about the price going in an upward direction. The price has already increased, so we're talking about an upward position, which is a static point that is higher than some other point.

ALTERNATIVES: "The price of gas has gone up". Of course, we can use the present perfect tense with the verb "to go", which is actually more "correct" than using the simple present tense with the verb "to be". In everyday speech, we can simply use the simple present tense and the verb "to be", at least in American English.

"The price of gas has risen." In this case, we don't use the preposition "up" at all. This is because the verb "to rise" implies the preposition "up". There are certain contexts where we can use the verb "to rise" with the preposition "up", but in this case it doesn't make any sense.

I live (up) on the tenth floor. This one is very similar to the example about the mountains, but we're simply talking about the height of a building. The reason why this sentence is in group two and not group one is because we're describing a static position (where my apartment is located). When we talked about the mountains, we were traveling upward into the mountains. There might be other floors that are higher, but the tenth floor is higher than the ground, so we can use the preposition "up". In this case, you can also use the preposition "up" (in order) to emphasize the height. If you do, we usually also add the word "way": "I live way up on the tenth floor."

Don't put your feet (up) on the table. Normally, your feet are at a lower point than the table (on the ground), so we can add the preposition "up" because you're raising the position of your feet compared to where they usually are. Remember, in all (of) the cases where "up" is not necessary, we can use it because it's logical, but it's also used in comparison to some lower point.

Hang your clothes (up) in the closet. When you hang something, the meaning of "up" is implied because that thing is hanging. When talking about clothes, it automatically means that the clothes are in an "upright position". They're also in an "upward position" because they're hanging above the ground, which is lower. So we have part 2 of the logic, but we also have part 1. How? In this particular sentence, we're not directly saying that the clothes are hanging, but they will be. We're saying "hang up the clothes", which is an action, so there's a movement in an upward direction as you raise the clothes to hang them on the bar in the closet.

Lastly, we also have part 3 of the logic. Specifically, it's the idea of "completion". We'll talk more about this in group four.

I think she looks better with her hair up. If someone has their hair "up", it means they have hair on their head that is long enough to make a ball or a pony-tail with it. Normally, hair hangs downward, but now it's put into a position that is higher than normal, so it's "up".

There's a "help wanted" sign (up) in the window of that restaurant. The sign might or might not be hanging (usually it

186

is). The important thing is that it's against the glass of the window and clearly visible from the outside. This means we have part 1 of the logic if it's hanging (an upward direction compared to what's below it). We have part 2 of the logic because it's upright and, if it's hanging, because it's in an upward position. And we also have part 3 of the logic because the preposition "up" is connecting to a positive/active state. What does that mean?

Think of it like "the hotel vacancy light is on". When a hotel has vacancies, it means there are rooms that people can stay in. The word "vacancy" is made with lights (or there's a special light next to the word "vacancy"), so when they turn on the light, you know that there are rooms that are available. When there are no available rooms and they're all filled by other people, either the light turns off or a "no vacancy" light turns on. If the restaurant is looking for new employees, then they have job openings, which means that someone can take/fill that spot. This is a positive/active state. If they don't need any more workers, then all positions are filled and there are no openings. This is a negative/inactive state.

So, if the sign is "up", it tells people that there are job openings, meaning that the light is "on" for those positions. This is how the preposition "up" is connecting to the preposition "on", and it implies the preposition "on", which is a positive/active state. It also has the added idea of "creation", because if a job is open, that spot has been "created" so that someone can take it. Of course, the first two parts of the logic work really well and we don't need the third part, but it can be useful to look at it this way.

ALTERNATIVES: "They're hiring." Obviously, this isn't the same thing. However, in this context, the sign is up because they're looking for workers. In other words, they're hiring new workers. So in this case, this is another way to express the same meaning, even though the words are very different. There is one necessary detail: the person who you're talking to has to see that there's a sign in the window. If they don't, then they might ask,

"How do you know?" The you'll have to say part of the original example sentence.

3) *Creation*

This group is all about "creation". Specifically, we're talking about something that's in a negative/inactive state and it moves to a positive/active state (see the positions of the prepositions "on" and "off" on the map (in order) to see this more clearly). This can include the idea of something coming into existence from non-existence. Note: the "creation" idea is more common in phrasal verbs, so we'll see more soon.

I have to open (up) Firefox. When talking about a computer program, the verbs that we usually use are "to open" and "to close". You can add the preposition "up" to give it an extra feeling of "creation" because you're <u>starting</u> the program. However, the verb "to open" is enough by itself. We just like to add the preposition "up" and it sounds very natural.

ALTERNATIVES: "I have to start Firefox."

"I have to run Firefox". The verb "to run" in this context means "to start".

"I have to bring up Firefox." We'll talk more about the phrasal verb "bring up" later. In this sentence, "bring up" can mean "to start", but it's more likely that the program is already started and it's currently in the background (which means that it's not the currently active window (program) that you see on the screen). So, you have to "bring it up" so that it's visible in front of the other windows (programs).

The servers are currently down. Do you know when they'll be (back) up? This is a very easy example. Of course, in this sentence, the word "servers" means computer servers. For example, the servers that hold data for a website. If a machine is "down", it means that it's off or not working somehow. If it's "up", it's on or working. Why? Well, the preposition "on" is a positive/active state and we know that the prepositions "on" and "up" connect in a special way. If the computers are "down", "off", "offline", or just not working in some way, then the computers are in a negative/inactive state. "Up", "on", "online", or just generally working properly means that the computers are in a positive/active state. So, if they're "down" right now, then we want them to be "up".

That's easy enough, but why do we use the prepositions "up" and "down" instead of "on" and "off"? Notice that the servers being "down" can mean "off", "offline", or just not working properly. So, the computers might be on, but not online. Or they might be on, but not working properly. When we talk about machines, the preposition "on" simply means that the machine starts, but that doesn't mean that it's working they way that it's supposed to. We use the prepositions "up" and "down" in this context (in order) to show that something is or isn't working properly. This means that both the preposition "on" and the preposition "up" can mean a "positive/active state". It just depends on the context. Usually, the preposition "up" is more about the connection between "on" and "off". This can be on and off (of) a surface/platform, but especially the connection between a positive/active state and a negative/inactive state. However, sometimes, "up" is a positive/active state (and "down" is a negative/inactive state). Again, it just depends on the context.

Ok, so now that we know all (of) that, why is this sentence in the "creation" group? We know from the previous example sentence that if we "open up" a computer program, it means that we're starting that program. In this case, we're talking about the servers being off or not working the way they're supposed to. Because we have to restore them, it's like you close a computer program and then open it again. You're "creating an instance" of that program. That sounds a little complicated, but it's a real expression in English when talking about computer programs or programming. Obviously, a computer program is different than an entire server and all the possible problems that might happen with a server, but the same basic idea of "creation" is being applied to this new context. Of course, we're actually talking about the servers being <u>back</u> up (meaning "working again"), so more specifically, we're talking about "re-creation" or creating again, but that's just because of the preposition "back" and it doesn't matter for the logic of the preposition "up".

Note: As you can see, the preposition "back" is in parentheses because it's not necessary. However, we often use the preposition "back" with the meaning of "again, "to return", or "to restore". In this example, the computers were working fine, and then there was a problem, so we want to return them to the positive/active state in which they're working fine again. It's not necessary to use the preposition "back", but it's very natural in this context. In fact, if the context isn't 100% clear (for example, if the first sentence is missing) and you don't use the preposition "back", it might sound like you're turning the servers on for the first time.

ALTERNATIVES: "Do you know when they'll be (back) up and running?" We have a phrase in English: "up and running". If the server is "up", then of course it's running (which means "working" in this context). So it's redundant (meaning repetitive and unnecessary) to say "up and running", but we use it (in order) to emphasize.

4) _Completion_

This group is all about "completion". In the "creation" group, we were talking about something that's in a negative/inactive state and it moves to a positive/active state. The idea of "completion" is the opposite: something that's in a positive/active state and it moves to a negative/inactive state. This can include the idea of something going out of existence. Note: the "completion" idea is more common in phrasal verbs, so we'll see more soon.

190

Finish (up) your dinner before it gets cold. In this group, the preposition "up" simply adds a feeling of "completion". The verb "to finish" means "to complete" or "to end", so we don't need the preposition "up", but we like to add it anyway.

Also, when you're going to eat dinner, there's food, which means that the food exists. When you finish eating dinner, all (of) the food is gone, which means that it doesn't exist anymore.

Can you fill this cup (up) with water? Here we have another example that doesn't need the preposition "up", but we like to add it. Obviously, if you fill a cup with water, it will be full of water. But we like to say "fill up" because it adds that little extra feeling of completion.

5) Positive state/Active State (rare slang uses)

Unfortunately, because the prepositions "up" and "on" share such a close relationship, there are some cases in which we use the preposition "up" with the meaning of "positive state/active state" instead of the preposition "on". This isn't common, and it seems that it only happens in slang phrases.

What's up? (What's wrong/happening?; also a common casual greeting) You're probably familiar with this phrase. If not, we usually use it as a casual greeting that means the same as "hi". In the US, we normally don't expect an answer when using these basic greetings and we just use it (in order) to be polite by acknowledging the other person. When we use it as a greeting, we're using part 3 of the logic (the connection to a positive/active state). This is one of the special cases where it's not just the connection to a positive/active state, but it actually IS a positive/active state. This is because of the meaning of the phrase, which is "What's wrong?" or "What's happening?". If something is happening, it's an active process. For example, your friend asks, "Do you have a minute?" You respond, "Yeah, what's up?" This means that you want to know what it is that they want to talk about, or "what's happening".

191

But here's another important thing: the preposition "on" is often a surface/platform and always a positive/active state. These two parts of the preposition "on" are closely related. If something is on a platform, it's at a higher point. When we say, "What's up?", we're using both parts of the logic of the preposition "on" because the thing that's happening is "active", but it's also like it's on an abstract platform, so it's "up" (part 2 of the logic of the preposition "up").

You might be wondering how a positive/active state applies to the idea of "what's wrong", because the word "wrong" is negative. Remember, if the red light is "on", it's in a positive/active state. "Positive state/active state" is neutral, not "good". The phrase, "what's up" can mean "what's wrong" depending on the context. It's basically a context-specific version of "what's happening".

ALTERNATIVES: "What's going on?" We can also use the verb "to go" with the preposition "on". The logic of "on" works as it normally does. This phrase can be a casual greeting like "What's up" and it means the same thing. If you don't use it as a greeting, then it means "what's happening" or "what's wrong", depending on the context, just like the phrase, "What's up?" In other words, "What's going on?" uses the preposition "on", which is what we expect because of the meaning and the logic behind the meaning. "What's up?" is slang that's based on the phrase "What's going on?", which means that "What's up?" is a newer use of the original phrase.

Hold up. I need to grab something before we leave. This phrase sounds very informal and it's definitely slang. It's exactly the same as saying "hold on", which means "wait". Again, we're using the preposition "up" in a casual context with the logic of the preposition "on". As I said, this only seems to happen in very casual/slang phrases. All the explanation for the previous example applies to this example, as well.

192

6) A "forward/closer to" direction

Part 1 of the logic covers the ideas of an "upward direction", a "northward direction", and a "'forward/closer to' direction". However, this last one is not as common and it's a little special, so it has its own group. What's the difference between "forward" and "closer to"? They're very similar and are really just two slightly different ways of looking at the same thing. The difference depends on the context.

(Standing in line:) Move up, please. The line is moving. Here we have the phrasal verb, "move up". Imagine that you're at the bank and there's a long line. As you wait in line, you start doing something on your phone. Because you're not paying attention, when the line moves forward, the person behind you says, "Move up, please. The line is moving." So, we have the verb "to move". Then we have the preposition "up", which in this case means "forward". When we put these two together, we have the idea of "move in a forward direction". Why? How does the logic work? We're talking about part 1 of the logic. The idea of an "upward direction" is shifted. Instead of meaning "upward", like toward the sky (which is a vertical (up-and-down) direction), we mean "forward", which is a horizontal (side-to-side; front-to-back) direction. So, we're using "upward" horizontally, which gives it the meaning of "forward".

ALTERNATIVES: "Move forward, please. The line is moving." Of course, we can just use the preposition "forward", but native speakers really like to use the preposition "up" as often as possible.

(In the back of a store:) I'll meet you up front. This means that I'm inside (of) a store, specifically in the back part of it and I'm telling you that I'll meet you in the front part of the inside. When we talk about the front of something, especially the front part of something that's inside, we often like to add the preposition "up".

193

But why do we say "up front"? How does the logic work? Well, we know that we're talking about part 1 of the logic. Remember that the idea of an "upward direction" is shifted to horizontal instead of vertical, which means we're talking about "forward"/"closer to". But there's an extra piece here: it's very natural to extend this idea to part 2 of the logic (an upward/upright position). So, where am I going to meet you? Inside the store, but specifically the part that is the front. This is because the words "forward" and "front" are almost the same, but the word "forward" is a direction and the word "front" is a static (not moving) point. I'm going to move forward (in order) to meet you at that point.

ALTERNATIVES: "I'll meet you in the front (of the store)." We can also use the preposition "in" because you are inside the store, specifically the front part.

Note: This is different than the sentence, "I'll meet you in front (of the store)" (the word "the" is missing). The phrase "in front of" means that you are outside of the store, but the part of the store that you are outside of is the front part. Interestingly, instead of saying "up front", the alternative for this is "out front" because you are outside of the store. The phrase "in the front of" means that you are are inside the store, but the part of the store that you are in is the front part.

They live up the road from here. The meaning of this sentence is: "They live at a point that is farther along than the point we are at right now". So, if you keep going forward, you'll find their house. We definitely have the idea of "forward", but we're also talking about moving closer to the destination, which is their house.

Interestingly, the prepositions "up" and "down" are interchangeable in this context; it just depends on how the speaker is thinking about it. There are a lot of interesting points related to this idea, but because it's more common with the preposition down, we'll discuss and compare all (of) the details about both of

194

these prepositions when we talk about the preposition "down" later in the book.

The bathroom is just up this hall. This example is very similar to the previous one. You and I are standing next to a hallway and you ask me where the bathroom is. I say, "It's just up this hall". We use the word "just" (in order) to emphasize that it's really close. We use the preposition "up" (in order) to talk about moving forward and closer to the bathroom. That's the simple version of the explanation. Like the previous example, we can use both the prepositions "up" and "down". We'll see this sentence again later when we talk about the preposition "down".

D) Verbs that usually take the preposition "up"

Finish up	Fold up	Open up
Pull up	Go up	Come up
Close up	Drag up	Stand up

E) **Phrasal Verbs.** Look up each phrasal verb and try to understand how the logic of the word "up" applies. Remember, a phrasal verb is basically a preposition put into action by a verb.

For this preposition, I've limited the number of phrasal verbs to 10 because there are so many and adding more would take up extra space in this book. Unlike the prepositions "of", "to", and "at", the preposition "up" is used in a lot of phrasal verbs.

(Mom:) Pick up your dirty clothes and put them in the laundry basket! The phrasal verb "pick up" is easy to understand because the meaning is literal: there's something on the floor (or some other surface) and you grab it. You're higher than the surface you picked it up from, so it moves upward. However, in some

195

cases, there's an extra meaning. This sentence isn't just about grabbing the items, but it implies "cleaning" or "organizing" of some kind. So, we have the literal meaning of part 1 (upward direction), but also the meaning of "completion" from part 3 because if you pick up all (of) your clothes and put them where they belong, you're done and you've cleaned that part of the room.

He came up to me and punched me in the face. This sentence doesn't mean that the other person is at a lower point than me (although it can mean that). It means that the person comes toward me and stops in front of me and then punches me in the face. From the perspective of that person, this is a forward direction. From my perspective, the person is coming closer to me.

Here we run into some of the details that I mentioned earlier about the prepositions "up" and "down". (In order) to explain this sentence, we need one of those details. In the mind of an English speaker, wherever you are is like the center of your existence and this center is sort of "raised" in relation to other things. This isn't something that native speakers are fully conscious of, but there's strong etymological evidence to support this idea and it explains why we say things like, "I'll meet you down at park", even if the park isn't at a lower position than you (we'll discuss this example later). When we say "he came up to me", the he's "down" (meaning "farther away") compared to your position and when they come closer to you, they move "up" or "upward" (meaning "closer to") until they occupy almost the same space that you do. If that's confusing, it will make a lot more sense later in the book.

Is there any way to warm up this room? "To warm up" simply means "to increase the warmth/make warmer". We've seen before that we can use the preposition "up" with the meaning of increasing something, which is an abstract upward direction. It can also be a connection to a positive/active state because if it's cold, there's a lack of heat. Add more heat into the room and now the heat is existing in the room.

196

What time do you get up in the morning? This is a phrasal verb that you probably know. Why do we use the preposition "up"? Obviously we're lying down and physically raise ourselves out of bed. This means we have part 1 (upward direction) and part 2 (upright/upward position). However, we also have part 3, and this time we can see both the ideas of "creation" and "completion", depending on how you look at it. It can be creation because (in order) to start your day, you have to get up. It can be completion because once you've gotten up, you've finished/completed the task of getting out of bed.

Can you help me set up my wi-fi? "To set up" is a perfect example of both "creation" and "completion". It's creation because you're establishing a connection to the internet where there was no connection before, meaning that you're getting it "up and running". After it is "up and running", it means that the connection has been established. In other words, the connection is "completed". Of course, it's also active.

I have a meeting coming up next week. If something is "coming up", it means that it will happen in the future. In this example, you can of course just say, "I have a meeting next week", but the "coming up" makes it feel a little different, like "it's happening soon", or "it's coming". It makes the event feel more like it's not just sitting in the future, but is actively coming closer to the present moment. Or you can look at it the other way: the present moment is coming closer to the meeting. This is exactly the same as "he came up to me" or "they live up this road". The only difference is that we're talking about points in time instead of space.

The preposition "up" in this sentence uses part 1 of the logic because we have the idea of moving forward in time or moving closer to an event that will happen in the future. It's also part 3 of the logic. Of course, we have the idea of "creation" because it's going to start/happen. However, we also see a very strong connection between the prepositions "up" and "on". When the meeting starts, it will be "on" (active), like a light. The

197

preposition "up" is helping to strongly connect the present moment with the event in the future as we move forward in time. Next week, when the present moment = the time of the meeting, we have officially moved "onto the platform" and the meeting comes into existence – in other words, it's now a positive/active state of existence.

NOTE: Don't confuse this with the preposition "in". We say "I'm in a meeting" because a meeting is a container. The example sentence isn't about being in a meeting. We're talking about when the meeting will start. So we're talking about the point in time that's currently in the future and is inactive.

I'm glad you brought that up. Let's talk about it. This example is very similar to the diver example that we saw in group one. However, in that example, we were talking about the physical surface of the water. Here, we're talking about the fact that someone mentions something. When you mention something, you bring it into the conversation and it becomes a topic. That topic was inactive but now it's active. We could also say that the topic was hidden under the abstract "surface" of your mind (like the surface of water) because it was first just a thought, and no one knows what you're thinking. When you mention it, it comes up to the surface and into existence as a topic to discuss.

Also, as you know, we can look at a topic as an abstract platform. So, "to bring something up" means that you grabbed it from inside your mind and brought it out into reality, then placed it onto the platform for discussion so now it's the active topic. And, as you know, because you introduced the topic into the conversation, you start talking about it, which gives us the idea of "creation". This is one of the clearest examples of how the preposition "up" is a connector to the preposition "on" and the idea of a positive/active state.

As a side note, you've probably noticed that we say "to talk about", not "to talk on". We'll see the preposition "about" later in the book, but this is a good example of where two

198

prepositions touch or overlap, but English doesn't like to use the preposition "on" with the verb "to talk". You can "give a talk on a topic", but that's "talk" as a noun and the preposition "on" goes with the word "topic". So this is an example of when you have to remember a special case for a particular verb.

(While running:) Can you slow down? I can't keep up with you! "To keep up with" someone or something means that you can maintain the same speed as that person or thing. In this example, two people are running and one person is faster than the other person. The second person is having trouble maintaining the same speed, so they can't "keep up". The verb "to keep" means "to remain the same", "to maintain", or "to continue".

Let's say that the first person is running at 15 miles per hour and the second person can only run 10 miles per hour. 15 miles per hour is the positive/active state ("current speed") of the first person that is compared to 10 miles per hour, which is the positive/active state ("current speed") of the second person. So, the second person's speed is not equal to the first person's speed, meaning the positive/active states (the speeds) are not the same. The second person can't "keep up" (maintain) the same positive/active state (speed) as the first person. Note that this isn't about "creation" or "completion" because we're talking about the maintaining of something that already exists and isn't starting or ending. In this special case, we're talking about the connection between two different positive/active states because we're comparing them and trying to keep them the same. So the verb "to keep" and similar verbs might seem strange when we talk about the logic.

Of course, we also have part two of the logic, which is a "forward/closer to direction". In this case, the idea of "forward" is what we're talking about specifically. The first person is ahead of the second person, so the first person is farther up or "more forward". The second person can't "keep up", so they can't maintain the same amount of forward direction (speed), which means that their location is behind the first person.

The bus never came, so I ended up walking home. "To end up doing something" is about the result of something. Because the bus never came, the result was that I walked home instead of taking the bus. The verb "to end", of course, means the end of something. The preposition "up" adds the idea of <u>completion</u> and gives us the meaning of "a result" when we combine it with the verb "to end". But why can't we just say, "I ended walking home"? That sounds more like you were walking home and then you arrived home, so the walking ended. In this case, we don't use the verb "to end". Instead, we use the verb "to finish": "I finished walking home". This clearly doesn't give us the meaning of "a result". It only tells us that some action ("walking") finished. So, the verb "to end" by itself doesn't mean "a result". However, we can use the preposition "up" (in order) to talk about the <u>creation</u> of a result that's due to some other action or event. The bus didn't come (action/event 1) → This is the cause. What effect/result did the cause <u>create</u>? I walked home (action/event 2).

ALTERNATIVES: The bus never came, so I walked home."

"Because the bus never came, I walked home." / "Because the bus never came, I ended up walking home." Because of the word "because" in these two sentences, we can clearly see the cause and effect ("result") relationship.

When I grow up, I want to be a police officer. The phrasal verb "to grow up" usually means "to become an adult", but it can also mean "to be more mature". For example, you have a friend who is thirty, but they're acting like a child, so you can tell them, "Grow up!", which means "stop acting like a child" or "be more mature".

How does the preposition "up" work with the verb "to grow" (in order) to create the meaning of "to become an adult"? Obviously, adults are taller than children, so we can apply part 1 of the logic. We can also apply part 1 in terms of becoming more mature (an increase in maturity), as well as becoming smarter and more experienced in life (an increase in knowledge and experience). Part 2 doesn't apply. What about part 3? Well, if we use the preposition "up" to mean "completion", it works. Of course, just because you reach the age of an adult (or older), it doesn't mean that you're done learning or growing mentally. However, physically, you've finished growing and your body is more or less fully developed.

F) Examples of idioms that use the preposition "up", with detailed explanations.

It's up to you. This means that I'm telling you to decide what to do. Let's say we want to go to a restaurant tonight. You ask me, "Where do you want to go?" I say, "I don't care. It's up to you". So I'm saying that you can pick the restaurant because I don't care which restaurant we go to. There's another meaning of this phrase, but we'll only talk about this meaning.

How does the logic apply? We know that we have collocations like "based on", to depend on", etc…, as well as phrases like, "He has to carry the weight of the world on his shoulders". That's the basic idea that's in the background. When I say, "It's up to you", I'm making you the basis for the decision and the "weight" is on you. Ok, so why do we use the preposition "up" and not the preposition "on"? In this particular context, you asked me, which means that you're putting the weight on me. If I decide where we go, then I carry the weight of the decision. But I don't care, so I remove the weight from myself (off (of) a platform) and move it onto you (onto a platform). So the preposition "up" is <u>connecting</u> between me being the basis/platform and you being the basis/platform. Of course, the ideas of "positive state/active state" and "negative state/inactive state" are working, as well, because the preposition "on" is always a positive/active state and the preposition "off" is always a negative/inactive state.

It might help to know that we also have the idiom "It's on you" (more commonly, "That's on you"). This idiom has more

201

than one meaning, but the important one in this case is "blame". If I say, "That's on you", it means that I'm blaming you because you decided to do something. Blame is a weight that you put on someone and it's negative, so it makes sense that we use the preposition "on". This is part of the reason why we say "up to you" and not "on you" or "on to you" when we want to talk about allowing someone else to decide something.

Time's up! This means that there's no time left for some activity. For example, you're taking a test and you have sixty minutes to complete it. After sixty minutes, the person who gave you the test says, "Time's up!", which means that you have to stop if you haven't finished yet. Why do we use the preposition "up"? Because we're talking about the <u>completion/end</u> of the available time.

BY

A) Example Sentences. Remember to follow the instructions in section A from previous prepositions.

1)

This book was written by my father.
I'm excited by the prospect of living in Japan.
We were amazed by his skill.
I was raised by my grandparents.
She's old enough to walk home by herself.
I'm very calm by nature. (My natural personality; NOT when I'm in nature)
"Mom, can I go to my friend's house?" "It's fine by me."

What does the word "by" mean in this group?

2)

You can travel all around the world by plane.
We walked to the beach by foot.
Are you paying by cash or credit?
I learned how to sing by watching videos online.

What does the word "by" mean in this group?

3)

The bank is by the park.
I live by the beach.
He drove by us on his motorcycle.

What does the word "by" mean in this group?

4)

Turn in the report by Friday.
I'll be home by seven.
My brother had already left by the time I arrived home.

What does the word "by" mean in this group?

5)

I get better at English day by day./I get better at English by the day.
I'm paid by the hour, but my friend is paid by salary.
Stock prices rose by 40 percent.
This room measures 15 by 18. (measurement of room size in feet)

What does the word "by" mean in this group?

B) The Logic

Key Idea(s): a path or a way

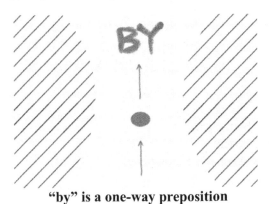

"by" is a one-way preposition

Explanation of the logic: The preposition "by" is probably the most abstract of all (of) the prepositions, and I had a lot of difficulty trying to find the exact logic and putting the feeling of it into words. There are two words that are very similar, but we usually use them in different contexts and different ways (for example, in this context, we don't say, "we use them in different paths"). Some of the example sentences fit both ideas, and you can (sometimes very abstractly) fit most of the uses of the preposition "by" into the idea of "way". However, there are some uses that are simply too abstract to realistically fit the idea of "way". So, we have the similar idea of "path".

The preposition "by" is naturally very abstract and you might have difficulties completely understanding it at first. Like all (of) the other prepositions, with enough exposure to English and enough practice, you'll eventually start to feel the preposition "by". It just might take you a little longer than the other prepositions.

Etymology notes: The etymology of the preposition "by" is extremely useful for English learners. "By" comes from the Old English "be-"/"bi", which meant what is now "near", "in", "by", "during", and "about". This originally came from the Proto-Germanic word "bi", which meant "around" or "about". Lastly, this Proto-Germanic word came from the Proto-Indo-European word "(am)bhi-", which meant "around". So we can see that over time, the original idea of "around" expanded to include many other meanings. This expansion (including new and different applications of the modern preposition "by") continued through Middle English and into Modern English. 10 This is why the preposition "by" is so abstract and why it touches or sometimes overlaps with many other prepositions. However, even though it's so abstract, it still has a logic and a feeling.

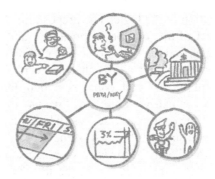

Now, go back to the example sentences and try to apply the logic. Ask yourself: "How is 'by' a path or a way?"

C) Detailed Explanations of the Example Sentences.

1) *an abstract medium that's a cause/source*

The preposition "through" isn't very difficult to learn, so it's not in this book. However, when we talk about a "way" or a "path", or just the preposition "by" in general, the idea of "through" often applies. Why? Because we can often use the preposition "through" with the meaning of "a medium through which something happens".

In this group, the mediums are abstract and they're the "cause/source" of what happens. The passive voice structure is very common in this group.

This book was written by my father. If we use active voice, this sentence is: "My father wrote this book". When we use passive voice, we use the preposition "by" to show who or what does the action. The logic works like this: it's like the action flows through the person or thing that does the action. In other words, that person or thing is the medium through which the action happens. That person or thing becomes the <u>path</u> that the action flows through, or the <u>way</u> that the action comes into existence. In this case, we have a book, and we're talking about writing a book. Who wrote the book? My father. Because he wrote it, the words in the book flowed from him, going through his mind and into the book, eventually resulting in a finished book that is now written. The book came into existence through my father, who was the "medium". Because my father created the book, he is the cause/source of the book coming into existence. We can also see that if someone else wrote the book, that person would probably write it in a different way. So, the way that my father wrote it also applies here.

I'm excited by the prospect of living in Japan. The active voice version of this sentence is: "The prospect of living in Japan excites me". The word "prospect" means the possibility of something. It's like saying "the thought of living in Japan", but it's not just a thought, it's an actual possibility that might happen. So, I have or might have the chance to live in Japan. When that thought enters my mind, I get excited. In other words, my excitement comes into existence or happens through that thought, meaning that the thought is the medium through which my excitement is created. In other words, the prospect of living in Japan is the cause/source of my excitement.

ALTERNATIVES: "I'm excited at the prospect of living in Japan." In this case, the prepositions "by" and "at" overlap. We saw sentences earlier like "He smiled at hearing her voice". In that sentence, the two actions happen at the same time and one action causes the other action. This alternative sentence is the same. When I think about living in Japan (and I know that it actually might happen), I become excited. So, the thought enters my mind (the first action) and when it does (at the moment that it does), I become excited at the same time. But the thought is also the cause of my excitement.

Note: it would be perfectly logical to use the preposition "for" (as a basis), as well, but in this context, that's the old use of the preposition "for" that we mostly use in poetry.

We were amazed by his skill. The active voice in this case is: "His skill amazed us". When we use the preposition "by", "his skill" becomes the path of our amazement, or the way that the amazement comes into existence. In other words, it's the cause/source of our amazement.

ALTERNATIVES: "We were amazed at his skill." This is exactly the same as the alternative for the previous example.

I was raised by my grandparents. Active voice: "My grandparents raised me". Notice that we have a phrasal verb that can replace the verb "to raise": "to bring up". We saw earlier the use of "to bring up" with the meaning of "to mention something". It can also mean "to raise a child": "I was brought up by my grandparents./My grandparents brought me up". Why does that matter? Because the logic of the preposition "up" in that phrasal verb is closely tied to the logic of the preposition "by". My grandparents taught me right from wrong and everything else that's related to raising a child. These things were a large part of what formed who I am today. How did I get where I am? Through the influence of my grandparents. Their raising me was the path or way that I became who I am. This is related to the preposition "up" because the preposition "up" is about connecting to a positive state/active state ("on") and as we've seen with previous examples, we're really talking about the path or way through which something comes into existence. You might also notice that, in an abstract way, my grandparents put (and kept) me "on" a certain path that led to who I am now. So, we can see how these prepositions are related in this sentence.

Basically, my grandparents are the cause/source of who I am, or at least the cause/source of what I was taught when I was a child.

She's old enough to walk home by herself. If you do something "by yourself", you do it alone. We use the reflexive pronouns (yourself, myself, etc..), and that's the key here. Whatever action it is, it happens through your own efforts without the help of someone else. In other words, you are the path through which the action happens. We can easily see how you are also the cause/source of that action.

I'm very calm by nature. When we talk about how someone is naturally, meaning how their personality is, we can use the preposition "by". Why? If something comes from nature, then nature is the source of that thing.

Another way to look at it is that it's similar to the preposition "through": you can also think of "calm" as a path that goes through the person. Or, more simply, you can say that that's the way the person is. It's part of the way that they exist.

ALTERNATIVES: "I'm naturally very calm."

"Mom, can I go to my friend's house?" "It's fine by me." If something is "fine by someone", it means that they're ok with that thing happening. However, just because I think that it's ok, doesn't mean that you think that it's ok. So maybe there's a mother and a father. The mother says, "It's fine by me", but the father disagrees. So, if the child decides to go based on the mother's perspective, it's fine.

ALTERNATIVES: "It's fine with me." We can also use the preposition "with". The child wants to go to their friend's house. That's an idea. The child asks their mother if they can go. The mother says, "It's fine with me", which means "yes". So, the question/idea about going their friend's house and the mother's opinion/permission go together.

2) mode/method (more specific versions of "way"); a concrete (not abstract) medium

You can travel all around the world by plane. When talking about modes of transportation, we often use the preposition "by" because the word "mode" is closely related to the word "way". This applies to cars, buses, ships, etc..., as we saw earlier with the

209

alternatives for the preposition "on". Whatever mode of transportation that you use, it's the way that you get from one place to another place.

We walked to the beach by foot. This is another example of transportation or travel, but I included it because it's not a vehicle. If you go "by foot", this is exactly the same as saying "on foot".

ALTERNATIVES: "We walked to the beach on foot."

Are you paying by cash or credit? Cash and credit card are methods of payment. They're the ways through which you pay for things.

ALTERNATIVES: "Are you paying in cash or credit?" We can look at the method of payment as a container that carries the value. Note that if we specify a particular currency (US Dollar, Mexican Peso, etc...), we don't use "by", only "in" because when you're in a particular country, you usually can't pay with the currency of another country.

I learned how to sing by watching videos online. When you do something by doing another thing, you are doing the first thing through the second thing. In other words, "watching videos online" is the method (way) that I used (in order) to learn how to sing. We can also say that watching videos is the path that I chose instead of taking classes or some other method/way.

ALTERNATIVES: "I learned how to sing through watching videos online." As we know, the meaning of the preposition "through" is often very close to the meaning of the preposition "by", but they're not usually interchangeable. In this sentence, they are interchangeable.

3) *Proximity (meaning that something is close to something else)*

The bank is by the park. When we say that the bank is by the park, it means that the bank is close to or near the park. It might be next to the park or it might not be, but it's in the same area. The preposition "by" in this context implies "within a close distance" of something. It could be next to, near, across the street, or even up the block (a short distance farther along the road). But how is this a "path" or a "way". The bank and the park are along the same path or close to the same path, but within a short distance from each other. Let's say you walk along 5th street. Eventually, you see the bank and next to it is the park. Or, after you see the bank, if you keep going, you see the park. It might not be a straight line, but they're both along or close to the same path. We can also think of it as a "way" meaning "direction". Go this way (direction) and you'll see the bank and then the park. It might help to imagine two trees and a road or a street (which are types of paths). One tree is on one side of the road and the other tree is on the other side of the road, so they're both found along the same path. Just remember that the preposition "by" doesn't tell us exactly where something is. It only tells us where something is within short distance from something else.

ALTERNATIVES: "The bank is near/close to the park."/"The bank is next to the park"/"The bank is (somewhere) around the park." These alternatives aren't exact synonyms of the preposition

211

"by". They imply a certain degree of distance that can be either the same as "by" or different than "by". First we have "next to", which is the shortest distance. Usually when something in next to something else, it means that they are side-by-side. The preposition "by" includes this idea, but it can be much bigger. "Near" is the same as "close to", and they're a little bigger than "next to". Again, the preposition "by" includes these two, but is still bigger. We can also use the preposition "around". It's very abstract in this context and means "in the general area of something", which means that it can be a little bigger than the preposition "by". If we use the preposition "around" (which is the least common option), we usually add some extra words, like "somewhere around here" or, in the case of our example sentence, "somewhere around the park".

I live by the beach. This is exactly the same as the previous sentence, except instead of saying where one thing is located based on its proximity to another thing, I'm talking about where I live based on my proximity to something.

ALTERNATIVES: same as previous sentence

He drove by us on his motorcycle. Here, we're using the preposition "by" with a verb of motion ("to drive"). The preposition "by" in this case is simply a synonym of the preposition "past", which means "farther than": "He drove past us on his motorcycle".

How is the preposition "by" a way or a path in this case? It's very similar to "The bank is by the park". The difference is that the bank and the park don't move, so in that case, we're talking about the fixed/static location of one thing in relation to the fixed/static location of another thing. Here, we're talking about our location, which is fixed/static, and his location, which is moving. He moves (drives) from a point that is behind us to a point that is farther ahead of us. He's on a path that at one point is next to or near us, but the path continues farther than the point

212

we're currently at. So we have the same logic, but with the added meaning of movement.

4) *a passage of time with a strict end point (limit point)*

Turn in the report by Friday. We know that the preposition "to" is about an end point. The preposition "by" can also be about an end point (in time), but the difference is that we include a period of time before the end point. If today is Monday and I have to turn in the report by Friday, it means that I can turn it in any time between now and Friday, including Friday.

Ok, so how is this a "way" or a "path"? Well, we can imagine an abstract path of time that starts on Monday and ends on Friday. The path leads to Friday, which is the due date (the "destination"). This is exactly the same as saying from my house to the beach, which creates a path. However, we need the preposition "from" (in order) to talk about the start point and the preposition "to" (in order) to talk about the end point. Remember that the "from/to" combination is usually focused on the start and end only. The preposition "by" starts now and goes to a certain end point in the future, but the path between the two points is also very important. Remember that if we're using the preposition "by", I can turn in the report on any day as long as it's not after Friday. So we're on a path of time, and I can turn in the report at any point along that path. Note that we have a phrase in English: "a passage of time", and the word "passage" has a similar meaning to the word "path".

213

I'll be home by seven. This is another example, but with a specific hour as the end point, instead of a specific day. I might be home at 4, 5, etc… but I won't be home later than 7.

My brother had already left by the time I arrived home. This sentence is a little more complex. It's the basic structure used for the past perfect tense. Remember that the past perfect is used to show that two actions happened in the past. The part of the sentence that uses "had done something" is the action that happened first, and the part of the sentence that uses "by the time" is the action that happened later. My brother left and later I arrived home. The preposition "by" in this case is being used the same way as in the previous two sentences, but it might be harder to see how. In a sentence like this, "the time" means whatever time the action happened (for example, 11:00), but the specific time isn't important. So, my brother leaves the house. Starting from that point, he isn't home anymore. Later, I arrive home. The time I get home is the end point. In this sentence, we don't know the specific time that I arrived, nor do we know the specific time that my brother left. Maybe he left five hours ago or maybe he left two minutes ago. All we know for sure is that when I arrived, we wasn't home anymore.

Note that you can simply replace the second part of the sentence with a specific time and it looks almost exactly the same as the previous sentences: "My brother had already left by 11:00"; or to make it even easier and more similar: "My brother left by 11:00". We don't know exactly when he left, but we do know that it wasn't later than 11:00.

5) a measurement (often a rate, which is a specific type of measurement)

I get better at English day by day./I get better at English by the day. "Day by day" and "by the day" mean the same thing: "each day". You can replace "day" with "minute", "hour", "month", etc… This is very similar to saying "little by little" (a

214

little more/less each time). It's very easy to see that we're advancing toward a goal little by little or step by step, and that's exactly how a path is traveled: step by step (one step at a time). In this sentence, each day is a step on the path to becoming a fluent English speaker.

This is a "rate" because we're measuring how quickly you're improving. Is it minute by minute (each minute) or hour by hour (each hour)? In this case, it's a little each day, so "day by day".

I'm paid by the hour, but my friend is paid by salary. If you get paid by the hour, it means for every hour that you work, you earn a certain amount of money. Literally, this can mean that you get paid immediately every hour, but in reality, you receive the money at regular intervals (usually every two weeks). The amount that you earn is measured in hours. However, if you get paid by salary, it means that you don't make money based on each hour. The amount that you earn is determined for the whole year, so if you work extra hours, you don't get paid extra money. This can be an abstract "path", but in this case it's easier to look at it as a "way". For example, we ask: "How do you get paid?" In other words: "In what way do you get paid?" In either case, we can see that there's an hourly rate vs a yearly rate, which means that "hourly" is one measurement and "yearly" is another measurement.

Stock prices rose by 40 percent. In this example, we're talking about an increase of 40%. You could also use dollars, for example: "Stock prices rose by $2". Think of the amount as a path. You start at $5, for example, and the price increases to $7. Between the two prices, we can draw a line: 5------>7. This is like a path between the two prices. In this case, we can say that the price increased by $2. So the path is "$2". Note that we can also talk about this with the prepositions "from" and "to": "The price changed/increased from $5 to $7". You can see that the preposition "to" and the preposition "by" touch sometimes. But remember, the preposition "to" is an end point and the preposition "by" is about the path from the start point to the end point. They touch because sometimes the path leads to an end point, such as in time ("due by Friday") or in price ("rose by 40%"). Of course, in this context, the percentage or amount that something increases by is a measurement: "How much did it increase?" In other words, how long is the path?

This room measures 15 by 18. Lastly, we have one of the most abstract example sentences. When measuring the dimensions of something (length, width, height), the measurement of each side is like it's own path. If we think of the length and width of a room, for example, we start from one corner and measure how far it is to the next corner (in order) to find the length of the room. The wall is a line that makes a path. Then we turn the corner and measure the width, which is another path. If we take the measurement of the two paths and multiply them (15 X 18), we get the total area of the room. So this example isn't about a "rate", just a basic measurement.

If that's confusing, there's another way that you can think about it. When multiplying two numbers (for example, 2 X 3 = 6), we say, "Two times three equals six". We have two 3's (3 + 3) or three 2's (2 + 2 + 2), which means that we're going through 3 two times or going through 2 three times. We lay out a path of that number, which leads to a total: 3_3→ 6; 2_2_2→ 6. In other words, if we think about this using the idea of steps, take 3 steps (1) and then 3 more steps (2) and the total number of steps is 6; or take 2 steps (1) and then 2 more steps (2) and then two more steps (3) and the total number of steps is also 6. Either way, you get the same total.

D) Some verbs that often use the preposition "by"

Be by (a location)	Walk by/drive by	Pay by
Go by	Use by (an expiration date)	Pass by
Drop by/stop by	Travel by	

E) **Phrasal Verbs.** Look up each phrasal verb and try to understand how the logic of the word "at" applies. Remember, a phrasal verb is basically a preposition put into action by a verb.

Note: the preposition "by" is not used in many phrasal verbs, but it is used as a connector sometimes.

Drop by if you're ever in town! The phrasal verb "to drop by" means the same as "to drop in": to visit, normally for a short time. When we use the preposition "in", it's because you're going into a building. When we use the preposition "by", it's because you decided to visit and the visit will probably be short, so it's like you don't actually stop and the building you're at is just one point along the path to where you we're going before stopping (in order) to visit. Because you don't plan to stay long, it's like you're just going past that place without stopping.

I need a job that pays more money. I'm so tired of just getting by! "To just get by" means that you only make enough money (in order) to survive and nothing or almost nothing more than that. As you know, the verb "to get" has many meanings. In this case, it's close to the verbs "to reach" and "to arrive". Imagine you're driving your car on a road (which is a type of path). Your car needs gas (in order) to work. If you make more money, you can pay for more gas, which means that you can reach a point that is much farther along the road than if you had less money. In the context of this sentence, your job is the car. If you only make enough money at your job (in order) to survive, then you can't buy things that you want. However, if you have extra money, it's like you're able to go farther along the path.

　　We can also think about it this way: imagine that there's a lion sitting at a certain point on the road. It's sitting at the point that equals how much you have to pay in bills. Let's say that you have to pay $500 every month (in order) to survive (meaning what you pay for rent, food, etc...). Now let's say that every mile or kilometer equals $100. The lion is sitting around the mile or kilometer that equals about $490. If you make enough to "get by", then you make it past the lion and you survive. If you don't make enough money, you'll be homeless or starve (the lion eats you).

During university, time just flew by. "To fly by" means to go very quickly. In this case, we're talking about how time can seem to go/pass quickly. This usually happens because you're having a good time (in English, we have the phrase: "Time flies when you're having fun!"). So this person really enjoyed their time attending university.

How is this a "path" or a "way"? Remember when we talked about the "passage of time"? We can look at time as an abstract path. First, the person starts attending university. From that point until the end of it (when they graduate), time seems to pass very quickly. It's similar to someone driving by on a motorcycle, except we're talking about time instead of space. This is because we often don't feel different as we get older, but many things in our lives change. In other words, those things "pass by" us as we get older.

Before we play, let's warm up by running around the court. Note that this is not a phrasal verb; the preposition "by" is just a connector. "To warm up" means "to increase your body temperature so that your body is prepared for physical activity (like sports).

This example is the same as the sentence, "I learned how to sing by watching videos online", so it goes into group 2. Let's warm up. How? By running around the court. The big difference between this example and the one about learning how to sing is that the other example is about using videos so that you can learn something, but this example is about using running so that you can warm up.

F) Examples of idioms that use the preposition "by", with detailed explanations.

We did everything by the book. When you do something by the book, it means that you do it in a way that follows certain official rules, especially if it involves the law. For example, if you want to start a business, there are certain things that you have to do and rules that you have to follow or the government won't allow you to have your business.

So, "by the book" is like a short way to say that you follow all those official rules, meaning that you do things according to what the rules say. If you do something according to something else, then it's your guideline, which is like an abstract path that you follow. If you decide to break one of the rules, then you are stepping off (of) that path. We can also see the idea of a "basis" here. When you follow the rules, you are making decisions based on those rules. They are the foundation for what you can and can't do.

By and large, his answer makes sense. The phrase "by and large" means "mostly" or "generally". In this case, someone asks a question and someone else answers that question. Then I use the phrase "by and large", so I mean that his answer mostly makes sense. It's only "mostly" because maybe there's a small problem with his answer or something that I just don't understand.

It's not hard to see that the word "large" is similar to the idea of "mostly". For example, if you have a pizza and you eat most of the pizza, then a large amount of the pizza is gone. In fact, we can also say, "Largely, his answer makes sense". But why do we use the preposition "by"?

We know that the preposition "by" is very abstract. It seems that it actually doesn't mean anything in this idiom, but we're using the abstract nature and feeling of the preposition itself. In other words, there is no "surface meaning". We're just adding it to emphasize the idea of "mostly" or "generally". This is especially true if we're not sure why his answer doesn't make complete sense. We just feel that there's something not quite right,

219

which gives us an abstract feeling because we're not sure what the exact, concrete detail is that's wrong. For example, we might naturally say, "By and large, his answer makes sense, but there's something missing."

FROM

A) Example Sentences. Remember to follow the instructions in section A from previous prepositions.

1)

The camp is a few miles from here.
I'm from the United States.
How far is it from here to Mexico?
He fell from the roof and broke his arm.

What does the word "from" mean in this group?

2)

Most people work (from) Monday to Friday.
He works (from) three to seven tomorrow.
The legend dates from the 15th century.
All (of) my favorite songs are from the (19)90's.
(From this day forward,) I will never speak to you again!
He's an old friend from my childhood.

What does the word "from" mean in this group?

3)

This cup is made from plastic.
All (of) our products are made from recycled materials.
This bread is made from wheat.

What does the word "from" mean in this group?

4)

He died from a heart attack.
I made all (of) my money (from) investing in stocks.

From what I can see, he's alone.
We can conclude from the evidence that Tom was murdered.

What does the word "from" mean in this group?

5)

This jacket will protect you from the wind, rain, and snow.
(In a thunderstorm:) Hurry! We can use my car as shelter (from the storm).
He stopped me from speaking.
They banned her from the building.
Keep that spider away from me!

What does the word "from" mean in this group?

6)

My language is very different from yours.
The fake painting looks so authentic, it's hard to tell the real one from the fake one.

What does the word "from" mean in this group?

7) Miscellaneous

I bought this car from my friend.
The phones in this store range from $50 to $600.
I lost so much weight that I went from a size 10 to a size 2. (pants)
I've translated the documents from English (in)to Spanish.

What does the word "from" mean in this group?

B) The Logic

Key Idea(s): origin point or start point

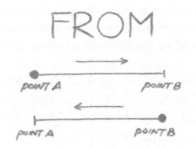

"from" is a one-way preposition

Explanation of the logic: The preposition "from" is about an origin/start point which can be physical (from France), temporal (from 9:00), or more abstract things, such as a "cause". The preposition "from" isn't very difficult, but it has many different uses. Note that the idea of a "start point" is actually a more specific version of an "origin point", but sometimes the idea of a "start point" works better. We have this hierarchy: "origin point" → "start point".

Etymology notes: The preposition "from" comes the Old English preposition "fram", which was used to show the idea of moving away from a point in time or space. Interestingly, this comes from the Proto-Germanic word "fra", which meant "forward" or "away from". 11 We'll see some specific examples where the idea of "forward" makes perfect sense, but the preposition "from" is not specifically about forward motion; it's mostly about the origin/start point of that motion.

Now, go back to the example sentences and try to apply the logic. Ask yourself: "How is 'from' an origin/start point?"

223

C) Detailed Explanations of the Example Sentences.

1) *Starting point/origin point in space (physical)*

The camp is a few miles from here. We're here, the camp is there, and the distance between is about three (a few) miles. So, starting from where we are now, that's how far away the camp is.

ALTERNATIVES: "The camp is a few miles away (from here)." Of course, we can always use the combination "far" + "away", in which case we imply the starting point based on the context. The preposition "away" basically just means "not near this location".

"The camp is a few miles off." We can use the preposition "off", as well. It's a little complicated – and we'll see many examples when we talk about the preposition "off" – but one of the surface meanings of that preposition is "removed from a center point/platform". We know that the preposition "on" usually deals with a surface/platform, so the preposition "off" is the opposite. The problem is that, though the logic is the opposite, there are surface meanings of "off" that don't have an opposite surface meaning with "on". As I said, we'll see more about this later, but for now, here's the reason why we can say, "The camp is a few miles off":We're here and the camp is there. "Here" is the implied start point, which in this case is also the central point/platform. The camp's location is "off" of and away from this central platform. In other words based on (platform) our current location, the camp's location is a few miles away.

I'm from the United States. When you talk about the origin of where a person or thing comes from, we use "from". In this case, the United Sates is my country of origin. I can also say, "I'm from San Diego", which is my city of origin. But why do we use the preposition "from"? This specific example is actually close to the logic of the preposition "of", but don't confuse these two. We generally think of being from a particular country as your origin. That's where you were born, so that's where you started your life.

224

ALTERNATIVES: As you probably know, we can also say, "I come from the United States". Be careful though. If you say, "I'm coming from the united States", for example, this does not mean the same thing. The example sentence, "I'm from the United States" is the most common way that we express this idea.

How far is it from here to Mexico? As you know, the preposition "from" is often used with the preposition "to". This is natural because "from" is an origin point/start point and "to" is an end point. So, when talking about a distance, we can use the preposition "from" (in order) to show the start point (from here, from there, from the store, from New York, etc…) and we can use the preposition "to" (in order) to show the end point (to Mexico, to here, to my house, to the beach, to there, etc…).

Note that we often say "from here to there", but we can also say "from there to here". Remember that it depends on the context and how you look at things. If we say "from here to there", the place where I am is the start point. If we say, "from there to here", we're just looking at "there" as the start point, but the meaning of the sentence is the same.

ALTERNATIVES: "How far away is Mexico?" It's possible to omit the word "away" sometimes, but we often use it, especially if the context isn't clear. This alternative sentence means the same thing as long as we're using my location ("here") as the implied start point, which is usually what we do.

Note: like the first example, you can use the preposition "off" and say, "How far off is Mexico?" However, in this specific context, it's less common.

He fell from the roof and broke his arm. He was on the roof and he fell off of the roof. The origin point or start point was the roof. In other words, where was he when he started falling? On the roof. From that point, he fell to the ground and broke his arm.

225

ALTERNATIVES: "He fell off (of) the roof and broke his arm." He was on (top of) the roof, which is a surface, so you can also say that he fell off (of) the roof. This is probably the more common way to say it.

2) *Starting point/origin point in Time*

Remember that a "point" is usually small and specific, but it can also cover a lot of time or space, like a really big dot.

Most people work (from) Monday to Friday. This group is extremely easy, but I've given different examples so you can see how it applies to many things. Here, we start work on Monday, so Monday is the start point for the week. Friday is the end point. When talking about the days that you work, the word "from" is optional because it's implied. So you can simply say, "Most people work Monday to Friday".

He works (from) three to seven tomorrow. This example works exactly the same as the previous one, except now we're talking about specific hours of the day. He will start working at 3.

The legend dates from the 15th century. Instead of talking about a range of days or hours of the day, here we're talking about the century in which the legend was created. So it's the origin point in time/history.

All (of) my favorite songs are from the (19)90's. We can also apply the idea of an origin point or a start point to a specific decade. This works exactly like the previous sentence.

(From this day forward,) I will never speak to you again! This one is also the same as the previous two, but in this case the origin point in time is today. Of course, if we say, "I will never speak to you again", that implies the idea of "from this day forward", so we don't have to say that part, but we can.

226

He's an old friend from my childhood. Lastly, we can use a particular time span of our lives as the origin point. I met him when we were children, so I met him in my childhood. Now we're adults. Our friendship <u>started</u> when we were children, so the origin/start of our friendship is in the period of time that we were children, which we call "childhood".

3) *original material; "made of"*

This cup is made from plastic. We know that we can use the preposition "of" when talking about the material that something is made of. We can also use the preposition "from". Why? Well, I have a cup. It's made of plastic. So in order to make it, someone took plastic and shaped it into the form of a cup. The cup came from the plastic. If I have a table that's made of wood, the table came from wood → "This table is made from wood". Whatever raw material we use, we shape that material into some item, so the item comes from that material. In other words, the item <u>originates</u> from that material. The cup was originally just plastic. The table was originally just wood.

ALTERNATIVES: "This cup is made of plastic."

All (of) our products are made from recycled materials. In this case, instead of talking about the specific material, such as plastic or wood, the products are made of whatever materials were recycled (in order) to create new things.

ALTERNATIVES: "All (of) our products are made of recycled materials."

This bread is made from wheat. We can also use the same idea when we talk about food. We take the wheat and make it into bread. What material/ingredient did the bread come from? Wheat.

ALTERNATIVES: "This bread is made of wheat."

227

4) cause/source; basis (as an origin point)

Note: This group touches the logic of the preposition "for". Remember that there's often more than one way to look at something, especially if we consider the context. The preposition "for" focuses on a basis or cause as a single, whole idea, meaning that it's the basis or cause itself that's important. The preposition "from" focuses on the basis or cause as the origin point or original event that leads to something else. In other words, the focus is on the result of that event.

Also, remember that the word "cause" is a more specific version of the word "basis". When talking about the preposition "from", we also have the closely related idea of a "source", which is also a more specific version of "basis".

He died from a heart attack. What was the cause or source of his death? A heart attack. A cause or a source can be an origin point. One thing happens and that thing is the original event that causes another event. In other words, cause and effect. He has a heart attack. That's the first event. From that event, the effect/result is death. We can say that the origin point of his death was a heart attack.

NOTE: We say this if the result is death, but we <u>don't</u> say it if he survives. So we don't say, "He lived from a heart attack." Instead, we say, "He survived a heart attack."

ALTERNATIVES: In this particular example sentence, we can also use the preposition "of": "He died of a heart attack". We

228

saw this sentence before with the preposition "of". When we use the preposition "from", we're not thinking about a "part" or "content". We're looking at things a little differently, but this is a perfect example of how we can look at the same idea in two different ways by using two different prepositions. The surface meaning in both sentences is the same, but the logic is different. In this case, the prepositions "from" and "of" overlap.

I made all (of) my money (from) investing in stocks. The source of my money was investing in stocks, so my investment in those stocks was the origin point that the money came from. This is an example where the preposition "from" is not necessary, but it's implied and still works in the background (this is true for all (of) the prepositions in the "alternatives" section below.

ALTERNATIVES: "I made all (of) my money (by) investing in stocks." Again, we don't need to say the preposition, but this is another possibility: the preposition "by". In this case, the prepositions "from" and "by" overlap. Why? In this context, "investing in stocks" is the path/way/means through which I made my money. So, we can look at "investing in stocks" as the source of money, or we can look at it as an activity that I did over time. This activity becomes the abstract "path", the "way" I made my money, or the means through which I made the money. Notice the word "source", which is close to the idea of "origin".

"I made all (of) my money (through) investing in stocks."

From what I can see, he's alone. You and a friend see a strange man sitting on a bench. He's been there for a while. You and your friend are curious, so you watch him to see if he does anything, but you don't want him to see you, so you hide in a nearby cafe. It's a little harder to see him from inside the cafe. Your friend, who can't see the man right now, asks you if someone has joined the man yet. You reply: "From what I can see, he's still alone." This is just one possible situation, but it helps to have a little more context (in order) to understand this example.

So, the phrase "from what I can see" means "based on what I'm able to see at the moment". This is followed by a conclusion: "X is true" → in this case, X = "He's alone". But maybe there's someone with him that you can't see for some reason. By saying "from what I can see", you're letting the listener know that you could be wrong and that what you're telling them is based on the (possibly limited) information that you have. But why do we use the preposition "from"? The conclusion that you make is based on that information. In other words, the information is the basis. Or we can say that the information is the origin point from which you make your conclusion.

ALTERNATIVES: "Based on what I can see, he's alone." You might have noticed that the preposition "on" is often used with the word "based". This use of the preposition "on" is close to the prepositions "from" and "by" in this kind of context. We use the preposition "on" with the word "based" because we are looking at the basis as a platform. You take some information as the base (platform) that you use to build more complex ideas and make certain conclusions.

So, we can look at the idea of a "basis" as an idea or item in itself (which is how we use it with the preposition "for"), as the origin point of something (which is how we use it with the preposition "from"), or as a platform (which is how we use it with the preposition "on"). Note that in the example sentence, "From what I can see, he's alone", you cannot use the preposition "for". The logic of the preposition "for" is close in this case and the basic meaning is there, but we don't use "for" here because that's the older use that we no longer use.

"Going by what I can see, he's alone." The phrase "going by" is another way to say "based on".

We can conclude from the evidence that Tom was murdered.
This example is similar to the previous one. The evidence that
we found is the basis (origin point) that we use (in order) to
reach the conclusion that Tom was murdered. Notice that we
have a phrase: "to reach the conclusion". It's like the conclusion
is the destination (end point), meaning that the logic of the
preposition "to" is working in the background. And what's the
opposite of "to"? "From", of course. So we go from the evidence
to the conclusion. When you look at it this way, it's very similar
to the examples about time and space.

ALTERNATIVES: "Based on the evidence, we can conclude that
Tom was murdered." This is the same as the alternative sentence
that we saw for the previous example sentence.

If you change the words a little, you can use the preposition "for":
"The evidence suggests that X happened. For that reason, we can
conclude that Tom was murdered." This isn't a common way to
express this idea.

5) *unable to accomplish something OR unable to start doing something*

This group is a little strange. Luckily, the surface meaning
itself isn't very hard to understand. Part of the etymology of the
preposition "from" is that it's related to the Old English word
"fremian", which meant "to promote" or "to accomplish". One
way to understand this group is to think of a barrier that
stops/prevents something. In other wards, that thing can't be
accomplished. This is an extremely important idea. Remember the
idea about using the preposition "to" when we want to connect
two actions/verbs ("I want to go")? We can use the preposition
"from" the same way, but instead of the first action pointing to the
second action, the preposition "from" kind of goes in the opposite
direction.

Common verbs that we use with this group are: prevent,
protect, stop, ban, and keep (away). All of these verbs stop

231

something from happening or being accomplished, which means that they pull the person who's trying to do that thing back to the start point. The specific application of this idea depends on the context and how you look at it. For example, something might not be able to <u>reach</u> an origin point, or the opposite, <u>leave</u> an origin point, which includes the idea of not being able to start something (because you can't leave the start point, so you can't start doing that action).

We'll discuss this in more detail in some of the examples below. However, this group isn't only about the connection between two verbs. For example, a jacket can protect you from the rain. Just like we can say: "want to go" (verb + verb), "respond to him" (verb + noun), and "a letter to me" (noun + noun), we can also say: "stop (someone) from speaking" (verb + verb) "protect (someone) from the rain" (verb + noun), and "a letter from me" (noun + noun). Not all of these fit into this group, of course, but the point here is that the logic of the preposition "from" can apply in all (of) these ways just like the logic of the preposition "to" can.

This jacket will protect you from the wind, rain, and snow. When we talk about protection, we usually use the preposition "from". Why? Because the thing that you're being protected from is kept away from you in some way. In this case, you have a jacket. If it's windy, the jacket will stop the wind from hitting your body, which will keep you warm. If it's raining or snowing, the jacket will stop the rain or snow from hitting your body (in order) to keep you warm and dry. Another example: "Bug spray protects you from bugs (insects)". You want to keep bugs away from you and off (of) your body.

In both cases, your body is the central point that is being protected, and that central point is the "origin" point because we're looking at it from the perspective of where your body is. The jacket and bug spray are barriers around your body. The wind, rain, etc... are kept at a certain distance from your body. The distance is very short, but it's enough. This is like saying "from here to there". For example, from the rain's perspective,

232

the rain is coming closer and trying to reach you, but it's kept outside of the jacket and it isn't able to touch your body because the jacket stops it.

ALTERNATIVES: "This jacket will protect you against the wind, rain, and snow." You can look at protection as something that pushes or keeps something else away. Because of this, we can also use the preposition "against" because the protection goes or pushes against the thing that you want to keep away from you so that you're protected. The prepositions "from" and "against" are not the same and they feel a little different, but in this case they both work.

(In a thunderstorm:) Hurry! We can use my car as shelter (from the storm). This is similar to the previous example. We're outside and a thunderstorm starts. It's raining. We need to find shelter (in order) to protect ourselves. I say that we can use my car as shelter, because inside the car it's dry and it will keep the rain outside and off (of) us. The rain will hit the car, but there's a space between us and the rain. From where we are (the space inside the car) to where the storm is (outside), there's something between (which is the car). So the car keeps us away from the effects of the storm and the space inside the car is the origin point. If we look at it from the perspective of the storm, it can't reach that point.

He stopped me from speaking. You can stop someone from doing something. The easiest way to think of this is that he stops me from starting the action of speaking. But let's look at some more details.

I want to speak. He stops me. So, he's keeping me away from speaking, which means that I can't "move forward" with that action. In other words, I can't accomplish that action. Imagine that you're walking. Someone else gets in your way and blocks the path, so you can't move forward in that direction. You can't reach the place that you want to go, so there's a gap between you and the destination (from here to there). This is

233

exactly what we're saying, except instead of a physical destination, you can't "reach" the action that you want to do. When he stops me from speaking, he's the barrier that keeps me "away from" the speaking.

But there's also something very interesting happening here. Remember that when we say, "I want to go", the preposition "to" is a special link that points from the first action to the second action. So, we have "want" (action 1/desire) + "to" (points to second action) + "go" (action 2). In other words, I have a desire, and that desire points to the action of going somewhere. When we say, "He stopped me from speaking", we get the opposite of the preposition "to": "stopped" (action 1) + "from" (points away from action 2) + "speaking" (action 2). In other words, my goal is to speak, but I can't reach/accomplish that goal because he stops me. It's like I try to walk forward, but he's behind me and pulls me back, which keeps me away from my destination. It's the same thing with actions/verbs. So, the origin point is "not speaking" because I'm currently not speaking. I try to speak (meaning that I try to reach/accomplish the action of speaking), but he stops me, so I can't reach/accomplish that action. The result is that I'm still not speaking. In other words, I'm still at the "origin point".

As I said, the easiest way to look at this is that he stops me from starting the action, so we have a start point that I don't leave. However, it's useful to look at these other details to see how the logic of the prepositions "to" and "from" are connected under the surface.

ALTERNATIVES: "He prevented me from speaking." In this case, the verbs "to stop" and "to prevent" are interchangeable.

"He wouldn't allow me to speak." This isn't exactly the same, but it's almost the same and you can use it in the same context. Of course, I'm sure that you noticed that we're using the preposition "to" and not the preposition "from" in this case. Why? We'll have to get into some basic grammar here.

234

"Stop from doing" means that the action doesn't happen. Even though the words "no" or "not" are not part of this, the verb "to stop" implies the negative of the action that I tried to do. In this alternative sentence, we have the words "would" and "not" ("wouldn't"), because the verb "to allow" doesn't imply a negative, it implies a positive. Normally, we just have "allow" + "to" + "speak", so we use the preposition "to" and it works like "want to", "have to", etc...

Verbs that imply positives use the preposition "to" because we are pointing to the second action (the end point). We have to negate these verbs with the word "not" (in order) to make them negative, but nothing else changes ("I want to go", "I don't want to go"). Instead of saying that my desire points to the action of going, we're saying that my desire doesn't point to the action of going.

But verbs that imply a negative use the preposition "from" because we're pointing away from the second action (meaning that we're pointing to the start point, which is before the second action happens). If you make a verb like "to stop" negative ("don't stop"), then the meaning becomes "positive" in the sense that we want the second action to happen, but nothing else changes ("He stopped me from speaking", "He didn't stop me from speaking").

In these cases, the prepositions "to" and "from" are just linking the two actions based on whether the first action/verb implies a negative or a positive. If we change the first action/verb using the word "not", it doesn't change the preposition because it's just a structure change that affects the verb. In other words, it's because of the grammar of English verbs.

They banned her from the building. The verb "to ban" means that you're never allowed to enter a place again. In this case, there's a building. She did something really bad in that building and now they won't allow her to enter anymore. So in this sentence, there's no physical barrier (except maybe security guards). The people who own the building decided not to allow her to enter, and that decision is the barrier that stops her from

235

being able to enter. If she tries, the security guards will stop her because that's what they were told to do. Although we're using the verb "to ban" instead of the verb "to stop", this sentence works the same way as the previous example sentence, "He stopped me from speaking". Let's say that she's outside the building right now. That's the origin point. From that point, she can't move forward if "forward" = "entering the building". Of course, this is also like the examples about the jacket and the storm, but she's kept outside of the building instead of inside the building. It's like looking at it from the rain's perspective: The rain is kept outside of the jacket and it isn't able to touch my body because the jacket stops it.

Note: There's a big difference between "ban from" and "stop/prevent from". A ban (the noun form of "to ban") is something permanent. It can be changed in the future, but the intention is that it will be permanent. So a ban is something that permanently stops you. If you are stopped/prevented from doing something, it's a single time. For example, if we say, "They stopped her from entering the building", it just means that one time. Maybe they'll stop her again the next time that she tries to enter, but there's no official "ban". Also notice that when we use the verb "to stop", we have to say "from entering the building" and not just "the building" because "The stopped her from the building" doesn't mean that they stopped her from entering. With the verb "to ban", we can say "from entering the building", but the verb "to ban" doesn't need another verb and it can simply be used with a noun, especially a location. Of course, if someone is banned "from a building", the implied meaning is that they aren't allowed to enter.

Keep that spider away from me! The spider is not on you or near you. Let's say that it's on the wall. So right now it's away from (not near) where you are now. From the spider's location to your location, there's a certain amount of distance. This sentence is simply about keeping distance between you and the spider because we're talking about your physical location, the spider's physical location, and not allowing those two physical locations to be the same. In other words, keep them separate.

But how exactly does the logic of the preposition "from" work? The same as all the other sentences in this group. The difference between this sentence and the previous sentences is that we're using the verb "to keep", so we're not only talking about preventing/stopping something in this case, we're also talking about maintaining the current state of things. The spider's location is the origin point/start point. The spider is already away from your location and you want the spider to stay away from your location. So we use the preposition "from" (in order) to point away from your location, which is where the spider already is. "Keep away" + "from" + "me".

6) *Comparison (from first thing (origin/start) to second thing (end point))*

My language is very different from yours. Let's say that I'm a Japanese speaker and you're an English speaker. I think about your language (English). Starting from that thought, I then think about my language (Japanese). I notice that they're very different. It's like saying "California is very far from New York", but we're talking about differences instead of distances. From English to Japanese, there are many differences. This is the same as saying, "There are many differences between English and Japanese". Either language can be the start/origin point, but in this case, it's English.

237

ALTERNATIVES: "My language is very different than yours." Of course, we can also use the construction "different than" instead of "different from".

"Japanese is very different from English." Instead of saying, "My language (Japanese) is very different from yours (English)", we can specifically talk about two languages. Of course, if we specifically name the two languages, then we're just comparing languages and it doesn't mean that I speak Japanese and that you speak English. For example, maybe your native language is Spanish, and you say, "Japanese is very different from English". You're just comparing two languages.

"Our languages are very different." This is a much simpler way to express this idea. The preposition "from" is implied: "Our languages are very different <u>from each other</u>".

The fake painting looks so authentic, it's hard to tell the real one from the fake one. The phrase "to tell something from something" is a very natural expression that's kind of common, but it's also a phrase that causes confusion for many English learners. The first thing you need to understand is that the verb "to tell" in this context does <u>not</u> mean that you are going to say words or tell someone something. It means "to notice", but the verbs "to notice" and "to tell" aren't quite the same, so they're not interchangeable. It's just the surface meaning of these verbs that overlaps. Next, we have the phrase, "the real one from the fake

238

one". Again, we can look at this like "from here to there", but we're talking about comparing differences instead of talking about a distance. One painting is real (authentically created by the original painter) and one is fake (not authentically created by the original painter). Because we're comparing them, we use the preposition "from". So, it's hard to notice what the small differences are between the original, authentic painting and the fake one.

7) *A general origin point/start point*

I bought this car from my friend. Who owned the car? My friend. It was in his possession. He sold it to me. The ownership went from him to me. My friend is the origin point or source that I got the car from.

The phones in this store range from $50 to $600. Just like we say "from Monday to Friday" or "from the US to China", we can use the preposition "from" to talk about a range. The start/origin point is $50. That's the lowest price for a phone in this store, so we set the start/origin point at $50.

I lost so much weight that I went from a size 10 to a size 2. (pants) Here we're talking about the size of pants. Before, this person fit into a size 10. That's the original size or start point in the context of this sentence. Then they lost a lot of weight. The new size is 2, which is the end point after losing all (of) that weight.

I've translated the documents from English (in)to Spanish. We have two languages. One language is the original and the other language is the one that I translated the original into. You can also say that English, not some other language, is the basis from which I translated the document into Spanish. For example, if I translated it from Japanese to Spanish, then Japanese would be the basis.

239

D) Some verbs that often use the preposition "from"

Prevent from	Protect from	Move from
Buy from	Make from	Stay away from
Go from	Take from	Keep away from

E) **Phrasal Verbs.**

The preposition "from" is not used in phrasal verbs.

F) Examples of idioms that use the preposition "from", with detailed explanations.

Speaking from the heart. / Speaking from experience. When you speak from the heart, it means that you are speaking honestly and expressing your emotions. This is because we think of the heart as the center of emotion, so you can "speak from" that center of emotion, but the extra meaning of honesty is also part of it. This sentence is very abstract, but your "heart" (meaning, your emotions) is the origin or starting point that words come from. You can also say that the words that you are going to say are based on your emotions, so your emotions are the source of your words or why you're going to say those word.

    When you speak from experience, it means that you've had some experience that is relevant to the current situation or topic. The logic works exactly the same as in the phrase "speaking from the heart".

Japanese is a far cry from English. The idiom "a far cry from" means that something is very different than something else. In other words, we're comparing Japanese and English. The word "far" in this idiom is the same as the word "very".

240

OUT

A) Example Sentences. Remember to follow the instructions in section A from previous prepositions.

1)

He took his phone out of his pocket and called his friend.
My wallet fell out of my backpack.
Don't stick your tongue out at people!
He jumped out (of) the window.
It's so hot (out) today! (The outside temperature is very hot)
Someone dropped by while you were out. (not at home or work)
He was voted out of office. (in a government election)
Please stop hiding and come out.
You sort (out) the laundry and I'll fold.

What does the word "out" mean in this group?

2)

It's too cloudy tonight. I was hoping the stars would be out. (visible)
Is his new book out yet? (Has the book that he's writing been released yet?)
In baseball, three strikes mean you're out.
After such a long day, I'm really tired (out).

What does the word "out" mean in this group?

B) The Logic

Key Idea(s): 1) an outward direction; 2) movement between existence and non-existence

"out" is a two-way preposition

Explanation of the logic: "Out" is a strange preposition. The basic idea is an "outward direction", which is the main part of the logic. This idea is always or almost always applied. "Outward" means a direction going from the inside of something to the outside of something, or it can be mean "away from". However, there are many cases in which the preposition "out" also deals with existence and non-existence, which are very closely related to the ideas of "positive state/active state" (existence) and "negative state/inactive state" (non-existence).

More specifically, the preposition "out" deals with a change of state from existing to non-existing <u>and</u> a change of state from non-existing to existing. For example, this includes the idea of something that's hidden becoming visible, the idea of something unknown becoming known, and the idea of something that's not yet finished/released (like a book) being finished/released. All (of) these are more specific versions of the abstract "existence" and "non-existence" idea. So you have to look at these two concepts in a flexible way. Because existence is closely related to a positive state/active state and non-existence is closely related to a negative state/inactive state, and because we're specifically talking about the change in state between the two, the preposition "out" can also use the ideas of "creation" and "completion". In fact, we'll see that the prepositions "on", "off", "up", "down", and "out" are all very closely connected in a special way. The idea of an "outward direction" is the basis for the idea of "movement between existence and non-existence". Why? Because something can go out of existence and into non-existence (like the flame on a candle) or something can go out of non-existence and into existence (like a book that's been written and published).

The most difficult part about this is that "existence" and "non-existence" are **both** containers, so when you enter one, you immediately leave the other at the same time. In other words, when you move something from one container to the other container, it starts inside the first container, which means that it's currently outside of the second container; as it leaves the first container, it starts entering the second container. Understanding this concept is the key to the preposition "out" and will make learning it much easier. If you remember the preposition "in", the logic of that preposition is "a container".

So why are we talking about containers with the preposition "out"? Well, as you know, in most cases the opposite of the preposition "in" is the preposition "out". The preposition "in" is about the general idea of containers, which might be physical (like a box) or abstract (like a bad mood). The preposition "out" deals with two special containers: existence and non-existence. But it's not about existence and non-existence directly. Instead, this preposition is specifically about the movement between existence and non-existence. This also means that the preposition "out" almost always implies the preposition "in" because both "existence" and "non-existence" are special containers.

If you look at the map of the prepositions in Appendix B, you'll see that the preposition "out" is located at the top and the bottom of the cone of existence and it has two arrows. One arrow points into the cone of existence. This means that something is being created or coming into existence (which also means that that thing is leaving non-existence). The other arrow points out of the

243

cone of existence. This means that something is ending, being completed, or simply going out of existence (which also means that that thing is going into non-existence).

Etymology notes: There are no useful notes for this preposition.

Now, go back to the example sentences and try to apply the logic. Ask yourself: "How is the preposition 'out' showing an outward direction or moving between existence and non-existence?"

C) Detailed Explanations of the Example Sentences.

1) *an outward direction*

This group is mostly about an outward direction. Most of the time, we can also apply the idea of moving between existence and non-existence in an abstract way, but the main idea is clearly an outward direction.

He took his phone out of his pocket and called his friend. This example is very simple. His phone is inside (of) his pocket and he takes it out of his pocket. His pocket is a kind of container, so, just like something that's inside (of) a box, for example, he simply takes it out of the container. We can easily see that his phone is moving in an outward direction: from the inside of his pocket to the outside.
    We can also look at this with the idea of "existence" and "non-existence", but it might be confusing. It makes logical sense, but if this way doesn't help you understand the example better, you can ignore it. Both existence and non-existence are special containers, so we have 1) inside of his pocket (the phone is existing inside the pocket, which also means that it's not existing outside of the pocket) → 2) outside of his pocket (the phone is not existing inside the pocket, which also means that it's existing outside of the pocket).

244

When you move something from one of these special containers to the other, it starts inside the first container and leaves that container, but at the same time it starts outside of the second container and goes into that second container. This means that what's happening at the same time is: 1) the phone is outside of the non-existence container (meaning that it's existing inside the pocket) → 2) inside the non-existence container (meaning that it's not existing inside the pocket, it's existing outside of the pocket).

ALTERNATIVES: "He took his phone from his pocket and called his friend." We can also use the preposition "from" in this case. The phone is inside of his pocket, meaning that's the origin/start point before he removes it and calls his friend.

My wallet fell out of my backpack. This is almost the same as the previous example. The difference here is that something is falling out on accident instead of being taken out intentionally. Here we can see the idea of an outward direction: the backpack is a container and the wallet falls out of it. All of the same information about "existence" and "non-existence" applies here, as well.

Note that we do not say, "My wallet fell from my backpack". Why? Because when we use the verb "to fall" with the preposition "from", it sounds like someone is on something and they are falling off of it → He fell off of the roof/He fell from the roof.

Don't stick your tongue out at people! Your tongue is inside your mouth, so your mouth is like a container. Normally, your tongue and teeth are inside your mouth. If you stick your tongue out, you are exposing your tongue and part of it is now outside of your mouth. You're making it clearly visible. This is clearly an outward direction.

We can also say that when your tongue is inside your mouth, its "existence" (location) is inside your mouth and it's not existing outside of your mouth. This is the normal state. But when you stick it out, you reverse those states: part of your tongue is

245

now outside of your mouth, so it left its existence inside of the mouth/container and went into what is normally non-existence for your tongue (outside the mouth/container). Inside mouth → outside mouth = inside of normal existence → outside of normal existence; simultaneously, inside mouth → outside mouth = outside of normal non-existence → inside of normal non-existence. Remember that "existence" and "non-existence" are both containers, so when you go into one, you go out of the other and when you go out of one, you go into the other <u>at the same time</u>.

A couple (of) useful notes: 1) Notice that if someone punches you in the face, for example, and one of your teeth is removed from its socket, you can say, "He punched my tooth out" or "He knocked my tooth out" because your tooth was inside your mouth and now it's not. 2) Notice that we use "<u>at</u> people" in the example sentence. This is because you are <u>targeting</u> a person who you want to stick your tongue out at. You are trying to "hit" them with the effect of it (which is to be disrespectful or maybe playful).

He jumped out (of) the window. Here we find something different. Obviously, he's not inside the window and then jumps out of it. When we say this, we mean that he exited the building by jumping through an open window. A window isn't the just glass, it's a hole. In fact, all you need is a hole (in order) to have what we call a window. So, what we're really saying is that he's inside the building and he's leaving, but through the window instead of the door (which is: "He walked out (of) the door"). The building is a container. Of course, since he's exiting the building, this is obviously an outward direction: from inside to the building and outward to the outside of the building. We can also say, "He jumped out of the building through the window", but "He jumped out of the window" is shorter and works just as well because of the context. Since the building is the container, all the same ideas as before of "existence" and "non-existence" apply.

246

It's so hot (out) today! (The outside temperature is very hot) This example is just about an outward direction because we're talking about the temperature/weather outside. The preposition "out" is completely optional because if it's a hot day, that heat obviously comes from the weather.

Someone dropped by while you were out. (not at home or work) If you're not at home or work, you're outside of the house or outside of the place where you work (usually a building). Of course, you can physically be outside and still be "at home" or "at work". For example, you're gardening in the backyard. In that case, you're outside, but not "out", because "out" means that you're away from home or work for some reason (lunch, errands, etc...). So this example isn't just an outward direction, but also "away from".

He was voted out of office. (in a government election) In elections, someone can be either voted in or voted out. "Voted in" means that they won the election, and because it's an election, people voted for that person to get the position, so he or she is entering an official government office or position. The result is that we say that the person is "in office". We combine the verb "vote" and the preposition "in" (in order) to show this idea. The opposite is also true: if someone is voted "out", they had the government position, but they lost the election and will no longer have that position in that government office. So in this case, the "outward direction" isn't physical, but it works the same.

Please stop hiding and come out. Here we see how the preposition "out" is used with something that's hidden. Let's say that you have a child and they're playing hide-and-seek. You don't have time right now to play, so you tell them to stop hiding and come out. They are inside a hiding spot (behind the couch or under the bed, for example), so the hiding spot is like a container. We can see that you want them to move in an outward direction from the hiding spot so that you can see them.

247

Also, because you can't see them, they are outside of your vision. You want them to move from inside the hiding spot (container of "non-existence"/hidden) and out of it (into the container of "existence"/"visible"). All this talk of existence and non-existence can be confusing, so remember that the ideas of "visible" and "hidden" are like more specific versions of "existence" and "non-existence". So, instead of saying "existence" and "non-existence", which we're using very abstractly, we can say "visible" (existing in your vision/awareness) and "hidden" (not existing in your vision/awareness).

You sort (out) the laundry and I'll fold. When you sort something, you're organizing it into different categories or groups. With laundry, we have pants, shirts, etc... So, let's say that I put all the pants into one pile, all the shirts into another pile, etc... I'm taking each item from the big main pile of clean laundry and separating them into different piles or groups. There's an outward direction here because I'm taking each item out of the main pile ("container") and putting it outward and away from the main pile into other piles ("containers"). Note that the preposition "out" isn't necessary because the verb "to sort" implies the outward/away from direction.

2) *movement between existence and non-existence*

This group is mainly about the movement between existence and non-existence. However, remember that both groups are very closely related, so the idea of an outward direction often still applies.

It's too cloudy tonight. I was hoping the stars would be out. (visible) This is just like the previous example, but instead of someone hiding, we're talking about the stars. Obviously the stars aren't hiding, but they are hidden behind the clouds. In other words, the clouds are hiding the stars, so we can't see them. You can think of this like the clouds are the lid of a big container, just like if you put something into a container with a lid that you can't

248

see through. This example isn't really about an outward direction because the starts don't move outward or away from anything.

Is his new book out yet? (Has the book that he's writing been released yet?) This sentence is similar to the last two sentences, but it's a little different. Here, we're not talking about something being hidden or visible. Instead, we're talking about a product being released or not. When you're writing a book (or writing a song, or creating a painting, etc...), the book doesn't exist yet. It's being created, which means that it's going from non-existence (no book) into existence (a completed book). So writing a book or creating any kind of product is just the process of moving something from inside the container of non-existence and into the container of existence (and remember that the opposite is true at the same time: from outside the container of existence and to outside the container of non-existence).

Also note that the logic applies to this sentence in two ways: 1) the book being created (from start to finish) and 2) the book being released (from not released to released). This is because you might finish/create something but not release it to the public. So first, you have to finish writing the book, which brings the book into existence. But then you have to release it to the public, meaning it goes from not publicly available (non-existence in the public, meaning private) to publicly available (existence in the public, meaning not private). Here we find that "public" and "private" can also be containers that are more specific versions of "existence" and "non-existence", except "public" can be both "existence" and non-existence" and "private" can be both "existence" and "non-existence". We see a close relation to the ideas of "positive state/active state" and "negative state/inactive state". Either the private light is on and the public light is off or the public light is on and the private light is off.

In this case, the idea of an outward direction also applies. If it's "out", then it's available to the public. If the author completes the book but never releases, then it's not "out". It's like you write a letter, but you never send it, so it doesn't move in an outward direction from where you are.

249

In baseball, three strikes mean you're out. When we talk about a game, we use the prepositions "in" and "out" in many ways, depending on the type of game and the context. For example, "in play" and "out of play". When we talk about baseball, we use "you're out" to mean that you can no longer try to hit the ball for now because you missed three times. So, you are currently "out of play", but we just say "out" in this case. A different example is poker (a card game that usually involves betting money). If you want to bet all (of) your money, you go "all in". If you give up because you don't think you can win with the cards that you have, you can say, "I'm out". So in the case of games, the preposition "out" means that you're currently not playing, so you're "out of play" or outside of the game. Again, we see a close relationship to the ideas of "positive state/active state" and "negative state/inactive state".

After such a long day, I'm really tired (out). In this case, the preposition "out" is optional, but it adds a little emphasis. We can use the preposition "out" because it's like all (of) your energy has left your body. It's like saying, "I'm completely tired and have no energy left". Your body is the container, and your energy has gone out of the container. So, we can see an abstract "outward direction", but this sentence is really about the "existence"/"non-existence" idea. If you have a lot of energy, then that energy exists in your body. If you're really tired and don't have any energy, then that energy doesn't exist in your body.

D) Some verbs that often use the preposition "out"

Fall out	Stick out	Take out
Stick out	Sort out	Jump out
Leave out	Cut out	Figure out

250

E) **Phrasal Verbs.** Look up each phrasal verb and try to understand how the logic of the word "out" applies. Remember, a phrasal verb is basically a preposition put into action by a verb.

Note: For this preposition, I've limited the number of phrasal verbs to 10 because there are so many and adding more would take up extra space in this book.

Look out! A car's going to hit you! When we say "Look out!" it means that you need to pay attention to the things that are around you. It's a warning that there's some danger and you need to look around (in order) to see what it is so that you can avoid it. It would probably make more sense if the phrasal verb were "Look around!", but we don't say that in this context. Why? If you're not paying attention, you're lost in your thoughts or something similar and so your awareness is either inward (focused inside) or narrowly focused on a particular thing (maybe listening to the music that's playing in your headphones or looking at your phone as you walk). In this case, you need to turn your attention outward to your surroundings so that you can see the danger. You can also think of it this way: the danger is simply outside of your awareness (not existing in your awareness), and the person warning you is trying to bring it to your attention (make it exist in your awareness) so that you can avoid it.

I've been going out with my girlfriend for three months. The phrasal verb "to go out (with)" means that you're dating someone. The meaning is based on another meaning of "to go out", which means to eat dinner or do some activity (like dancing) away from home, usually at night. When you date someone, you usually go out to dinner, go dancing, and/or other activities, so we simply extend the basic meaning of "to go out" to include the meaning/context of dating someone. Notice that we have both the outward direction and the "away from the inside" (of the house) ideas.

251

Keep out/Stay out of the basement. If I want you to keep out or stay out of the basement, it means that I don't want you to enter the basement. So, you're already outside of the basement and I want you to keep it that way. In most cases, the preposition "out" involves exiting something or going outside of something from the inside, but this sentence is about not entering in the first place. Your physical location/existence is already outside of the basement (meaning an outward from the perspective of inside the basement) and I want you to stay outside.

Check out that guy in the pink shirt! The phrasal verb "to check out" has several different meanings. In this case, it's similar to the phrasal verb "to look out", which I explained earlier, and the logic applies in the same way. The big difference is that when we use "to check out", there's no danger. It's exactly like saying, "Look at that guy in the pink shirt!" I'm just trying to draw your attention to something interesting or funny that I want you to see.

(Talking about a stain on my shirt:) I can't get this stain out. If you have a stain on your clothes and you try to wash the clothes but the stain won't go away, then we say that it won't come out or that someone can't get it out. You're simply trying to remove the stain ("remove" is often part of the preposition "off"). This one is a little strange because notice that we say "I have a stain **on** my shirt", not "in my shirt". This is because we don't think of the stain as being part of the fabric, it's just on the surface. In reality, this isn't 100% true, but that's how we think about it. If you talk about the fabric itself (the material that the shirt is made of), then you can say that there's a stain in the fabric, but we're not talking specifically about the fabric, we're talking about the shirt as an item. So in this specific case, we see that the opposite of the preposition "out" is the preposition "on"

The logic of the prepositions "out", "in", "on", and "off" are a little tangled together because they're so closely related, and we find situations like this on rare occasions. Language isn't always perfect, but you can see that the logic still applies to the prepositions "on" and "out" in this context. If you want, you can

252

think of the preposition "on" or the preposition "out" in this context as an exception.

Either way, we definitely have the idea of moving from existence to non-existence. The stain exists and you are trying to remove it so that the stain doesn't exist on your shirt anymore. Also, if we think about the stain being inside the fabric, you are trying to get the stain out of the fabric, so we have an abstract outward direction.

We ran out of milk. Can you buy some more? The phrasal verb "to run out" is very strange. It can literally mean to run from the inside of something to the outside, for example, "He ran out of the building". In that case, it's pretty easy to understand. But what about "We ran out of milk"? Did the milk run away? Were we inside a giant glass of milk and we ran out of it? Of course not. When you run out of something, it means that that thing has been completely used and that there's no more. This is for things that have a limited amount. You buy a gallon of milk and eventually you'll use all of it. Or let's say you buy napkins for a party, but the guests use all of them. Well, you ran out of napkins.

You have to think of the verb "to run" like we use it with computers. When you start a program on the computer, you are "running" that program. So we're using the verb "to run" in a way that means "a process is active" (again, something connected to the preposition "on"). Process is the keyword. If you have milk, that milk exists in your possession. Using the milk over time is a process. You start with a full gallon, then you use a little, and then next time you use some more, etc…

So you can see that from a full gallon to an empty gallon, there's a process of emptying. When you "run out" of milk, the process is over and all the milk is gone. It no longer exists in your possession and you need to buy more. So the idea of existence ("full") and non-existence ("empty") works well here, but of course there's also an abstract "outward direction" as the amount of something decreases. In the case of milk or liquid specifically, you can say that there's a literal outward direction because the

253

liquid is in a container and you pour it out of the container, but this doesn't work with other things like napkins, for example.

I held my breath so long that I passed out. If you "pass out" is means that you lose consciousness. The traditional verb that we is "to faint". I held my breath so long that my brain wasn't getting enough oxygen and I lost consciousness. My conscious awareness went from container 1) "active" and existing (conscious and aware) to container 2) "inactive" and non-existing (unconscious and not aware). This is very similar to when we say, "the fire went out" or "blow the candle out". We use the verb "to pass" in this case because you're conscious awareness is "passing" ("moving") into unconsciousness.

We found out (that) he's been lying to us. "To find out" means that there was some information that you weren't aware of and now you are aware of it. In an abstract way, the information was "hidden" from your awareness (or, at least, it was outside of your awareness). You "find" the information and now it's no longer hidden. There is a difference between the verb "to find" and the phrasal verb "to find out". For example, you can find information, such as if you search online. The exact use of "find" vs "find out" can be difficult to explain because it partially depends on the context. The "out" part is usually applied to something hidden in the sense that you thought one thing, or didn't know what to think, but the truth was something else. So, if someone lies to you, at first you don't know that their lying to you. But later you discover that they did lie to you, so you "found out".

Why do you always have to point out when I make a mistake? "To point (something) out" means to bring someone's attention to something. In other words, it's like saying, "Look at that". If I make a mistake, you say, "That's not right", or something that makes me notice that I made a mistake. Depending on the context, you might literally point at something with your finger, but even if it's something that's not physical, like a mistake, you can "point" to it abstractly. We use the preposition "out" because we're

254

making something known, visible, or noticeable. If I make a mistake, I might not notice, but if you point it out, now it's clear for me to see and it's in my conscious awareness.

My friends and I like to hang out at my house. This final example sentence is strange. The phrasal verb "to hang out" means to spend time with one or more people in a casual and relaxed way. Because it's casual and relaxed, there's no concentrated focus or purpose. You can all do the same activity, like playing a video game or something, but basically you're just having fun and/or relaxing, not working. So the "out" part is about not being focused on a particular purpose or objective and instead being free to do whatever you want with your friends or family. The word "diffuse" describes this really well. The "hang" part is a little trickier. The verb "to hang" means "to suspend", like you hang your clothes in the closet. You can also think of a door, which is suspended by brackets in a way that allows it to freely swing open and closed. The idea here is "free motion". So, "to hang out" is basically "to casually spend time with one or more people with no particular purpose while being free to do whatever you want".

Ok, but how exactly does all that fit the logic of the preposition "out"? When you have a purpose, you put your effort into that thing, which means that thing is in your conscious awareness. If you're hanging out, you don't have a particular purpose or focus, so your attention is "diffuse", or spread out among many different possible things, or simply not focused on anything in particular. Also, not everyone has to be doing the same thing, so maybe one person is on the computer, two people are playing a video game and another two people are having a conversation. This means that the whole group isn't concentrated in a particular spot or on a particular thing. In an abstract way, we can say that not everyone is "in the same box" (container). And that's a key idea here. The preposition "in" is a container. But there's no particular container that all the people are in, so they're just freely and casually associating with each other and/or doing their own thing in the same general area (such as a house). In contrast, if you go to a business meeting, you're all "in a meeting", which has a particular purpose and objective, so you're all "in the same box" (container). The meeting could even be at your house, but you're not hanging out because you're in a meeting.

F) Examples of idioms that use the preposition "out", with detailed explanations.

You must be out of your mind! This idiom means "You must be crazy!" In this case, the word "must" doesn't mean that they have an obligation to be crazy. This is another meaning of the modal verb "must" which means that you think that it's the only logical answer because of something they did or said. If I say, "I want to jump out of an airplane" (go skydiving), some people think that that's crazy, so they might say to me, "You must be out of your mind!" Reason/logic/rationality is supposed to be located in your mind. But if you do or say something that seems illogical/irrational, then it seems like the thing that you do or say is outside the boundaries of what's logical. Usually, but not always, we use this phrase if something seems both illogical AND dangerous, or if it's something that can't be reasonably expected. For example, you ask someone who hates you for help. They respond: "You must be out of your mind if you think I would ever help you!"

John let the cat out of the bag. This idiom means that someone told a secret that they were trying to pretend was something else. For example, you and your family are going to have a surprise birthday party for your sister. You pretend that there won't be a surprise party (or any party at all), because you want it to be a surprise. But then your brother accidentally says something about the surprise party while he's talking to your sister. So, your brother "let the cat out of the bag".

It was a secret, meaning that it was hidden from your sister. So, this information wasn't in her conscious awareness, meaning that she didn't know about it. The use of the preposition

256

"out" should be clear: now that the secret is known, it's out in the open. It's not hidden from your sister anymore. The reason that we use the word "cat" doesn't matter, but it probably comes from a French expression. 12

(On the phone:) I can't hear you. You're cutting in and out. When we say that someone is "cutting in and out" it means that the connection is very weak. One second, you can hear them speaking, the next second, you can't, then you can again, etc... When they "cut in", you can hear them. When they "cut out", you can't hear them. So, it's like the words that they're saying exist in your awareness/hearing (in) and then they don't exist in your awareness/hearing (out) and then they do again (in), etc...

WITH

A) Example Sentences. Remember to follow the instructions in section A from previous prepositions.

1)

I'm with my friend right now.
How long have you been with the company? (been working at/for the company)
We're having problems with our son.
Her face was covered with chocolate. (A lot of chocolate was on her face.)
We can win! Who's with me? (supports me or agrees with me)
Do you mind? I can't focus with you watching me.

What does the word "with" mean in this group?

2)

I made a cake with vanilla frosting.
A short man with blue eyes gave me a dollar.
Did you see the man with a Spanish accent? (He has that accent.)
I finished the project with two hours to spare. (two hours remaining)

What does the word "with" mean in this group?

3)

The victim was stabbed with a knife.
I threw the ball with all (of) my strength.
I'm American, but I can speak with a British accent. (I can use that accent.)
Are you busy? I could use your help with something.
Can you fill this cup (up) with water for me?

B)The Logic

Key Idea(s): together

"with" is a one-way preposition

Explanation of the logic: The preposition "with" brings two or more things together. This can be people, items, or more abstract things like emotions or the ideas of using something or having something. We can use the preposition "with" in many different contexts and many different ways, but it's always somehow about to the basic logical idea of two things together.

Etymology notes: The history of the preposition "with" is very interesting. In fact, it originally meant the opposite: separate or against. There are still a few words that use "with" as part of the word (withdraw, withstand, etc). These words use the older meaning and are a lot less common than the preposition "with" by itself. Like many things in English, the meaning changed in Middle English, which was likely because of the French and Latin influence on English at the time, as well as influence from the Old Norse word "vidh". In Old English, the preposition "mid" was used instead of "with", which survives today in other Germanic languages (for example, the German word "mit"). In modern English, we still have some words that use "mid", but only as a prefix, for example in the words "midwife" and "middle". Because the preposition "mid" disappeared, the preposition "with" took its logic and replaced it. 13

Now, go back to the example sentences and try to apply the logic. Ask yourself: "How does the preposition 'with' bring these two things together?"

C) Detailed Explanations of the Example Sentences.

1) *Together*

This is the simplest and most basic use of the preposition "with". Sometimes, you can use the word "together" instead of the preposition "with". The first example is very simple, but the other examples are more complex and abstract. This group is simply about the general idea "together".

I'm with my friend right now. If you're with your friend, then the two of you are together in the same location.

ALTERNATIVES: "My friend and I are together right now." This way is much less common, but perfectly fine. Notice that the placement of the word "I" changed. This is because instead of saying "I am" + with someone/something, we're saying "My friend and I are". In other words, "we are". So if I say "we are with", that means there's a third person or thing: "We are with Tom." Word order is important.

How long have you been with the company? (been working at/for the company) This example is a little less concrete, but if you're with a company or other organization, then you work at/for that company or organization. Because you're an employee, you're "with" the company or the people who work there, and not on some other company's team. So, you and the company are together because you're part of that company's team. You work with the other people who work there.

ALTERNATIVES: "How long have you been (a) part of the company?" You're an employee, so you're part of the company. This is part 1 of the logic: you are one member (more specific word for "part") of the company or the company's employees.

"How long have you worked for this company?" Here, it's more natural to say "this company" instead of "the company", but it depends. We can use the preposition "for" because the company hired you. In other words, they are the basis of your employment (which means that they are the reason why you have a job). You can also look at it another way: The work you do is for the purpose of the company's profits and benefit.

"How long have you worked at this company?" When we talk about where someone works, it's a location. We're talking about the company as a whole, but if you work at a company, you usually only work at a specific store that the company owns, so the preposition "at" works.

We're having problems with our son. This sentence does NOT mean that our son and us are having problems together. It means that our son isn't listening to what we tell him and that's causing problems BETWEEN us and him. Another example: "I'm having problems with my computer". My computer isn't working properly, which is causing problems. So, in the first case, the son and the problems go together, so we have to deal with those problems; in the second case, the computer and the problems go together, so I have to deal with those problems.

262

ALTERNATIVES: "Our son is causing (us) problems." / "Our son is causing problems (for us)".

"We're having trouble with our son".

Her face was covered with chocolate. (A lot of chocolate was on her face.) In this case, her face and the chocolate are brought together and the chocolate is covering the whole surface of her face.

Note: Depending on the context, this could also mean "using" (group 3). If we just want to say that the chocolate is on her face, then there's no special meaning and it fits in this group. If I intentionally use chocolate as a tool (in order) to cover her face, then the surface meaning is the idea of "using". Either way, the logic is the same.

ALTERNATIVES: "Her face was covered in chocolate." Normally, the face is a surface, but if you use something to cover it, now we can also say that that surface is in(side) a container. Think of the word "cover". It's like a lid, so now the face is contained inside the chocolate, which is the cover/lid.

"There was chocolate all over her face." Of course, we can use the phrase "all over", as well, because the chocolate is applied to the entire surface of her face, just like if there are clothes all over the floor. We'll see this idea using the preposition "over" soon.

"Her face had chocolate all over it." This is the same as group 2.

We can win! Who's with me? (supports me or agrees with me) If someone is with you in this context, we don't mean physically together. This means that my idea and your idea are together. In other words, we agree and/or you support my idea. If you want to do something, and someone supports you, thinks that it's possible, or helps you do it, then they are "with" you (together) in that effort.

263

Do you mind? I can't focus with you watching me. In this example, we're bringing together two actions: focusing and watching. I'm trying to focus on something (like homework) and you're watching me do it. When we combine/bring together both actions, we can use the preposition "with" because they're happening at the same time and are connected to each other.

ALTERNATIVES: "I can't focus while you're watching me."

2) to have

This group is easy, but a little more complicated than the basic idea of "together". In this group, the idea of "together" is more abstract and the application of the logic gives us the surface meaning of "having something".

I made a cake with vanilla frosting. "Frosting" is the sweet stuff that you put on top of a cake. You can make a cake without frosting, but if you use frosting, then the frosting is part of the cake, just like wheels are part of a car. If I make a cake with vanilla frosting, it means that the cake has vanilla frosting. These two things go together. So, just like a car has wheels, a cake usually has frosting. This sentence can also go in group 3 ("to use" → "I made a cake using vanilla frosting"), but the meaning might change. It can mean the same thing, but it can also mean that the whole cake is made of vanilla frosting. Note that we cannot say, "I made a cake having vanilla frosting", but we can say, "I made a cake that has vanilla frosting".

ALTERNATIVES: "I made a cake that has vanilla frosting."

A short man with blue eyes gave me a dollar. If someone has a particular feature or characteristic, then you can often use the preposition "with". This is especially true for physical characteristics (color, shape, size, etc...), but can also be used for some abstract things. For example, "I like people with smart

264

minds." There are other ways to say this: "I like people who have smart minds", "I like people who are smart", or simply, "I like smart people". The exact context in which you can and can't use the preposition "with" for abstract characteristics varies. In our example sentence above, if the short man has blue eyes, you can say, "A short man with blue eyes". Just like the vanilla frosting, the man and the color of his eyes go together because the color is just a particular feature or part of his eyes, which are a part of him. It's almost exactly like saying "a man with glasses", which means a man who has/is wearing glasses, except the glasses aren't (a) part of his physical body.

Note that even with physical characteristics, it depends on the structure of the sentence. You <u>can't</u> say, "The man is with blue eyes" or "He's with blue eyes". That sounds like there's someone or something else that's called "blue eyes", maybe as a nickname for a second person that the man is currently with.

ALTERNATIVES: "A short man who has blue eyes gave me a dollar."

Did you see the man with a Spanish accent? (He has that accent.) This example is like the previous one, but instead of talking about eye color, we're talking about someone's accent in a foreign language. When the man speaks English, the sounds that he makes are influenced by his native language (Spanish). So, the words that he says are English words, but they have a Spanish sound. When he speaks English, the Spanish sounds and the English words come out together and it makes what we call an accent. The man "owns" that accent and the accent is part of his speech, so the man and the sounds that he makes go together, as well. It's one of his characteristics, or at least one of the characteristics of his English speech.

ALTERNATIVES: "Did you see the man who has a Spanish accent?"

265

I finished the project with two hours to spare. (two hours remaining) If you have an amount of time to spare, it means that there is still time remaining. For example, you have to finish the project by 5 (PM), but you finish it at 3. There's still two hours until the deadline, so you have two hours to "spare". In the example sentence, let's also say that your boss or teacher gave you the project at 9 (AM). This means that you <u>have</u> a total of 8 hours (in order) to finish the project. If you finish at 3, you still <u>have</u> two hours until you have to turn in the project. Of course, you could turn it in now, but that doesn't matter.

How does the logic ("together") work here? Well, the project and the amount of time to finish it (which includes the deadline (the end point)) go together. There's something that needs to be done and there's an amount of time to finish it. Your boss or teacher gives you both of these things, so not only do the project and the time limit go together, but you possess (have) both of them. This is more abstract than the previous examples, but I hope it's clear how the logic applies.

ALTERNATIVES: "I finished the project and I <u>had</u> two hours to spare." This isn't the most natural or common way to say it, but it works.

3) to use

The victim was stabbed with a knife. The third surface meaning of the preposition "with" is "to use". We can change this example and instead say, "The victim was stabbed using a knife". But how does this connect with the logic? Knife + stabbing (action) + victim. You bring all these things together and we get a victim who was stabbed, and the person who stabbed them used a knife.

ALTERNATIVES: "The victim was stabbed using a knife"

I threw the ball with all (of) my strength. "I threw the ball using all (of) my strength". Simple. I bring the ball and my strength together (in order) to throw it as far as I possibly can.

ALTERNATIVES: "I threw the ball using all (of) my strength".

I'm American, but I can speak with a British accent. (I can use that accent.) Remember in the last group we saw a sentence about a Spanish accent with the meaning "to have". You can also use the preposition "with" meaning "to use" (in order) to talk about accents. In this case, when I speak English, I don't have a foreign language accent. My American English accent is a native accent and it's a natural variety of expressing sounds in English, as opposed to the non-native influence of Spanish sounds. If I decide to speak English but I want to sound British, I can use a British accent. I'm bringing that accent together with my words, but instead of "having" the accent, I'm just "using" the accent because I can stop using it whenever I want. The British accent isn't part of me because I normally speak with an American accent, but I can use a British accent, just like I can use a computer, for example.

ALTERNATIVES: "I'm American, but I can speak using a British accent."

Are you busy? I could use your help with (moving) the couch. I'm trying to do move the couch, which is heavy, so I need help. I'm bringing together the task ("moving the couch") and your effort (help) so that I can achieve the task. Notice that this one is a little different. We use the verb "to use" in the sentence, and it's not correct to say, "I could use your help using moving the couch". So in this case, the meaning of "use" isn't implied, it's directly stated in the sentence. But what if we say, "Could you help me with (moving) the couch?" Now we're not using the verb "to use", but the surface meaning of "to use" is still applied indirectly.

267

Can you fill this cup (up) with water for me? When we fill a cup with water, for example, we are using the water (in order) to fill the space inside of the cup.

D) Some verbs that often use the preposition "with"

Go with	Take (something) with	Work with
Stay with	Connect (something) with	Do (something) with
Come with	Fill (something) with	

E) **Phrasal Verbs.** Look up each phrasal verb and try to understand how the logic of the word "at" applies. Remember, a phrasal verb is basically a preposition put into action by a verb.

Note: The preposition "with" is another preposition that isn't often used in real phrasal verbs, though you will see it more often than some of the other prepositions. Even when it's required to make the phrasal verb, the nature of the preposition "with" means that it's always just a connector, anyway, because the logic is "together". Remember, the point is that it doesn't completely matter if something is a phrasal verb or not; the logic always applies. The only reason that phrasal verbs exist in the first place is because of the logic and feeling that is at the core of each preposition.

We came up with an idea to solve your problem. ("With" is part of the phrasal verb) This phrasal verb is a little complicated because of the preposition "up". "To come up with" an idea or something similar means that you create/think of an idea, usually to solve a problem. The preposition "up" in this case is connecting to the preposition "on", which is a positive state/active state and is applied in the background of the sentence. The easiest way to remember this is to think of it like

268

diving under water in a lake or an ocean (which represents your mind). You dive down trying to find something (an idea) and when you find it, you come to the surface and bring it with you. Even though the preposition "with" is required (in order) to make the phrasal verb, it doesn't have any special meaning and it just brings together the idea and the process of finding the idea.

I don't have to put up with your stupidity! ("With" is part of the phrasal verb) "To put up with" something is basically the same as "to deal with" something, but there is a slight difference between them. Most of the time, they're interchangeable. The preposition "up" in this case is, again, a connection to a positive state/active state, but in this case it's also specifically a surface/platform. The thing that I have to "put up with" or "deal with" is like a weight on me, which is a burden (something that's negative/inconvenient for me). In other words, your stupidity is a weight/burden that I don't want to carry and I have no obligation to carry it. The preposition "with" is required, but, like in the last example, it just connects two parts: the weight (your stupidity) and the carrying of that weight (put up).

She came down with the flu last night. ("With" is part of the phrasal verb) In the first example, we saw "to come up with". Now we see "to come down with". This means "to become ill". Notice something very interesting: we have a phrase in English: "to fall ill". This sounds much more formal, so we usually use the phrasal verb "come down with" and it's obvious that the words "down" and "fall" are related. We won't talk about the logic of the preposition "down" right now, but you can easily see that if you're healthy, it's like you're "up", which is connected to "positive/active". If you're sick, then your health is "down" or weakened, which is more closely related to the idea of "negative/inactive". What about the logic of the preposition "with"? Well, it's like the flu brought her (or her health) down with it. Health + flu (together) = a negative/inactive state of health ("off", which connects to the preposition "on" through the preposition "down").

269

F) Examples of idioms that use the preposition "with", with detailed explanations.

Tom's very popular with the ladies. This sentence means that most women are physically attracted to Tom. So, "to be popular" + the source of that popularity = "to be popular with something/someone". This one is a little strange and different, but we can see how the preposition "with" simply joins the popularity and the source of the popularity. Another example: "This game is very popular with children".

You passed the test with flying colors. When we're talking about a test, the phrase "with flying colors" means "a perfect score". So, you can also say, "You passed the test with a perfect score". We can see that in both cases, the preposition "with" brings two things together, but we can also see that the surface meaning is close to group two ("to have").

ABOUT

A) Example Sentences. Remember to follow the instructions in section A from previous prepositions.

1)

Think about trees.
This is a book about Gandhi.
I'm worried about you.

What does the word "about" mean in this group?

2)

He's about five feet tall. (1.5 meters)
I'll be home (at) about five.
The project is due in about a week.
It took me about six months to write my first book.
I think he makes about $50,000 a year. (per year)

What does the word "about" mean in this group?

3)

I'm about to go to the beach.
I was about to finish my homework when the phone rang.
My daughter's four, which means she's about ready to start school.
I think I'm about ready to go to bed.

What does the word "about" mean in this group?

271

B) The Logic

Key Idea(s): a scope (the numbers are for the surface meaning groups)

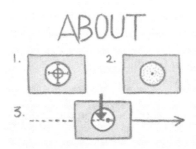

"about" is a one-way preposition

Explanation of the logic: The preposition "about" has three surface meanings, but they all fit into the idea of "a scope" (similar to a microscope or a telescope, for example). We'll see specific details in the examples. This preposition is naturally very abstract, but in most cases, it's not very difficult to understand. Because it's very abstract, like the preposition "by", it's difficult to find a single word or phrase that fits this preposition perfectly. One of the meanings of the word "scope" is "everything that's involved". For example, "The specific uses of the present perfect tense are beyond (outside) the scope of this book." A word related to "scope" is "focus", and the preposition that we use with the verb "to focus" is usually "on". As we'll see, there's a close relationship between the prepositions "on" and "about" in group one. So, the scope idea is more or less about the scale of focus, but the exact size of the scope depends on what we're focusing on. For example, we can go from a small scope to a large scope: "leaves", "trees", "nature", "the earth", "the universe".

The numbers in the picture are each of the groups instead of different parts of the logic. Group one is a general scope, which sometimes overlaps with the preposition "on" and is closely related to the idea of a "topic". Group two is about an approximate

272

scope (approximate amount, size, age, etc…). Group three is about verbs, specifically the point right before something happens. In this group, we'll see how the "to" + "action/verb" idea works with the scope idea (in order) to gives the idea of "close to starting an action", "close to finishing an action", and "almost ready".

Etymology notes: The preposition "about" originally comes from the Old English word "abutan", which came from the word "onbutan", which meant "on the outside of", "around the circumference of", "near", and "from place to place". Later in Old English, it gained the meaning of "approximately", which really means "near in time, number, etc…." By the 1300's, it was being used like the preposition "around", which is one reason why these two prepositions are so similar. Also around the 1300's, the idea of "about to do" developed, which means that you are intending to do something/close to starting an action. 14 You can see that the scope idea is closely related to the words "near" and "close to" (which are synonyms), but the preposition "about" isn't exactly the same as "near" or "close to". They're just closely related ideas.

The prepositions "about" and "around" are very similar and it took me a long time to identify the keywords for them. It seems that the preposition "about" might have come from Proto-Germanic, the language that Old English came from. However, we also have the preposition "around", which might have come from Latin. Both of these words are very similar in meaning, and there are some cases where they are 100% interchangeable, but they clearly feel differently and their logic is different. In many of the cases where they're interchangeable, "about" is generally more common in Britain and "around" is more common in America.

Now, go back to the example sentences and try to apply the logic. Ask yourself: "How is 'about' a scope?"

C) Detailed Explanations of the Example Sentences.

1) *topic; general "scope"*

Think about trees. Because the preposition "about" is a scope, the verb "to think" often uses it. As soon as I tell you to think about something, your mind focuses on that thing. Of all the possible things that you *could* think about (meaning everything and anything in existence and in your imagination), you're narrowing your focus to trees. You might ask, "What about trees?" "Think about the branches." "What about the branches?" "Think about the color of the branches" or "Think about the leaves that are on the branches".

As you can see, we can zoom in, going to smaller and smaller levels. We can go the other way, too. Instead of saying, "Think about trees", I can say, "Think about a forest". Now we're zooming out to a bigger level. So, just like we have microscopes to see super small things and telescopes for the giant night sky, we can adjust the scope of our focus. Also notice something interesting: if I say, "Think about trees", or even just the word "trees", you immediately see trees in your mind. If I say the word "cat", "dog", or "pink elephant", those things appear in your mind and not other things, like people, cars, or the ocean, for example.

As a quick note, both the preposition "about" and the preposition "on" are used for topics. The difference is that the preposition "about" is a scope and the preposition "on" is a platform or positive state/active state (remember that we often say "focus on something"). Sometimes, they overlap, like in the next example sentence. In a case like that, they are 100% interchangeable. However, the preposition "about" is the preposition "about" and the preposition "on" is the preposition "on", so unfortunately they're not always interchangeable, even if we're talking about a topic. This is usually just because of the

274

particular preposition that a verb takes. For example, we say "talk about", but we don't say "talk on". "Talk on" can be used, but it's a phrasal verb that's not common and means "continue talking", usually said with annoyance.

This is a book about Gandhi. In this case, you can say, "This is a book about Gandhi" or "This is a book on Gandhi" and they're exactly the same. Books, speeches, and other such material can use both of these prepositions when we're talking about their topics. When we use the preposition "about", we're talking about the scope of the topic that's covered. What's the focus of the topic or the boundaries of the topic? It's not trees. It's not science. It's Gandhi. Because the book is about Gandhi, it limits the scope to him and his life.

ALTERNATIVES: "This is a book on Gandhi." If we think of this sentence in a very literal way, it might mean that there is a book that is physically on top of Gandhi's body. Of course, that's not what we mean. Gandhi is the topic, and a topic can be an abstract platform.

I'm worried about you. Though we can use the preposition "about" with a topic, usually we use "about" as a general "scope". In this case, we can't say, "I'm worried on you", because the word "worry" often uses the preposition "about", but not the preposition "on". Here, we can simply say that "about" is being used to show the scope of my worry. Am I worried about the world? Am I worried about being late for work? No, I'm worried about you. If nothing else, you can simply remember that the word "worry" usually goes with the word "about" because if you're worried about something then we want to specify what you're worried about, which is naturally a scope that narrows our focus to a certain thing. There are other options that can be used depending on the specific context, but these two usually go together, so remember them as one unit.

275

2) *"approximately"; 100% interchangeable with "around"*

This group is simple and in all of these sentences, you can replace the preposition "about" with the preposition "around". This is because they both have the same surface meaning in this context. We'll see all of these exact same example sentences when we talk about the preposition "around" later. This group simply means "approximately", which means "near/close in number, time, age, etc... The words "approximately", "about", and "around" are almost always 100% interchangeable when talking about any type of measurement, amount, or similar concept. The only difference in this case is that the words "approximately", "about", and "around" all feel a little different.

Notice that I said "almost 100% interchangeable". There are rare exceptions. For example, earlier we saw the sentence, "The bank is (somewhere) around the park." This was a close alternative to the sentence, "The bank is by the park." In this case, we do not say, "The bank is (somewhere) about the park." That sounds more like saying, "Banks are about making money". In that sentence, the meaning is that the focus of banks is to make money. So if we say that the bank is about the park, it sounds like the focus on the bank is the park. In other words, we usually use the preposition "around" when talking about approximate physical locations, but it depends on the specific context.

For example, if you're following a map and trying to find someone's house and you're close, but you don't see it yet, you can say, "His house should be right about here". You can also say, "His house should be right around here". These are extremely specific contexts that you just have to get used to. The problem is that the prepositions "about" and "around" are not the same, so sometimes when we use "about", we're using a different surface meaning that's specifically based on the logic of the preposition "about" and not the preposition "around".

He's about five feet tall. (1.5 meters) In this case, we're talking about height. He's either a little shorter than five feet, exactly five feet tall, or a little taller than five feet. We don't know his exact height until we measure him. The scope idea works because we're focusing the scope on that specific measurement (five feet).

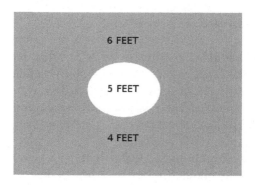

ALTERNATIVES: "He's approximately five feet tall." "He's around five feet tall."

I'll be home (at) about five. Here we're talking about the time. I might be home a little before five, at five, or a little after five. The scope is zoomed in on five o'clock.

ALTERNATIVES: "I'll be home at approximately five." Notice in this case that we have to use the preposition "at". When we use the prepositions "about" and "around", they can replace the preposition "at" when we talk about time, but we can also keep it and use "at around" or "at about". The word "approximately" is not a preposition, so we have to keep the preposition "at". However, this isn't the most natural/common way to express this sentence. Using "about" or "around" are much more common.

"I'll be home (at) around five."

The project is due in about a week. I don't remember the exact date that the project is due, so I'm simply saying that it's approximately 6-8 days from now. The scope is focused on those days.

ALTERNATIVES: "The project is due in around a week." "The project is due in approximately a week." Note that both of these alternatives are possible, but "about" is probably the most common in this case.

It took me about six months to write my first book. Again, I don't know the exact amount of time, but it was more or less six months. Maybe 5.5, maybe 6, maybe 6.5. This is a much larger scope, but it's still a scope. We're just zooming out: instead of "about 5 o'clock" or "about a week", it's "about six months".

I think he makes about $50,000 a year. (per year) Here, we're talking about an amount (not a year). Maybe he makes $45,000, maybe $50,000, or maybe $55,000. Again, it's just a number that's close. Here, the scope is centered on that amount ($45,000-$55,000).

3) *close to starting/finishing an action; almost ready to start/finish an action*

This last group is a little different than the other two. When we use the preposition "about" in the structure "to be about to do", it means that you have the intention to do that action and you are close to starting that action or you have the intention to finish that action and you are almost finished. This structure and use of the preposition "about" is extremely natural for native English speakers and it's very common.

I mentioned earlier that the "to" + "action/verb" idea works with the "scope" idea. If you put these two together, this group will be very easy to learn and remember. Let's look at some specific examples.

I'm about to go to the beach. So, let's say that I'm about to go to the beach. I'm either ready to leave or getting ready to leave and you call me on the phone. You ask, "Hey, are you busy?" and I reply, "Well, I'm about to go to the beach." This let's you know that going to the beach was my intention and that I was either

278

preparing to go or I was close to leaving. Note that if you call me after I leave, I would say, "I'm going to the beach" or "I'm on my way to the beach". Also note the connection between "about to go" and "on my way". We'll come back to this in a moment.

The first question is: how is the preposition "about" a scope in this sentence? Well, in this group the idea of a scope is very abstract and it means the nearness in time between starting an action and the action itself. Think about it this way: there's the moment that I leave (in order) to go to the beach and the moment right before I leave. Imagine that you look into a microscope or a telescope and you see two things that are close to each other. That's basically what's happening here, but instead of physical objects, we're using a scope of time and looking at two things that are close to each other (leaving and the time right before leaving). This brings these two things together in a special relationship and we can say that they fit into the same scope because of how close they are to each other in time.

The second question is: how does the "to" + "action/verb" idea work with the "scope" idea in this case? We have "about" + "to" + "go" (or "leave", depending on how we're talking about it; to make this easier, we'll use the verb "to leave": "about" + "to" + "leave"). We know that the preposition "to" is pointing to the action of leaving. Instead of having two verbs ("want to leave"), we have a preposition and a verb ("about to go"). This means that instead of the first action/verb pointing to the second action/verb, we have a preposition pointing to an action/verb. Specifically, we have the idea of a "scope" (scope of time) pointing to the action of "leaving". In other words, the present moment ("I am") and the action of leaving is put into the same scope, and because the scope idea in this context is very similar to the idea of "near/close to" (in time), we get the combined idea of "close to leaving".

Lastly, I mentioned earlier that there's a connection between the phrases "about to go" (before the action starts) and "on my way" (after the action starts). We now know that "about to go" means that I'm close to starting the action of going/leaving. This means that going/leaving is "inactive" because I haven't left

279

yet, but it's close to becoming "active". When we say "I'm on my way", it means that going/leaving is "active". We can clearly see that we have another close connection between the prepositions "about" and "on".

I was about to finish my homework when the phone rang. This particular sentence structure is extremely common and useful. We use it when we want to talk about what was close to happening when something else happened, which usually stops or interrupts the first action. In other words, my homework was almost finished at the time that the phone rang. The idea of a "scope" and the idea of "to" + "action/verb" are the same as in the previous example, but with two differences: here we're close to finishing something instead of starting something, and we're describing something was close to happening in the past instead of the present.

ALTERNATIVES: "I was almost finished with my homework when the phone rang." Notice that we can't say "almost to do", so we have to change the sentence a little. Sometimes it's not possible to use the word "almost", like in the previous example sentence.

My daughter's four, which means (that) she's about ready to start school. When we add the word "ready" between the preposition "about" and the verb, we get a slightly different meaning. Instead of the action being close to happening, you are almost ready to start the action. So, if she's *about to start* school, that means that the school year is starting soon and she'll be attending. If she's *about ready* to start school, that means that the school year might or might not be starting soon, but she's almost ready to start either way. Most sentences that use "about ready" can also use "almost ready", but there's a small difference in how they feel.

In a sentence like this, the scope idea is the same, but instead of the two things being the action and the point right before the action, the two things are the state of being ready and

280

the point right before that state, meaning the point right before you're ready. In other words, we're adding the idea of "ready" into the scope. The idea of "to" + "action/verb" also works the same here, but the small difference is that the words "about" and "ready" are like one unit that point to the action/verb: "about ready" + "to" + "start".

ALTERNATIVES: "My daughter's four, which means (that) she's almost ready to start school."

I think I'm about ready to go to bed. This is an example like the previous one, but it also helps to show the small difference between the words "about" and "almost". Specifically, the word "almost" sounds a little more like we're talking about the steps involved in getting ready for bed. For example, you might turn off the TV, brush your teeth, and change your clothes. If you haven't done those things, you aren't ready. If you do all of them except one, then you're almost ready.

We usually use "about ready", especially in this context, to mean that you feel like you want to go to bed very soon. You might not actually go to bed soon because maybe you get pulled into reading social media or you can't stop watching videos online, but you feel tired and know that you should go to sleep. Most of the time, though, when we say this, we're telling the listener that we want to go to sleep.

You can still use "about ready" and "almost ready" interchangeably because they're extremely close in meaning, but this slight difference in how they feel does exist. All (of) the ideas from the previous example ("scope", "ready", "to" + "action/verb") are the same.

D) Some verbs that often use the preposition "about"

Think about	Talk about	Tell (someone) about
Dream about	Cry about	Say (something) about
Worry about	Ask about	Lie about (meaning "to tell a lie")

E) **Phrasal Verbs.** Look up each phrasal verb and try to understand how the logic of the word "about" applies. Remember, a phrasal verb is basically a preposition put into action by a verb.

The preposition "about" is not used in phrasal verbs, but it can be a connector.

He was going on and on about his new car. It was so boring. The phrasal verb "to go on" can be extended into the phrase "to go on and on". This means that something takes a very long time to end. Literally, something "continues and continues". In this case, we're saying that someone was talking about his new car. So, we use the preposition "about" because he's talking about his car. If we want to say this without the phrasal verb, it would be: "He kept talking about his new car." When we use "go on and on", it sounds stronger, but you can see that the verb "to talk" is just being replaced, so we keep the preposition "about", which is connected to "his new car", because that's the topic.

F) Examples of idioms that use the preposition "about", with detailed explanations.

I was out and about when I ran into Tom. The phrase "out and about" means that you are away from home and doing different things. It could be errands (things like going to pay bills, do the grocery shopping, mailing letters, etc…) or it could be that you were walking around town with some friends, for example. The

282

"out" refers to being outside of the house. In a sentence like this, the preposition "about" specifically means "here and there with no fixed direction" according to the *Online Etymology Dictionary*. We know that this inside the scope of something (like a city, for example), and this is related to the meaning of "from place to place" that we saw in the etymology notes earlier. This means that while you were out, you didn't just go to one place or that you didn't just have one thing planned. Unfortunately, this meaning of the preposition "about" isn't normally part of "about" and it's almost always part of the preposition "around", as we'll see later. So we're using the preposition "about" when we should use the preposition "around", which means this is a very rare exception to the logic, but that's probably because these two prepositions are extremely similar. Strange things like this sometimes happen in idioms, and it's always best to memorize idioms as one chunk.

But how does the logic work in this case? Well, the scope is the general area of the city or town that you're in. Again, this is usually expressed using the preposition "around", but without the idea of a scope. So we can see that the surface meaning is strange for the preposition "about", but it's just a special/uncommon application of the logic.

All of his clothes were lying about the room. This is another sentence where we use the idea of "here and there with no fixed direction", as well as the idea of "from place to place" (but each "place" is a different part of the room). In this case, British English uses the preposition "about", but American English uses the preposition "around" → "All of his clothes were lying around the room". However, in contexts like this, both are acceptable and Americans can use both versions. They feel a little different and Americans usually prefer to use the preposition "around", but you can choose either one. The meaning of the preposition "about" in this case overlaps with the preposition "over". For example, we can say, "His clothes were lying all over the room". We'll talk about the preposition "over" next, but the preposition "around" also deals with this idea, which is why we can use "around", as well.

283

How does the logic work in this sentence? The scope is the room, and because we're saying that the clothes were all around the room, they aren't in one single location (place) inside the room. Most likely, they're all over the floor. So there's a shirt by the door and some socks in the middle of the room and a shirt by the wall, for example. The clothes are simply located anywhere and/or everywhere inside the scope (the area) of the room.

OVER

A) Example Sentences. Remember to follow the instructions in section A from previous prepositions.

1)

The door had a sign over it that said "Hotel Tokyo".
A helicopter was flying over us.
You have no control over me./You don't have control over me.

What does the word "over" mean in this group?

2)

He threw the bag over the fence.
Do we have to go over the bridge? I hate bridges.
A plane was flying over us.
The doctor put a bandage over his wound.
Has she gotten over the flu yet?
I sent the file to him over the internet.
The meeting will be over at eleven.
Let's buy a pizza. If we have any money left (over), we can get a soda, too.

What does the word "over" mean in this group?

3)

I tripped over the wires.
A tree fell (over) on(to) his car.
The car drove over (the edge of) the cliff.
(I have an injured hip:) I dropped my phone. Can you bend over and pick up it for me?

What does the word "over" mean in this group?

4)

I don't want a computer that costs over $1,000. That's too expensive.
(For a roller coaster:) Children over (the age of) ten can ride without an adult.
He's a little over four feet tall. (1.2 meters)
I worked here for over five years.
We walked (for) over twenty miles! (32 kilometers)

What does the word "over" mean in this group?

5)

They always fight over/argue over stupid things.
She took him to court over the damages. (She sued him for damaging her property.)

What does the word "over" mean in this group?

6)

Let's talk about your business plan over dinner.
I'll be in Japan over the winter.
I worked there over five years. (notice: not "for over")

What does the word "over" mean in this group?

7)

My computer crashed and I had to do my essay over.
The teacher made the students write their names over and over (again).
The seasons come and go, over and over (again).

What does the word "over" mean in this group?

8)

(Two people in the same bed:) Can you roll over, please? I don't have any space.
The phone is face-down on the table. Turn it over.

What does the word "over" mean in this group?

B) The Logic

Key Idea(s): 1) an arc shape (like a bridge) that goes from one point to another point (in order) to get to the other side of something;
2) a cycle or circular movement;
3) more than (like the top of the arc)

"over" is a one-way preposition

Explanation of the logic: The preposition "over" is generally easy to understand, but it has a lot of surface meanings. In other words, the logic has a lot of applications, making this a very useful and common preposition. The preposition "over" has a very clear and distinct feeling for native speakers. It usually feels like some kind of arc-shape or semi-arc-shape, meaning that it gives us a clear feeling of movement. This movement can happen in space ("over the bridge"), time ("over the winter"), an argument

287

(from one person to the other person and back), or a cycle/repetition ("do it over" → "again").

However, there a couple (of) uses of the preposition "over" that are static positions (not moving). These cases are like the top of the arc in an abstract way, but the surface meaning is always "above" (example group one) or some version of "more than" (example group four), which includes "older than", "more expensive than", and "higher than". Another way to look at group four is "past a certain point", which is connected to part 1 of the logic.

Etymology notes: There's not much useful here, but the preposition "over" originally comes from the Old English "ofer", which meant "beyond", "above", "upon", "in", "across", and "past" ("past" meaning "farther than", not the past tense). 15 Most of these meanings still exist in Modern English, plus a few newer ones.

Now, go back to the example sentences and try to apply the logic. Ask yourself: "How is the preposition 'over' related to the idea of an arc-shape?"

C) Detailed Explanations of the Example Sentences.

1) *above (a point/position higher than something else)*

This group is very simple. In many cases, the prepositions "over" and "above" are interchangeable in this group. This group is actually a subgroup of group four, but I put it here because it helps to learn and understand group two.

The door had a sign over it that said "Hotel Tokyo". Since the preposition "over" usually feels like some kind of arc, you can think of this as the highest point of the arc, but if that's confusing, then don't worry about it. As I said, this is the most basic meaning and is very easy to remember. In this case, there's a door. Above the door is a sign. So, we can say that the sign is "over" the door.

ALTERNATIVES: "The door had a sign above it that said "Hotel Tokyo".

A helicopter was flying over us. Again, this is the same meaning as before, but there's an added part when we talk about something like "flying". In this group, we talk about a helicopter because a helicopter can hover in place. (Also, notice that the word "hover" is like "h" + "over", except that the pronunciation changes). In the next group, we'll talk about a plane, which can't hover. If something is hovering or flying over something else, then we can use "over" or "above", just like when something is over a door.

ALTERNATIVES: "A helicopter was flying above us."

You have no control over me./You don't have control over me. Here we have something a little different. It seems that it fits best in this group, but it's more abstract. In this sentence, we *cannot* use "above" because we're not talking about a physical point that is above something. However, in an abstract way, if you have control over me, it means that you're above me in position or power, meaning you can influence or maybe even control what I do and don't do. For example, you might be my manager at work, or maybe you brainwashed me so that I'll do whatever you tell me. You're in a position that's more advantageous. Notice that we also say, "He has an advantage over me", which doesn't mean exactly the same thing, but the basic idea of the preposition "over" is the same.

2) *from one side of something to the other side (above + movement)*

The idea of this group is: starting from one point, you go to another point which is on the other side. The difference between "from"/"to" and "over" in this context is that the preposition "over" is more about the distance that's between the two points, which emphasizes the journey between the two points instead of just the start point or the end point, plus the idea of an arc-shape. We saw this with the preposition "by" earlier, but the preposition "by" is about the distance that's between two points with an emphasis on not going past the end point, where the preposition "over" feels like an arc that goes from one side, up, over to the other side, and then down. Why? The preposition "over" in this group is similar to the preposition "above", but with the added idea of movement from one point to another, particularly (in order) to reach the other side of something. This includes the idea of "past a certain point". It's also useful to note that the idea of the preposition "across" is very similar, but "across" doesn't include the feeling of an arc.

He threw the bag over the fence. This example clearly shows an arc-shape. The fence is an obstacle, so (in order) to get to the other side, you either have to go around it, or you have to go over it, which means that you have to go up to the point that's directly above it and then down to the other side. Again, it's like "above" + movement as we go from one point to another point so that we can reach the other side.

Do we have to go over the bridge? I hate bridges. When we talk about bridges, we're talking about going from one side of something, such as a river, to the other side using the bridge as the connection. Specifically, we're going over ("above") the river while driving on top of the bridge, but we extend the idea of "over" to the idea of the bridge because a bridge is something that allows you to go over something else, so we simply say "over the bridge". A bridge doesn't have to be an arc-shape, of course, but it helps if you imagine an old bridge with an arc-shape that you might find in a forest.

A plane was flying over us. Ok, we know that if a helicopter is flying (meaning hovering) above you, you can use the preposition "over". But that belongs to group one. This example belongs to group two because we're also talking about movement. A helicopter can also fit into this group if it's not just hovering and instead actually flying from one point to another point. Again, we have "above" + movement. In this example sentence, it might not seem like the plane is trying to reach some point that's on the other side of point A (where it started). However, that's what planes do. They start at one location and fly in the air for a long time until they reach the second location. In the process, they "reach the other side" of everything that they flew over. It's like a really big bridge.

The doctor put a bandage over his wound. This is another example that emphasizes the idea of "from one point to another point", except we're not talking about a single straight line. We're talking about covering something, which means we're moving from left to right and from top to bottom. In other words, cover ("c" + "over") means that we're going over something in at least two directions (you can also include the diagonal directions (like top-right corner to bottom-left corner)), which allows us to cover the entire surface of something.

We can also see the idea of "reaching the other side of something" because we want to cover the entire wound (or whatever surface that we're talking about). If we use the bottom of the bandage as a starting point, for example, then we want to place the bandage on top of the entire wound, which means that the bandage has to extend from the bottom of the wound to the top of the wound. This means that we're trying to "reach the other side" of the wound so that it's completely covered.

ALTERNATIVES: "The doctor put a bandage on his wound". In this case, we can also use the preposition "on". Why? Because the bandage is physically being placed on top of the wound. After the bandage is there, it stays there, unlike the car that can travel over any terrain.

Has she gotten over the flu yet? The phrasal verb "to get over" means you are no longer affected by something negative. This could be the flu, an old relationship ("Has she gotten over her ex-boyfriend yet?"), etc... So, if you're over the flu, then you're no longer sick (ill). In this case, the flu is like an obstacle or wall that stands between you and being healthy. Just like a real wall or fence, we can apply the idea of "over" with the verb "to get" (in this case meaning, "to reach") (in order) to show that she reached the other side of the wall and is healthy again.

Because it takes time to recover from an illness, we can also look at this from the perspective of time. There was the point when she wasn't sick, just like the point before you start going over a wall. Then there's the movement up and over, which is when she was fully sick. This is the duration of time that she's sick, just like it takes a certain amount of time to climb a wall. Finally, there's the point when she's no longer sick. This is the other side of the wall.

I sent the file to him over the internet. We've seen before that when we talk about the devices that are part of communications systems – such as phones, TVs, and the internet – we can use the preposition "on" because the communications system is a platform that allows us to communicate. Well, we can also use the preposition "over" when we talk about these things. Why? Because something is going from point A to point B, usually over a long distance. Notice: "*over* a long distance". This naturally gives us an arc feeling.

ALTERNATIVES: "I sent the file to him online." It's much more natural in this case to say "online" instead of "on the internet".

"I sent the file to him through the internet." This alternative works, but it's probably not common. We can use the preposition "through" because the internet is the medium that I sent the file through. Unfortunately, we cannot use the preposition "by" in this case. If we say, "I sent the file to him by internet", it doesn't sound too bad, but we simply don't say that in this context. This is probably because the preposition "on" is very closely connected to the idea of the internet. So you can say, "I spoke to him over the phone", "I spoke to him on the phone", and "I spoke to him by phone", but the internet is special because we're "online". After the internet was created, we just never started saying "by internet".

The meeting will be over at eleven. The preposition "over" in this sentence means "finished". You might think that this use of the preposition "over" doesn't fit in this group because it's different. It is different, but the way in which the logic applies is the same as the other examples in this group. The meeting has a starting point and an ending point (in this case, eleven). Instead of talking about physical start and end points, we're talking about points in time. This sentence talks about the journey from point A to point B like the other examples, but in this case, the end point is the focus.

Ok, so we're going from one point to another point with the purpose of saying when the meeting ends. But this group also has the idea of "(in order) to reach the other side". Well, that's the whole point of this sentence: to tell the listener what time we reach the end point. In other words, the start of the meeting is one point, and we want to get to the other side of the meeting (in time), which is the end point (eleven o'clock). When we reach that point in time, the meeting ends, so we've reached the other side. So, if the meeting "is over", then it means that the meeting has finished.

ALTERNATIVES: "The meeting will end at eleven." "The meeting will be finished at eleven". "The meeting will be done at eleven".

Let's buy a pizza. If we have any money left (over), we can get a soda, too. In this final example, we have another use of the preposition "over" that's not physical, but this one isn't about time, either. It's about an amount. If we have $20 and the pizza costs $15, then there's money remaining ("left"). The preposition "over" is optional, but the idea is still there in the background. We start with $20, after the pizza we end with $5, so we can use that $5 (in order) to get a soda if we want to. So that's the end amount that we still have. Although we don't say it this way, it's like saying, "When buying the pizza is over (finished), how much will we have left?" Note that we cannot say "remaining over". The words "left over" together mean "remaining", but we can omit the word "over" because it's implied.

The idea of "reaching the other side" is there, too. We buy the pizza. After we buy the pizza, the purchase is completed, meaning that we've "reached the other side of the purchase" (although we don't say it that way).

3) *from one point to another point in a half-arc shape (usually starting from the top of the arc ("above"))*

This group is about half-arcs, not full arcs. The start position is a point "above" or "higher than" and the subject of the sentence usually starts in a vertical (up-and-down) position.

I tripped over the wires. This group is exactly the same idea as the previous group, except the starting point isn't on one side of something. Instead, we start from the "above" point, usually in a vertical position. In this sentence, I was walking, meaning I was in a vertical (upright) position. When I tripped, it means that my

294

foot got caught on the wires and it made me fall forward. My head, which is the top of the half-arc (the "above" point), goes forward and downward toward the ground, which makes a half-arc shape.

A tree fell (over) on(to) his car. Same as the last example. The tree wasn't moving because trees don't walk, but it was standing upright (vertical position). When it falls, we can see that the top of the tree creates a path downward that is a half-arc shape. In this case, the preposition "over" is optional because if a tree falls, it's not falling from the sky. It can only fall over, so it's still implied in the background.

The car drove over (the edge of) the cliff. This one's a little bit different, but it's the same basic idea. In this case, the car was in a horizontal position (front to back instead of left to right). If the car isn't going very fast when it falls, then it will probably make a ninety degree angle instead of a curved half-arc, but we can see that the basic idea is still there. In the context of going over the edge of something, what we're really saying is going past the edge and then falling downward. Another example: There's a plate on a table. I push the plate over the edge, meaning that it falls off (of) the table and onto the floor.

ALTERNATIVES: "The car drove off (the edge of) the cliff." We can also use the preposition "off". This is possible because something can be on the edge. Specifically, let's say that the car stops, but only enough that it doesn't fall and the front wheels are hanging. In this case, the car is on the edge of the cliff. However, it doesn't have to be sitting in that position. We can still apply the idea of the preposition "off" when it's moving because for a moment, it's on the edge, and then it falls over the edge, so we just extend the idea.

(I injured my hip:) I dropped my phone. Can you bend over and pick up it for me? In this case, you're standing (upright/vertical position) and you bend forward, which means

295

that your feet stay where they are, but your waist bends so that you can reach toward the ground.

ALTERNATIVES: "Can you bend down and pick up it for me?" There is a difference between "bend down" and "bend over", but they can be used interchangeably if you mean "bend at the waist". However, "bend down" can also mean to bend at the knees, in which case you're moving downwards, but not forwards, so there's no arc or half-arc shape. You can still use "bend down" when you mean "bend at the waist" because you move downwards, but you also move forwards, which doesn't matter in that case.

4) *more than (the point at the top of the arc; or a point that's past another point)*

This group is very simple. The preposition "over" in this group means "more than", and these two are 100% interchangeable. However, we don't always use the word "more". It depends on what we're talking about. For example, if we're talking about age, we say "older than" instead of "more than". This group is almost the same as group one ("above"), except group one is (almost always) about a point that is physically above something. This group is like "above", but it's about an amount, an age, a height, etc… instead of a physical point. The reason this group is it's own group and not part of group one is because group one simply means "above" and doesn't have the meaning of "more than".

We can also look at the examples in this group as "past a certain point". This is related to group two because we're going farther than a certain point, meaning that we've "reached the other side" of that point. The specific examples below will make this idea clearer.

I don't want a computer that costs over $1,000. That's too expensive. I'm willing to pay as much as $1,000 for a computer, but I don't think any computer is worth more than that, or maybe

296

I just don't have enough money to afford it. So, $1,000 is the limit-point (this is the limit point that the preposition "to" uses; the price for a computer can go up to $1,000, but if the price goes higher, then I won't buy it). So, if we look at the amount of money as increasing (going higher), then it's like the top point of the arc. But let's say that we create a line that goes from left to right. We put $0 on the left and $2,000 on the right. $1,000 is in the middle. If the computer costs $1,200, for example, then the cost of the computer is "past" $1,000 because we have gone farther than that point and reached the other side of it. Normally we don't say "past $1,000", but you can see that the idea still works.

ALTERNATIVES: "I don't want a computer that costs more than $1,000."

(For a roller coaster:) Children over (the age of) ten can ride without an adult. This is the same as the previous example, but now we're talking about an age instead of a price. If a child is at least eleven years old, they can ride without an adult. If they're ten or younger, they need an adult (in order) to ride. The ideas of "the top point of the arc" and "past a certain point" both work here.

ALTERNATIVES: "Children older than ten can ride without an adult."

He's a little over four feet tall. (1.2 meters) This one is the same as the previous examples, but now we're talking about height.

ALTERNATIVES: "He's a little more than four feet tall." "He's a little taller than four feet."

I worked here for over five years. Notice that in this sentence, we have two prepositions: "for" and "over". Pay attention to this because in group six we're going to see how the meaning changes when we don't use the preposition "for". The best way to look at this sentence is "I worked here for five years" + "over/more than". We're talking about the total amount of time, which is more than five years. Remember, in this group, the preposition "over" and the phrase "more than" are the same. So, you can just replace the preposition over: "I worked here for more than five years." Five years is the amount of time that we're talking about, but it wasn't just five years. It was more than five years and less than six years (we know that it's less than six because if it were more than six, we would say "more than six years" instead of "more than five years"). We don't care about the exact amount of time (five years and three months, for example), so we simply use the preposition "over" (in order) to show that when I stopped working that job, the total amount of time that I worked was some point past the five year mark.

ALTERNATIVES: "I worked here for more than five years."

We walked (for) over twenty miles! (32 kilometers) Now we're talking about distance. In a sentence like this, the preposition "for" is optional, but it's still in the background. The reason it's optional is because when talking about a distance, the meaning doesn't change with or without the preposition "for", but the meaning does change when talking about time. In reality, the same change happens in both cases, but when we talk about a distance, we don't usually think about the second meaning (group six below). So, there's the start point and then twenty miles from the start point. We walked past that point, so we use the preposition "over".

ALTERNATIVES: "We walked (for) more than twenty miles."

5) *disagreement; arc-shape bouncing back and forth between two points (volleyball)*

This group is a little strange. Normally, we use either the preposition "about" or the preposition "on" when we talk about a topic. However, we can use the preposition "over" if there's any kind of disagreement between two or more people. It often depends on the verb that we use. The examples below will help make this idea clearer, but imagine a game of volleyball.

They always fight over/argue over stupid things. If you fight or argue about something, there are two sides. One person says or does something and then the other person says or does the opposite or something different, so there's a back and forth between the two people. In other words, from one point to another point and then from that point back to the first point (or to the next point that the first person will mention). The best way to imagine this is like volleyball. One person hits the ball over the net, then the other person hits it back to the other side, and so on. This makes it very clear that we also have an arc-shape.

ALTERNATIVES: "They always fight about/argue about stupid things." We can also use the preposition "about" and the meaning doesn't change. We cannot use the preposition "on". Why can we use "about" but not "on"? Because these two verbs ("to fight" and "to argue") can use both the preposition "over" and the preposition "about", but they <u>don't</u> normally use the preposition "on". So in this case, it's just about what prepositions these verbs use. The logic of the preposition "on" still works, but the English language just doesn't allow us to use "on" here. It might help to remember that the preposition "on" is always a positive state/active state and usually a surface/platform, but the preposition "about" is a scope. The verbs "to fight" and "to argue" don't use the platform idea, but they do use the scope idea. Notice that we have a phrase: "What's the scope of his argument?" This sounds a little formal, but we can see that the idea of "scope" and "argue" naturally work together.

She took him to court over the damages. (She sued him for damaging her property or reputation.) In this example, we can't replace the preposition "over" with the preposition "about". The reason here is because of the volleyball idea. We can apply

299

the scope idea of "about" in the previous sentence, but only the volleyball idea can be applied here because we're not talking about the damages, we're talking about the process of going to court (in order) to get compensation for the damages. So, instead of overlapping with the preposition "about" as a scope or a topic, here we're overlapping with the preposition "for" as a purpose.

6) time: during + whole

This group is also very simple. It simply means "during". In most cases, we can use both the preposition "over" and the preposition "during", but there's a small difference in meaning, and this difference might be important depending on exactly what you want to say. The preposition "during" simply means that something happens at some point while something else is happening. It might last the whole time or it might only last a small part of the time. The preposition "over" in this case, however, means from point A (the start time) to point B (the end time). In other words, the whole time. Now, in reality, it might not last the *whole* time, but the emphasis is on the whole and not just some part. The preposition "over" can also imply a purpose when we use it this way, but the preposition "during" doesn't.

Let's talk about your business plan over dinner. In this example, if we use the preposition "during", we're simply saying that I want to discuss your business plan at some point during dinner. We might also discuss other things, or spend the rest of the time just eating, but it's just one thing that we *can* do while we eat dinner. Also – and this is a very important point – when we use the preposition "during", we already have the plan to eat dinner. If we use the preposition "over", I'm proposing that we eat dinner with the purpose of discussing your business plan. There was no plan to eat dinner in the first place. So we're not having dinner just so that we can eat. Instead, we're going to have dinner specifically so that we can discuss your business plan. This is very common between two potential business partners who don't normally eat dinner together, but if we use

300

the preposition "during", it's much more likely that you're eating with someone that you normally eat with. Lastly, we also get the arc-shape for the same reasons as before: from point A (the start of the dinner) to point B (the end of the dinner). This creates an abstract "bridge". When you use a bridge, the purpose is to get to the other side. If the purpose of having dinner is to discuss business plans, then the dinner (or the time that you spend eating dinner) is like a bridge with the purpose of talking about the business plans. The preposition "during" feels like it's inside the length of time, but the preposition "over" feels like "above" + movement and not inside the length of time.

ALTERNATIVES: "Let's have dinner (in order) to discuss your business plan." Here we can clearly see that there's a purpose because we're using the special version of the preposition "to": "in order to".

I'll be in Japan over the winter. Again, the preposition "during" sounds like it will only be part of the winter. The preposition "over" sounds like you'll be spending the whole winter in Japan.

ALTERNATIVES: "I'll be in Japan for the winter." The preposition "for" in this context can create two slightly different meanings. 1) The reason (purpose) that I'm going to Japan is because it will be winter and I want to be there in the winter for whatever reason. For example, maybe I like the snow and/or the winter festivals. 2) I'm simply saying that during the whole winter I'll be in Japan (using the preposition "for" as a duration).

I worked there over five years. (notice: not "for over") This is the example I mentioned earlier in group four. In this case, we're not using the preposition "for". Without it, we simply mean "during", but for the whole five years. This creates a "bridge of time".

ALTERNATIVES: "I worked there for five years." Interestingly, if you use the preposition "for" without the preposition "over", it

301

means the same thing as the example sentence. So, you can say, "I worked there for five years" and there's no difference in meaning, though it does feel a little different (there's no arc-shape). This is a point where the prepositions "over" and "for" overlap. We saw earlier in the dinner example that we were using the preposition "over" to imply a purpose, and it also involved a duration. We also saw in the example about Japan that we can use the preposition "for" with the meaning of "the whole winter". The preposition "for" is a purpose, basis, or distance/duration. Most of the time, the prepositions "for" and "over" are not interchangeable, but sometimes they can be. Please note that the preposition "for" cannot be used in the dinner example because we use "for dinner" when we're talking about what we're going to eat. So, we can see that when we talk about a duration using the preposition "over", sometimes the preposition "for" overlaps and is interchangeable, sometimes the preposition "for" isn't used to mean the same thing, and sometimes the preposition "for" can't be used at all. It depends on the context and the purpose of the sentence.

7) again/repetition (a cycle; most common with phrasal verbs)

My computer crashed and I had to do my essay over. When we say that a computer crashes, it means that it stops working and you have to restart it. In this sentence, you were writing an essay and then your computer crashed and you hadn't saved your work. So everything that you wrote was lost and you had to start writing the essay again. In this sentence, the preposition "over" and the word "again" are interchangeable. Why? Because we can use the preposition over to talk about a cycle or repetition, though it doesn't work in all contexts. For the logic, imagine the arc-shape going from left to right and then downward from right to left. This creates a circle and gives us the feeling of repetition or "again".

ALTERNATIVES: "My computer crashed and I had to do my essay again." Note that this can mean the same thing, but it can also mean something slightly different. We know from the context that "again" means "start again" because I lost the data. The preposition "over" specifically means "start again from the beginning" in this type of sentence, but the word "again" can mean either "start again from the beginning" or "do something one more time". For example, if I say, "I want to go to the beach again", I cannot say, "I want to go to the beach over". It doesn't make sense. But when something happens that you have to restart from the beginning, we can use either the preposition "over" or the word "again".

The teacher made the students write their names over and over (again). In this case, we have a lot of repetition because we're saying "over and over". The word "again" is optional and the sentence will sound good with or without it. In the previous example, we saw that when you do something over, it means that you do it again, which makes a circle. In this example, we're making a circle and then making the same circle again. You only have to say "over and over", but the actual number of times that the action repeats can be more (three times, five times, ten times, etc…). If you want to emphasize that you repeated the action again and again and again many times, you can simply add the preposition "over" more times (in order) to make it stronger: "We had to write our names over and over and over and over and over (again)".

ALTERNATIVES: "The teacher made the students write their names again and again." Of course, instead of saying "over and over", you can simply say "again and again".

"The teacher made the students write their names repeatedly."

The seasons come and go, over and over (again). Every year, we have the same seasons: spring, summer, fall (autumn), and winter. Spring "comes" and then it "goes" when it changes into summer; now that summer has "come", it will "go" when it changes into fall (autumn); etc… This cycle (a repeated process) happens every year.

Note: Americans usually use the word "fall" instead of "autumn", but both are fine.

8) *a circular/rolling motion*

This group is similar to the previous group, but in this group we're not talking about repetition. We're talking about moving in a way that creates a circular shape. This can't be used in every context and it's most common to use it with the meaning of "from side to side". In this case, the "circle" that we get from the two arc-shapes is physical.

(Two people in the same bed:) Can you roll over, please? I don't have any space. In this example, two people are lying in the same bed. One person is taking too much space and the other person is pushed to the side. So we can say that instead of one person using half the bed and the other person using the other half, the first person is using about ¾ of the bed, which means that the second person doesn't have a lot of space and they can't sleep comfortably. So the second person says to the first person: "Can you roll over?" This means that they want the other person to roll sideways so that they aren't taking so much space on the bed. This movement of the body creates an arc-shape.

ALTERNATIVES: "Can you move over, please?" This isn't exactly the same, but in this context, these two sentences are interchangeable. The verb "to move" doesn't mean "to roll", but the person can still roll over because rolling is a type of movement. Instead of rolling, they might decide to just move their body to the side without rolling.

The phone is face-down on the table. Turn it over. We saw an example earlier in which a phone was face-up. "Face-down" is the opposite, which means that we don't see the front of the phone (the screen), we see the back of the phone. If you want to see the phone screen, you can turn the phone over. This means

304

that you rotate the phone (turn the phone sideways) so that it's now face-up on the table. This movement creates an arc-shape.

ALTERNATIVES: "The phone is face-down on the table. Turn it face-up."

D) Some verbs that often use the preposition "over"

Turn over	Come over	Go over
Fall over	To be over	Get over
Bring over	Look over	Argue over/fight over

E) **Phrasal Verbs.** Look up each phrasal verb and try to understand how the logic of the word "over" applies. Remember, a phrasal verb is basically a preposition put into action by a verb.

He ran over my bike! "To run over" means "to drive on top of something, usually causing damage or an injury". In this case, he was in his car and he drove on top of my bike, which damaged it in some way. This is similar to the example about the vehicle that can travel over any terrain, but we're talking about doing damage to some object: a toy, a person, a bike, etc... However, you can also run over a rock. In that case, you probably won't damage the rock, but the rock might damage your car.

I like the plan, but I have to talk it over with my wife first. "To talk something over" means "to discuss something", but with the purpose of making a decision about it. For example, someone offers you a great deal on a sailboat, but you're not sure if your wife will approve. "Talk" + "over" = "discuss" because you are going through all the details and the pros and cons of something (in order) to make a decision. So in an abstract way, you're going from the start point (the question: should we do it?) to the end

305

point (the answer: yes/no). As you discuss the issue, there are many different points that you might talk about (Do we need it? Can we afford it? Etc…), but you're also thoroughly going through each point, so there's this repetition/review quality to make sure that all (of) the details are considered and you can make the best decision.

Please stop trying to talk over me. In this case, we have "talk over someone or something", instead of "talk something over (with someone)". This means that while I'm talking, you're trying to talk at the same time, but louder. You can also talk over music, for example, if you're at a party and the music is really loud. So the meaning of "over" in this case is "more than" (higher volume).

My art project fell in the water. Now I have to start (all) over. This sentence is like the sentences in group seven and simply means "again". We can add the word "all" to a sentence like this if we want emphasize.

Can you go over/look over my essay with me? Both of these phrasal verbs mean "to review" and maybe also "help to improve". The essay is already written, or at least partially written, and you want the other person to read what you've written. When you read something, you start at the top of the page and your vision slowly goes down the page as you read each line. Remember, the preposition "over" almost always deals with some kind of motion. So, from point A (the start of the essay) to point B (the end of the essay). In this particular example, we don't have an arc-shape feeling, but we do have the feeling of a "cycle" (review/repetition).

F) Examples of idioms that use the preposition "over", with detailed explanations.

What you did was over the line! If something is "over the line", it means that what someone does is unacceptable behavior. We have a related phrase: "What you did went too far!" There's a limit to what behavior is acceptable and what isn't. If you go past that limit, then you're "over the line". Imagine a line that's on the ground. You're not supposed to go past it.

"Hey! You took my seat!" "Get over it." This one's a little more complicated. When we say, "Get over it", we mean to stop complaining and just accept the situation. A phrase that means the same thing (depending on the context) is: "Deal with it". The use of the preposition "over" in this example is the same as group two ("above" + movement). Something happens that you don't like and don't want to accept. This is an obstacle (like an abstract wall or fence) that's between you and what you want. The other person is telling you to just accept it even if you don't like it, meaning that there won't be an obstacle and the result is that you reach the other side of the wall, but you still didn't get what you wanted because you have to accept that you can't have it. This might seem like it should be the opposite, but think about it this way: you're ok and there are no problems. Then something happens that you don't like. If you get what you want, everything returns to normal. If you don't get what you want BUT you accept not getting it, then you're ok again and everything returns to normal. Of course, in real life, you'll probably be upset even if you accept it, but that doesn't matter. The intention of the phrase "Get over it" is that the other person is simply telling you to accept it even if you don't want to. How you feel about it doesn't matter.

But there's another interesting detail here. We know that the idea of "past a certain point" is part of the idea of '"above" + movement (in order) to get to the other side'. So you have to "get past" how you feel and accept it. We have a phrasal verb that's very closely related to this idea: "move on", which we saw earlier. Remember that it means that you're moving forward and onto

307

something else. For example, a new topic. But how is the phrasal verb "move on" related to "get over it" or the idea of "past a certain point"? If we're talking about topics, for example, then the topic is a platform, but if we're talking about getting over something, we can think of that thing as a point. In other words, it's possible to look at something as a platform ("on") or a specific point ("at"), depending on the context. If it's a specific point, we can go over (meaning "past") that point.

For example, let's say that a married couple got divorced last year. The husband is still in love with his ex-wife, so he's suffering. We can say: 1) "He hasn't moved on." 2) "He hasn't gotten over her." Both of these sentences mean exactly the same thing. These two ideas aren't interchangeable in every context, but we can clearly see that they're related.

Now, let's move on to the next preposition. (Note: here we probably wouldn't say, "Let's get over to the next preposition". It's possible, but it sounds more like going from here to there (physical locations). Normally when we use "get over" (and we're not talking about something that's physical), it means some negative (bad) emotional state. Different context, different application.)

AROUND

A) Example Sentences. Remember to follow the instructions in section A from previous prepositions.

1)

They all sat around the campfire.
The earth takes 365 days (in order) to go around the sun.

What does the word "around" mean in this group?

2)

"You're in the way." "So? Go around me."
We have to go (around) to the other side of the building.
Don't turn around! There's something behind you...
(While driving:) I forgot my wallet, so I had to turn around. (Go back to the place that I left it.)

What does the word "around" mean in this group?

3)

He's been walking around the city all day.
I traveled (around) the world for many years.
Wash your hands often. The flu is going around. (Spreading through contact between people.)

What does the word "around" mean in this group?

4)

He's around five feet tall. (1.5 meters)
I'll be home (at) around five.
The project is due in around a week.
It took me around six months to write my first book.
I think he makes around $50,000 a year. (per year)

What does the word "around" mean in this group?

B) The Logic

Key Idea(s): 1) a circle that's surrounding a specific point;
2) semi-circle that's surrounding a specific point;
3) within the general area of a specific point

"around" is a one-way preposition

Explanation of the logic: The circle/semi-circle is the edge of the general area of a particular point. In other words, we can use the preposition "around" to either talk about the area inside the circle or the edge of the circle itself. The circle doesn't have to be a perfect circle, and sometimes the circle might be more of an abstract idea.

Etymology notes: The historical meaning was "in(side) a circle" or "on every side" (number 3 in the picture). Later, the

310

meaning of "on or along a circuit" was added (number 1 in the picture). 16

Now, go back to the example sentences and try to apply the logic. Ask yourself: "How is the preposition 'around' about a circle/semi-circle or the general area of a specific point?"

C) Detailed Explanations of the Example Sentences.

1) A circle that's surrounding a specific point

This group is extremely easy and it's the most basic use of the preposition "around".

They all sat around the campfire. The campfire is the center point and the people are sitting in (the shape of) a circle. It doesn't have to be a perfect circle. If there are only three people, for example, two people might be close to each other and the third person is on the other side of them. If there are many people, we can easily see how a circle starts to form. It can actually be a square shape in this case, too, but the main idea is that the people are surrounding the campfire, which creates the "circuit".

ALTERNATIVES: "They all sat near/close to the campfire." This isn't exactly the same because we might not have any kind of circle.

"They all sat by the campfire." Of course, we can also use the preposition "by". Like the previous alternative, there might not be a circle.

The earth takes 365 days (in order) to go around the sun. In the previous example, the campfire was the center point. Here, the sun is the center point and the earth travels along a path ("circuit") that surrounds that point.

311

ALTERNATIVES: "The earth takes 365 days (in order) to revolve around the sun." Notice that the verb "to revolve" naturally uses the preposition "around", because when something revolves around something else, it means that the first thing goes around/travels around the second thing.

2) *A semi-circle that's surrounding half of a specific point*

"You're in the way." "So? Go around me." We saw before that we can use the preposition "over" if there's an obstacle that you need to get past. For example, a fence or a river. Well, going over something is one way to get to the other side. The other way is to go around. In this case, there's someone in my way, meaning that they're an obstacle in my path (the first part of number 2 in the picture).

The person tells me to go around them. So, I'm walking straight, I step to the side and move forward, and then step back onto the path/line that I was walking when I get to the other side of that person. Imagine you have a fence that has an opening at one end. Instead of going over it, you can go around it. The shape that's created by adjusting my path around the obstacle create a semi-circle of some kind. It might not always be a prefect semi-circle shape, but the idea is the same.

We have to go (around) to the other side of the building. This is like he previous example, but instead of going around a person, you're going from the front of the building, around the side of the building, and to the back of the building, or from the back of the building, around the side of the building, and to the front of the building. You can also go from one side to the other, passing the front or the back on the way.

Note: if you don't use the word "other", then you are only going to the side: "We have to go (around) to the side of the building". The preposition "to" is about and end point, so now your destination is the side of the building, which means not the front or the back and you're not going around from one side to the other side. In this case, the preposition "around" still works

312

because the circle is actually divided into fourths, so the path is probably only half a semi-circle (¼ of a circle), but the same basic idea is there.

Don't turn around! There's something behind you... This sentence is slightly different. We still have the basic semi-circle idea, but the distance between the center point and the edge of the circle is very close together. In fact, the edge of the circle is the width of your body. When you turn around, you turn 180 degrees so that you are now facing the opposite direction. This movement creates a very small semi-circle.

(While driving:) I forgot my wallet, so I had to turn around. (Go back to the place that I left it.) Here we have an example that's similar to the last one. When we say "turn around" in this context, it means to go back to the place that you were previously. It doesn't have to be an exact semi-circle. For example, you might drive half way across the city before you realize that you forgot your wallet. However, the idea of going one direction and then back the other way is the same basic idea of a semi-circle. More specifically, it's a "semi-circuit". Either way, this one uses the logic in an abstract way.

ALTERNATIVES: "I forgot my wallet, so I had to go back." "Go back" means "to return to the place that you were at".

3) *something that's within the general area of a specific point*

Note that in this group, the idea of "circle" doesn't matter, as we'll see.

He's been walking around the city all day. A city probably isn't a perfect circle, but it doesn't have to be. We're saying that he's been walking within the general area of a specific point (number 3 in the picture), which is a city in this case. As we'll see in the next example, a specific point or general area don't have to be small and can really be any size.

313

I traveled (around) the world for many years. The world is very big, but compared to the solar system, the galaxy, or the whole universe, it's a small point. Notice, however, that we can also say "I traveled (around) the universe for many years". In that case, the whole universe is the general area, and the center of the universe (or the general center of the part of the universe in which I traveled) is the specific point. So, in this sentence, the world is the specific point and you can travel around the general area of that point. You can also say, "I traveled around the United States for many years". The US clearly isn't a circle, but it has borders, and as long as we're inside those borders, we can use the preposition "around" because there's no specific direction. We're simply inside the general area of the country.

Note that in this sentence, the preposition "around" is optional.

Wash your hands often. The flu is going around. (Spreading through contact between people.) This example is a little more abstract than the previous two. Here, "going around" just means in general from person to person. The general area could be in a city, a country, or even the world. Again, there's no specific direction.

4) (means "approximately"; 100% interchangeable with "about")

As I mentioned before, the prepositions "around" and "about" are almost 100% interchangeable. There are only some rare exceptions.

He's around five feet tall. (1.5 meters) This group was explained when we talked about the preposition "about". But how does "around" apply? The same as group three. We have a specific point and a general area, but instead of being a physical location or area, it's a measurement, amount, etc... So, five feet is the specific point, and we're saying he's approximately five feet tall, meaning that he might be exactly five feet, but any measurement

314

that's close to that specific height can work. "Close to" in this case means that it's "within the general area (meaning general measurement)" of that height.

I'll be home (at) around five. Five o'clock is the specific time. Any time that's close/within the general area (general time) of that specific hour can work.

The project is due in around a week. Remember, this means approximately 6-8 days. So, a week (7 days) is the specific due date, but any date that's close within the general area (within a couple days) of that specific date can work.

It took me around six months to write my first book. Here, we're talking about a larger general time frame of approximately 5.5 to 6.5 months. Six months is the specific amount of time, but any amount of time that's close/within the general area (general time frame) of six months can work.

I think he makes around $50,000 a year. (per year) Finally, this sentence is talking about an amount of money. So, $50,000 is the specific amount of money, but any amount of money that's close/within the general area (general amount) of that specific amount can work.

D) Some verbs that often use the preposition "around"

Turn around	Walk around	Go around
Get around	Sit around	Get around

E) Phrasal Verbs. Look up each phrasal verb and try to understand how the logic of the word "around" applies. Remember, a phrasal verb is basically a preposition put into action by a verb.

Note: The preposition "around" is not used in many phrasal verbs.

I'm shopping around for a new phone. (To look in different stores and compare prices) If you're shopping around, it means that you're trying to find the best price for something. Of course, this is often done online these days, but you can still use this phrase. In this case, we're talking about a general area, which is all the stores, both online and offline. Remember, the important thing here is that we're not talking about a specific direction or, in this case, a specific destination. Imagine that all the stores are located in one place. You're going from store to store to store to store looking for the best price, so you're going around (in order) to find the best price.

I'll ask around to see if anyone has seen him. (To ask many people the same question) I'm going to ask different people that I see. I might not ask every person I see, but it's possible. So, just like in the example sentence that we saw about the flu going around, I'm going to ask the question within the general area of where I am (in order) to find an answer.

I can't get around very well because I broke my leg. (To be able to go from place to place) Again, we have another example that's talking about a general area. The general area could be as small as my bedroom or as large as the city.

Now that I'm on vacation, I can get around _to_ painting. (To find the time to do something) Here we see an example that fits into group two (a semi-circle that's surrounding half of a specific point) (number two in the picture). It might not seem like it fits into group two because it's a little abstract, but think about it. The

316

meaning is "to find the time to do something". Let's say you work 80 hours per week and you have a family. Clearly, it's very difficult to find time to paint in that situation. However, this month you're on vacation, which means you have a lot more free time. So, before the vacation, work and everything else was an obstacle that prevented you from painting. While you're on vacation, the biggest part of that obstacle (work) is gone, so now you can finally get around to the other side of the obstacle and reach your "destination" (goal/objective) of painting. Pretty cool, right?

Note: We don't say, "I can get <u>over</u> to painting". Why? Well, we know that we can use both the prepositions "around" and "over" when we want to talk about reaching the other side of an obstacle, but when we use the phrasal verb "get over", we don't apply this particular surface meaning.

F) Examples of idioms that use the preposition "around", with detailed explanations.

Wow, you have him wrapped around your finger. The idiom "wrapped around your finger" means that the person will do anything for you. Imagine you have a piece of tape and you wrap it around your finger. Now it's attached to your finger, so it's almost like it's part of your finger. This idiom doesn't make a lot of sense if we look at it literally. The main reason that we use the preposition "around" is because of the verb "to wrap", which often uses the preposition "around".

Stop beating around the bush and get to the point. "To beat around the bush" means that you're slowly trying to introduce a question or some information. "To get to the point" means to just say what it is that you want to say and stop giving unnecessary background details and things like that. But why do we say "beat around the bush"? This is a strange one, but it probably comes from gardening. Imagine that there's a bush that you want to trim. If you just take a blade a hit this point and that point, you might remove parts of the bush, but the result will be an ugly, uneven bush. Instead, you should be precise and cut the bush exactly where you want to, which will make the process faster and the result will be a nice, even looking bush.

Because we use this idiom when we want someone to get to the point, we're basically saying, "I don't want to hear this little detail and that little detail. Just tell me the important information or ask your question. In other words, we don't want you to "talk around" the point, we just want you to be precise and direct.

OFF

A) Example Sentences. Remember to follow the instructions in section A from previous prepositions.

1)

Take the keys off (of) the table.
Keep off (of) the grass.
Please take your shoes off before entering the house.
Wipe that chocolate off (of) your face.
He cut all (of) his hair off and became a monk.
Spider! Get it off (of) me!
"Where are you getting off (of) the bus?" "Main street."
Everything in the store is (on sale for) 50% off. (a 50% discount)

What does the word "off" mean in this group?

2)

Can you turn the light off, please?
Don't turn the car off on the freeway! (stop the engine)
(As a verb:) The gangsters offed him. (killed him)
(To a roommate:) The food that I buy is off-limits. (My roommate isn't allowed to eat it.)
I finally paid off my student loans.

What does the word "off" mean in this group?

3)

That's the wrong answer, but you're not far off. (the answer is almost correct)
"Shouldn't you be practicing?" "The piano competition is so far off. I have plenty of time."
It's an island (that's) off (of) the coast of China. (close to China)
This area is closed off for public safety. (Not allowed to enter)

What does the word "off" mean in this group?

4)

I'm off to work. (I'm leaving for work.)
(When a race starts:) And they're off!
Be careful! If one domino falls, it will set off a chain-reaction.

What does the word "off" mean in this group?

B) The Logic

Key Idea(s): ALWAYS: a negative state/inactive state; USUALLY ALSO: removed from/not on a surface/platform

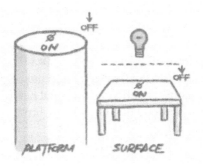

"off" is a one-way preposition

Explanation of the logic: The logic of the preposition "off" is just the opposite of the logic of the preposition "on". The surface meanings of the preposition "off" are usually the opposite of the surface meanings of the preposition "on", but there are some surface meanings that aren't the opposite.

Etymology notes: The prepositions "off" and "of" look very similar because the preposition "off" was originally a form of

320

the preposition "of" that was used for emphasis. It eventually separated from the preposition "of". Part of the earlier meaning of the preposition "of" was "away from"/"farther", but when the preposition "off" separated, it took these meanings. 17

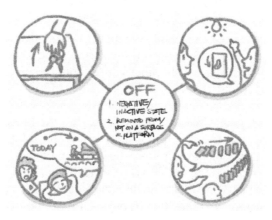

Now, go back to the example sentences and try to apply the logic. Ask yourself: "How is 'off' a negative state/inactive state in this sentence? Is it also removed from a surface or a platform?"

C) Detailed explanations of the example sentences.

1) *removed from a surface or a platform*

Take the keys off (of) the table. Here we have a normal surface. This is the most basic use of the preposition "off". The keys are on the table, which is a surface, and you're removing them from that surface.

ALTERNATIVES: "Remove the keys from the table". Notice the "move" part of the verb "to remove". We use the preposition "from" with this verb because the preposition "from" is an origin/start point. The keys are on the table, so that's the start

321

point. From that point, move them off of the table. This works with other prepositions, as well. For example, if I buy a new computer, it comes in a box, so "in a box" is the start point. I can take the computer out of the box, or I can remove the computer from the box. Both of these mean the same thing.

Keep off (of) the grass. This example is very similar, except you are already off the grass (which is the surface) and someone wants you to stay off the grass. In other words, don't go on the grass at all.

Please take your shoes off before entering the house. We saw before that we use the preposition "on" for clothing. This includes shoes. So, you put your shoes on, and the opposite is to take them off. Remember that you physically put your foot into a shoe, but when your foot is inside and you are now wearing it, the shoe is on your foot. It's not physically on top of your foot, but it's "on" your body.

Wipe that chocolate off (of) your face. If there's chocolate on your face (which is a surface), then you have to remove it.

He cut all (of) his hair off and became a monk. If you remove all (of) the hair from your head, then you're bald. When we talk about head hair, we use the preposition "on". For example: "That man doesn't have a single hair on his head." You might think that it's better use the preposition "in", but we use the preposition "on" because your hair is more like a hat that sits on top of your head, even if the reality is that the hair grows out from the inside of your head. It's the same as the way that we look at shoes.

Spider! Get it off (of) me! I notice that there's a spider on me and I get scared. I yell, "Spider! Get it off me!" The spider is on my body or clothing, which are surfaces.

"Where are you getting off (of) the bus?" "Main street." Remember that when talking about large transportation vehicles,

322

we usually use the preposition "on" because those vehicles are like platforms that transport many people. So, we use the preposition "off" (in order) to talk about the opposite (getting off (of) a platform).

Everything in the store is (on sale for) 50% off. (a 50% discount) We know that everything is on sale. This means that the sale is "active". You can also imagine that there's a special platform/surface labeled "sale" that all the items are placed on.

We know that the sale is active, but how much is the sale for? In other words, how much is being removed? The preposition "off" is always a negative state/inactive state, which means that 50% of the price is removed or not existing/not being applied. You can also use the platform/surface idea, which makes this idea very clear: imagine that the price of a bed is $100. There's a 50% discount, so now it costs $50. At first, you put $100 on the table (in order) to buy the bed, but the seller tells you that it's 50% off, so you remove $50 from the table, just like taking the keys off (of) the table in the first example.

Don't be confused by the fact that the prepositions "on" and "off" are in the same sentence and talking about the same thing. The preposition "on" is connected to the word "sale", and the preposition "off" is connected to the amount (50%). In this case, we can see how these two prepositions can actually work together.

ALTERNATIVES: "Everything in the store is at a 50% discount." Saying it this way probably isn't common, but it works. We know that we can use the preposition "at" to talk about a specific point of measurement. If there's a sale and 50% of the price is removed, it means that the amount of the discount is 50%. That's similar to a measurement: How much? 50%. So, we can say that whatever is on sale is at a 50% discount.

2) *Negative state/Inactive state only (no surface or platform)*

Can you turn the light off, please? When a light is on, it's in a positive state/active state. If we turn it off, it's in a negative state/inactive state.

ALTERNATIVES: "Can you turn the light out, please?" In this specific case, we can also use the preposition "out". This is probably because before electricity, people used candles. You light a candle and when you want it to stop burning, you blow the candle out. The flame was active/existing, and you literally blow it out of existence so that it's inactive (not burning).

Don't turn the car off on the freeway! (stop the engine) When we talk about vehicles, you can turn a vehicle on and off. In this case, we use the preposition "on" when we talk about starting the car's engine and the preposition "off" when we talk about stopping the car's engine. This is just like a computer.

   Notice that the sentence says "off on". The preposition "off" is attached to the verb "turn": "to turn (something) off". The preposition "on" is attached to "the freeway": "on the freeway".

(As a verb:) The gangsters offed him. (killed him) When we use the word "off" as a verb, it means "to kill". However, this sounds very informal and it's not used in everyday speech. It's much more common to say, "The gangsters killed him". This example is just to show you that the logic still works even when we use the word "off" as a verb. In fact, we can only use it this way because of the logic.

   Specifically, when someone kills someone else, they are ending that person's life. If someone is alive, then they exist, which means their life is in a positive state/active state. When we say that the gangsters offed him, we're saying that the person's life is now in a negative state/inactive state because they are dead (not existing).

324

(To a roommate:) **The food that I buy is off-limits. (My roommate isn't allowed to eat it.)** If something is "off-limits", it means that you aren't allowed to do that thing. In other words, that thing is forbidden. In this case, I'm telling my roommate that the food that I buy belongs to me and they're not allowed to eat it. The food is "off-limits".

But why do we say "off-limits"? It seems like it doesn't make sense. A "limit" is something that you can't go past, but then we have the preposition "off", so the limit is removed. So "off-limits" should mean that there is no limit and you <u>can</u> do something. But when we use it, it means the opposite, and there's a reason that it means the opposite.

According to the *Online Etymology Dictionary*, "off-limits" was first used in the American military in the year 1851. 18 A soldier has certain things that they are allowed to do and certain things that they aren't allowed to do because they have to follow orders. This means that there are certain <u>limitations</u> <u>on</u> their behavior/actions. Remember that the preposition "on" can use the idea of a "weight", "burden", or some other negative thing that is placed on top of them. In this case, the "weight" is the limitations, which restrict/<u>limit</u> what soldiers are allowed to do. The original use of "off-limits" was when a soldier did something that they weren't allowed to ("Soldier, you're off-limits!"). The limitations are supposed to push them down, which makes perfect sense because there are people in the military with more power than them, meaning that those people are in a higher position than them, which is where the "weight" comes from. In fact, as we'll see later, we have a related idea with the preposition "under": "The general has 10,000 soldiers <u>under his command</u>."

So, the original use of the phrase was that the soldier took the limitations off of himself. This means that they removed the limitations, but they're not allowed to remove those limitations, so the result is that they did something that was forbidden (not allowed).

So when I tell my roommate that the food that I buy is "off-limits", it means that he's not allowed to eat it. I put a limitation on the food, and that limitation is that only I'm allowed to eat it. If my roommate eats any of the food that I buy, he's removing the limitation, but he's not allowed to remove the limitation, so I'll be angry.

I finally paid off my student loans. "To pay off" has a couple of meanings, but in this case, we're talking about some kind of debt (student loans). A student loan is money that university students borrow from the government or some other source (in order) to pay for school. "To pay off a debt" or "to pay off student loans" means to completely repay all the money that was borrowed. Notice the word "completely". If you p<u>ay</u> (for) a student loan, it might mean that you paid part of it or all of it, but we don't know. When you add the preposition "off", we know that you paid the entire amount that was remaining. This is a negative state/inactive state because you are negating/removing the entire debt. In other words, the debt no longer exists.

As a final note, it's very useful to know that "pay off" is exactly like "turn off". The only difference is that the two verbs are used in different contexts because they have different meanings, but the logic of the preposition "off" is exactly the same. Instead of turning off a light, it's like you're turning off the debt. How do you do that? You pay for it. So, we say "pay off".

3) *"away from" a center point/to the "side" of a center point*

Remember in the etymology notes it says that the preposition "off" was originally part of the preposition "of", but when it separated, it took the ideas of "away from" and "farther" from the preposition "of". We'll see how these apply in each example sentence below.

That's the wrong answer, but you're not far off. (the answer is almost correct) If I ask you, "What's 2 + 2?" and you say, "3", your answer is close to the correct answer, which means that your answer isn't far off. In other words, your answer isn't far away from the correct answer. If you say, "4", then your answer is spot on (a phrase which means 100% accurate).

"Shouldn't you be practicing?" "The piano competition is so far off. I have plenty of time." In this case, we're talking about a point in time. The present moment (meaning "now") is the center point because it's active. But something in the future is currently inactive, so it's "away from" the present moment. Let's say that the competition is six months from now. That's not close to now/today. So, it's far off.

It's an island (that's) off (of) the coast of China. (close to China) China is the center point. When we say that there's an island off the coast of somewhere, it means that the island is closest to that location (in this case, China) compared to other locations (for example, the US). What we're saying here is that based on that central point (China), the island is to the side of it.

This area is closed off for public safety. (Not allowed to enter) In this example sentence, the area is closed off, which means that no one is allowed to enter. We use "closed off" instead of just "closed" because the preposition "off" gives us the extra meaning of "away from a center point". Let's say that there's a crime scene and the police create a barrier so that people know that they can't enter that area. The area is the center point. Because the police don't want people to enter the area, they create the barrier (in order) to keep people away form that center point. People can go close to the area, but they aren't allowed to cross the barrier and enter the area.

ALTERNATIVES: "This area is off-limits (to the public)." Because members of the public aren't allowed to enter the area, we can also say that the area is "off-limits" (to the public). Let's say that the police made this decision. The police put a limitation on the area, and that limitation is that the public can't enter. If someone who's not a police officer enters the area, they are removing that limit, which they aren't allowed to do.

327

"This area is closed to the public." In this case, we're not using the preposition off. Why? If we say that something is "closed to the public", we're saying that the public can't access that area. The preposition "to" points to the specific group that can't access the area. In the example sentence, if we omit the preposition "off" and say, "This area is closed for public safety" it sounds a little different. It sounds like something that can be open, like a business. But we're not talking about a business that's open during business hours. There are subtleties here and it really depends on how you're looking at things, but that's the general idea. One of the biggest differences here is that if something is just "closed" (for example, a business closes at night and reopens in the morning) or if there's some kind of barrier that's physically marking (off) an area as "closed". In the second case, we usually use "closed off". In fact, notice "marking off". This phrasal verb works very similarly.

4) *starting to move away from a central point*

This is a special version of the previous group. The previous group was about the position of something compared to a central point. This group is about starting to move away from a central point. You might notice that this is very similar to the idea of "creation". That's true, but not completely. It's actually the start of the "creation".

I'm off to work. (I'm leaving for work.) If you say, "I'm off to work", you're saying that you're leaving the house (in order) to go to work. In other words, you have started the action of leaving and your destination is work. That makes sense, but how is this a negative state/inactive state or removed from a surface/platform?

You can think of this as getting off of a surface/platform, which in this particular case is also connected to the preposition "down", as we'll see later. Basically, in this case, your home is like the central platform of your life because it's where you live. Think of it as your headquarters in life. When you go to work,

328

you're stepping off of that central platform and going to another location. This is where the idea of "away from" is very useful. Specifically, you are going away from your house, which is your central platform, (in order) to go to work. So, when you say, "I'm off to work", you are stepping off of that platform and moving away from it, which is the start of your trip to work.

We can also see the connection to the idea of "creation". You go from "on" your central platform to "off" of that platform, which begins the action of arriving at work (the preposition "down" is also working in the background). In other words, it begins your journey to the place that you work. After you arrive at work, the act of working becomes "active".

(When a race starts:) And they're off! This is the same idea as before, except instead of leaving the house, the racers are leaving their starting positions and beginning the race.

Be careful! If one domino falls, it will set off a chain-reaction. Again, this is like the previous examples, but we're talking about the start of a chain-reaction, which means that when one thing happens (a domino falls), it will cause many other things to happen (the other dominoes will fall). So we're using the preposition "off" (in order) to talk about the start of an action that leads to more actions, which is the start of a process or a series of events.

D) Some verbs that often use the preposition "off"

Take off	Be off	Turn off
Drop off	Put off	Come off
Keep off	Cut off	

329

E) Phrasal Verbs. Look up each phrasal verb and try to understand how the logic of the word "off" applies. Remember, a phrasal verb is basically a preposition put into action by a verb.

"What time do you get off ((of) work)?" "I get off at 5." **(finish working for the day)** When we talk about work, we often use the preposition "off". You can use this to express the time that you stop working for the day or for a day that you don't work. In fact, we call a day that you don't work a "day off". Or you can say, "I'm off (on) Friday". The word "work" is implied. So, the time or day that you're "off" means that you aren't working. In other words, your work is in a negative state/inactive state because it's not active. This is similar to a light that's off.

Unfortunately, we don't use the preposition "on" to talk about when you work, unless it's the day of the week. So, you can say, "I'm working on Monday", but this is really "on Monday". The preposition "on" is simply attached to the word "Monday". However, you cannot say, "I'm on tomorrow". It's just not something that we say.

(In a story:) I can't believe they killed (off) my favorite character. (The writers killed a character) In this example, the preposition "off" isn't required, at least in this context. The character is being removed from the story, which is kind of like the way we might remove something from a table.

The thieves drove off with the money. This is an example of the "start moving away" idea. They stole the money and drove away with it. So, not only do we have the idea that they start leaving or escaping, but that also implies that they're removing themselves from the location (in this case, escaping from the scene of the crime). This is similar to the "off to work" example that we saw earlier.

"Ow! You hit my leg!" "You're fine. Just walk it off." (walk (in order) to help remove the pain) If you get an injury on your legs or feet, but it's not a serious injury, the common advice is to "walk it off". This way you keep that part of your body moving so that it doesn't have time to tense up or swell up and start hurting even more than it already does. So basically, you're walking (in order) to remove the pain and other things that are related to the injury.

The soccer match was called off due to rain. (the match was canceled) When something is "called off", it means that it's canceled, usually before it starts. The soccer match or the plan to start the soccer match was active (active state), but the rain made the conditions on the field too bad to play in, so it was canceled (made inactive).

All I said was "hi" and he went off. (He got really angry.) The phrasal verb "to go off" has a few different meanings. This meaning is related to exploding, which is based on a bomb going off (exploding). When a bomb goes off, it means it explodes, but the emphasis is on the starting or causing of the explosion. If we use the phrasal verb "to blow up", there's no special emphasis, but both of these phrasal verbs are interchangeable in this context. When someone gets really angry, we can also use both of these phrasal verbs because if someone is really angry, it's like anger/rage explodes out of them.

I have to drop the kids off at school. (take them to school and leave them there) "To drop off" is a common phrasal verb and we can use it with both things and people. The verb "to drop" is used because you're not staying. Instead, you're just driving them there, letting them out, and then leaving. The idea is that you're only quickly passing by, so it's like you "drop" them at that location.

Why do we use the preposition "off"? We know that when we're talking about buses and other large vehicles, we use the preposition "on", and that's because they're like large platforms with the <u>purpose of transporting</u> many people. We use the preposition "in" when we talk about cars and trucks because these are smaller, personal vehicles that we look at as containers. But

331

when you drop someone off, you're driving your car for the purpose of transporting someone.

Note that we never say "get on the car" or "get off (of) the car" unless we're talking about being physically on top of the car. But notice that in this sentence, we're not even talking about a car. The purpose of this sentence is to show the idea that I am going to take the kids to school, which means that we're talking about the purpose of transporting them, but we're not talking about driving a car specifically. So, we can combine the idea of "quickly passing by" ("drop") and the idea of "getting off (of) a transportation platform" ("off") when we want to say that I am going to drive someone to a location and let them exit the vehicle. From that point, I will return to the place I came from or continue to another location that I have to go to.

I have to create a presentation, but I keep putting it off. (to postpone something/not do it now) If you put something off, it means you postpone it, which means that you don't do it. Notice the verb "to postpone". The verb "to put" comes from the same root as the Spanish verb "poner", which comes from Latin. The word "post" in this context means "after" or "later". So, "postpone" literally means "to place after something" or "to place at a later point in time". You plan to do the presentation today, but then you say that you'll do it tomorrow, so you're putting the action into the future.

We use the phrasal verb "put off" with the verb "to keep" when we want to say that you postpone something over and over (which means "again and again"). Tomorrow comes and you don't want to do it, so you say that you'll do it the next day or later in the day, but you don't do it then, either. This process can continue many times.

Also, remember that we say: "work on something". If you're not working on it when you should and you decide to do it later, then you're putting it off. In other words, you're literally putting it into a negative state/inactive state.

F) Examples of idioms that use the preposition "off", with detailed explanations.

Don't give the kids too much sugar or they'll be bouncing off the walls. If you give a child too much sugar, it will give them a lot of extra energy. Because children usually have more energy than adults, and because children can't control themselves as well as adults, if you give them too much sugar, the result is that they will be running around, yelling, and doing all kinds of crazy things. They don't literally "bounce off (of) a wall". The idea is that their behavior will be crazy, unstable, and hard to control, so it's like they're bouncing around the room. You've probably seen cartoons in which a character bounces off the wall, then the ceiling, then the floor, then the wall again, etc... That's the idea. Of course, the logic of the preposition "off" in this case is simply the idea of a surface.

DOWN

A) Example Sentences. Remember to follow the instructions in section A from previous prepositions.

1)

Put it (down) on the floor.
He walked down the hill.
When the sun goes down, we turn the lights on. (when the sun sets)
Hold him down! (Don't let him get up)
I'm too sick to eat. I can't keep anything down. (I throw up (vomit) anything that I eat.)
The military downed an unknown plane. (verb: to make something fall out of the sky)
I'm visiting friends (down) in Mexico. (I live in the US.)
He comes from a country (that's) down south. (South of where I am)

What does the word "down" mean in this group?

2)

The cost of gas has gone down.
Turn that music down! Some people are trying to sleep!
(while gambling:) I'm down $100. (I've lost $100)
(while gambling:) I'm down to $100. (I only have $100 remaining)
How fast can you count down from 50?

What does the word "down" mean in this group?

3)

The website is currently down. (offline and not accessible)
After the hurricane, the power grid went down. (The city's electricity stopped working)
Young people these days. They can't put their phones down for two seconds!

What does the word "down" mean in this group?

4)

I put $300 down on a new car.
They nailed down the furniture in preparation for the tornado.
Please write down your email address.
The building burned down.

What does the word "down" mean in this group?

5)

I'll meet you down at the park.
I'm walking down Main street.
"Where's the bathroom?" "Down this hall and to the left."
The ring was passed down in his family for a hundred years. (given to each younger generation)
The legend comes down to us from the 2nd century.

What does the word "down" mean in this group?

B) The Logic

Key Idea(s): 1) a downward or southward direction; or a downward position;
2) an away from direction (and sometimes a backwards direction);
3) changing to a negative state/off of a platform OR changing to a positive state/onto a platform

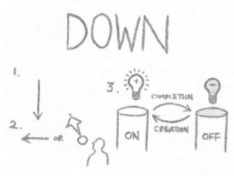

"down" is a two-way preposition

Explanation of the logic: The preposition "down" is usually the exact opposite of the preposition "up". However, it's not so simple. Both the prepositions "up" and "down" can be a connection between a "positive state/active state" and a "negative state/inactive state", but in different ways and different contexts (also, if you look at the map, it shows that the arrows connecting "on" and "off" are reversed). Remember that "upward" and "downward" are vertical (up-and-down) directions. We know that "forward" is like the horizontal version of "upward", and now we can see that "backward" is the horizontal version of "downward". However, it's much more common to just use the combination "back down" (with the meaning: "to return to a lower point") instead of saying "backward" and "backward" often doesn't mean the same as "downward". This is because "backward" usually means that you are moving in the direction that your back is facing

337

without turning around. Also, just like the preposition "up" can mean "closer to", the preposition "down" can mean "farther away from".

Etymology notes: We'll talk about the etymology in group five.

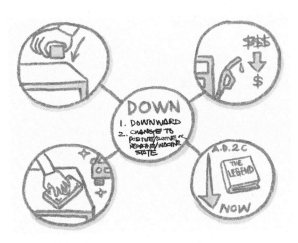

Now, go back to the example sentences and try to apply the logic. Ask yourself: "How is 'down' about one of those directions or about the connection between a positive state and a negative state?"

C) Detailed explanations of the example sentences.

1) *A downward/southward/away from direction*

Put it (down) on the floor. This is the most basic meaning of the preposition "down". It simply means a downward direction. In this case, I'm putting something on the floor. When I'm carrying it, it's higher than the floor. So, when I put it on the floor, it goes in a downward direction.

He walked down the hill. We was (up) on the hill, and we walked down so now he's not on the hill (in fact, he's off of the hill, but don't worry about that in this group). In reality, he might only walk halfway down the hill, but in cases like that, we usually specify how far down someone goes. The main point here is that he's moving in a downward direction.

When the sun goes down, we turn the light on. (when the sun sets) When we talk about the sun setting (meaning when day turns into night), it looks like the sun is going "down", meaning a downward direction. The opposite, when the sun rises (the start of the day), is "the sun comes up". Notice something that's extremely important here: we say "the sun goes down" and "the sun comes up". We don't say "the sun comes down" or "the sun goes up". Why? Notice number 2 that's in the picture in section B above. There's a person looking at something that's away from them. This is an "away from" direction. If you look at the picture for the preposition "up", you'll see the opposite.

The exact use of the verbs "to come" and "to go" is complicated, but the basic idea is that "to go" means "away from where the speaker is located" and "to come" means "closer to/toward where the speaker is located". So it's natural that we say, "the sun goes down", because as the position of the sun in the sky goes lower and lower, it feels like it's going away from us, especially because it's the end of the day and when the sun "leaves", the night starts. The opposite is also true. When the day starts, the sun starts to rise in the sky. The sun has returned and it feels like it's coming "closer" to us. We'll talk more about this idea in group five.

This also deals with the ideas of "creation" (start of the night) and "completion" (end of the day). Both happen at the same time in this case. When the sun goes down, the day is completed and is now inactive. At the same time, the night starts and is now active. When the sun comes up, the opposite happens. We'll see more about "creation" and "completion" in group four.

But wait. When we looked at the preposition "up" earlier, we saw this sentence: "What goes up must come down." As I said,

339

the verbs "to come" and "to go" are a little complicated. Remember that if something goes up, gravity will pull it back down, so we're talking about an upward (and then downward) direction. Let's say I throw a ball straight up into the air. The ball goes upward from the perspective of where I am, which is the ground. In other words, it's going away from the ground and toward/closer to the sky. We say that the sun goes down partially because it looks like the sun goes in a downward direction, but the sun mostly goes from one side (East) to the other side (West). Let's look at it this way:

We say that the sun comes up because it looks like it's coming closer to us (side to side) while it's moving upward. "Come" + "up" = "closer to us" (side to side) + "closer to us" (upward from the horizon)

We say that the sun goes down because it looks like it's going away from us (side to side) while it's moving downward. "Go" + "down" = "away from us" (side to side) + "away from us" (downward toward the horizon)

Notice that as the sun travels through the sky from morning to night, it creates an arc-shape (but because it moves so slowly, we usually don't say that it travels "over" us). When the day starts, the sun moves upward and closer to us. At noon (12:00), the sun is directly over us (we can also say that the sun is "overhead"). From that point, the sun begins moving downward and farther away from us. It's this combination that creates the arc-shape from East to West.

But if I throw a ball straight up, it doesn't move side to side. It only moves upward and downward. So when the ball goes up, it goes away from the ground. "Go" + "up" = "away from the ground" (upward) + "closer to the sky" (upward). In other words, when we say that the ball goes up, we mean that it's getting closer to the sky and farther away from ground at the same time. This is because it doesn't move from side to side.

340

When the ball comes down, it comes closer to the ground. "Come" + "down" = "closer to the ground" (downward) + "away from the sky" (downward). In other words, when we say that the ball comes down, we mean that it's getting closer to the ground and farther from the sky at the same time. Again, this is because it doesn't move from side to side.

So we can see that the verbs "to go" and "to come" can be very complicated depending on the context, and this can make things confusing with the prepositions "up" and "down". Just remember, you can use both prepositions with both verbs, but it depends on exactly what you want to say. This might seem very complicated, but in real life you'll always have a specific context, which will make this a lot easier. These are just two examples with two different contexts so that you can see how things work.

Hold him down! (Don't let him get up) In this case, someone is already down in some way. This can be sitting or laying down. If you hold him down, you don't allow him to stand (up). So, he's already in a downward direction (position in this case).

I'm too sick to eat. I can't keep anything down. (I throw up (vomit) anything that I eat.) This sentence can also fit in group four (creation/completion), but there's a reason it's in this group instead. I'm sick. When I eat, my body doesn't accept the food and I vomit (throw up). When you eat food, it goes into your mouth, down your throat, and down into your stomach, so we have a downward direction. But in this case the food comes back up, so you can't keep it down (keep it in your stomach so that it can be digested).

The military downed an unknown plane. (verb: to make something fall out of the sky) Here we see the word "down" as a verb. This particular use of the verb is most often found in the context of the military shooting a plane that's flying. In fact, we can say, "The military shot down an unknown plane". The verb "shot" by itself only means that they hit the plane, but it doesn't

341

mean that the plane fell out of the sky. "Shot down" tells us that the plane was hit AND it fell because of it. Obviously, in this case the plane moves in a downward direction.

An interesting note: before the plane was hit, it was flying (the process of flying was active state). When the plane is hit and it crashes, it's not flying anymore (the process of flying is now inactive). So we can also see in this case that we're connecting from a positive state/active state to a negative state/inactive state.

I'm visiting friends (down) in Mexico. (I live in the US.) Just like we can use the preposition "up" (in order) to talk about a northward direction, we can use the preposition "down" (in order) to talk about a southward direction. In this case, I live in the US, so if I'm talking to someone on the phone who's in the US, for example, it's very natural to say "down in Mexico" because I'm describing my position compared to their position.

He comes from a country (that's) down South. (South of where I am) This is like the previous example, but a little different. Instead of talking about my location (currently to the south of where I live), I'm talking about the location of the country, which is to the south of some other point (for example, my current location or where I live; it depends on the context).

2) *A decrease*

The cost of gas has gone down. This is simply a decrease in price. In other words, the price is going in a downward direction to a lower number.

Turn that music down! Some people are trying to sleep! Here we have a decrease in the volume of music that's playing.

(while gambling:) I'm down $100. (I've lost $100) In this example, we have a decrease in the amount of money I have. Specifically, how much money I've lost while gambling.

(while gambling:) I'm down to $100. (I only have $100 remaining) Remember that the preposition "to" is an end point. So, if we use the same sentence as the previous example, but we add the preposition "to", the meaning changes. Instead of saying how much money I've lost, this is how much money I have remaining now. Let's say I had $400. In the process of gambling, I lost $300 (which means that I'm down $300). The decrease stops at $100 because that's how much I have remaining. So, "down to $100" means from $400 to $100. $100 is where the decrease stops, so that's the end point. In the previous example, we don't know how much money I had before gambling and we don't know how much money I have now. That sentence is only about the amount that I lost while gambling.

How fast can you count down from 50? In this example, the preposition "down" means "decreasing". We start at 50 and count down: 50, 49, 48, 47, etc... We can use the preposition "down" because 49 and all the other numbers are smaller than 50, so it's like we're going downward until we reach the number 0.

ALTERNATIVES: "How fast can you count backward from 50?" Not only can we look at counting numbers as going up and down, but we can also look at it as going forward and backward.

3) inaccessible/inactive (moved to a negative state/inactive state)

The website is currently down. (offline and not accessible) Just like we can say that the website is "up (and running)", which means online, we can say that it's "down", which means offline. This is one point where the prepositions "up", "down", "on", and "off" are very closely connected. If a website or server is offline, then it's in a negative state/inactive state. In this context, we can say that the website is "down", but we can't say that it's "off". The reason in this case is because we're not talking about the machinery. A website can't be "off", but it can be "offline" (remember the information about "online" and communication systems (on + line)). A server (a special computer that holds

343

website information) can be "off", meaning that it's not on ("running"). However, it's possible that the computer (server) is on and there's some other problem that is making it inaccessible. That's why the preposition "down" means "offline" instead of the preposition "off".

After the hurricane, the power grid went down. (The city's electricity stopped working) This is very similar to the previous example, but instead of being offline/inaccessible, we're saying that the power grid (which gives the city electricity) changed from an active state to an inactive state.

Young people these days. They can't put their phones down for two seconds! It might seem like this sentence should be in group one. There is usually a downward direction, but in this context "put down" can be "put in your pocket", for example. It's not only about a downward direction. When you're using your phone, the process of using it is "active". When you "put the phone down", it means that you're not using it, so the process of using it is "inactive".

4) *creation/start and completion/secure*

Interestingly, the preposition "down" can also be used to express the ideas "creation" and "completion". When we use the preposition "down", both "creation" and "completion" usually happen at the same time, but one of them is usually the main meaning. This use of the preposition "down" isn't as common as with the preposition "up". Also, the idea of "completion" is sometimes closer to the idea of "secure" and we can abstractly connect these two ideas.

I put $300 down on a new car. When you put money down on something, it means that you pay a certain amount of the total cost first and then make payments over time (in order) to pay for the rest. This is common when buying very expensive things like a car or a house.

344

Why do we use the preposition "down"? It's like you're putting money down on top of a table at the place where you're buying the thing. For a car, you walk into the car dealership, choose a car, and put $300 down on top of the table. How we actually express this isn't with a table, but the item that you're buying: "on a new car". Notice that a table is a surface, or it can be an abstract platform in this case. Also, when we say "on a new car", the car (or specifically buying the car) is the abstract platform. This shows us that we can use the preposition "down" (in order) to move to a positive state/active state or onto a surface/platform, just like the preposition "up". That's one reason why these two prepositions are so special, because they actually do a lot of the same things, but they're often applied to different contexts.

Ok, so how is this sentence about "creation" and "completion"? "Creation" is obviously the main idea because you're <u>starting</u> to make payments on something that you want to own. It's also creation because usually you can <u>start</u> using that thing (for example, you drive the car home). For the idea of "completion", the first payment (which we call the "down-payment") is completed. Also, you have secured the car (this is something that we actually say in English), meaning that you have made it certain that you will be able to use it.

They nailed down the furniture in preparation for the tornado. Obviously, when you use a hammer and nails (in order) to nail something into the floor, there's a downward force that's applied to the nail so that it will go into the wood.

But we also have the ideas of creation and completion. In this case, completion is the main idea. This sentence is about making something secure, which is partially related to the general idea of "completion". This is easier if you think of the phrase "completely secure". Think about it: a tornado is coming, and a tornado can easily move the furniture that's inside the house if it gets close enough. So, they nail down the furniture to make sure that it doesn't move. They want to <u>keep</u> it where it is. In other words, <u>maintain the positive state/active state</u> of where the

345

furniture is currently existing/located. So, they're securing the furniture in place. This is also "creation" because they're creating that secure state.

Please write down your email address. This example is very similar to the previous one, but instead of nailing something down (in order) to keep it in place, we're writing something down so that we don't forget it. If I don't write it down for you, you might forget it, meaning that it's not "secure". Of course, this is also "creation" because we're physically writing words on paper.

The building burned down. This sentence is a little different because it's not about securing anything, but the main idea is still "completion". If we say, "The building burned", that sounds like only part of it burned. Maybe a room was destroyed, but not the whole house. When we use "to burn down" it means that the building was completely or almost completely destroyed. Maybe some the basic structure is still standing, but you can't live in it and it probably doesn't even have walls anymore. Notice the phrase "the basic structure is still standing", meaning that it's "up", so this is also a downward direction because the material of the house falls to the ground/the house collapses. Lastly, we have a negative state/inactive state, as well as the movement from a positive state to a negative state. The movement is because the house was standing and whole, but as the fire burned, it changed that. The result of the fire is a negative state/inactive state, because now the house isn't standing anymore.

5) *"ofdune"*: *away from "the central platform/central location"*

I highly suggest that you read the description of this group, take a break, come back, and look at the example sentences and their explanations, and then read this description again. This group might be very difficult to understand at first, but if you can master the logic and feeling of it, it will help you deeply understand the preposition "down" (and also the preposition

346

"up"). It will be a lot clearer when we see the examples below, but first let's look at the etymology.

This is the most important information about etymology in this entire book. The Modern English preposition "down" comes from the Old English noun "dun", which meant "down", "height", and "hill"/"mountain".The dative (indirect object) form of "dun" was "dune" ("from the hill"). If we add the Old English word "of" to the word "dune", we get "ofdune", which meant "downward". 19 We already know that in Old English, the meanings of "away from" and "farther" were originally part of the Old English word "of" but these meanings later become part of the word "off" when it separated. So: "hill" → "from the hill" → "downward". If you're on a hill and you want to go from the hill to another location, you have to get off of the hill, which means that you have to go downward. This information is extremely important and it's the key to fully understanding the preposition "down" (and "up"). This is why the meaning of the preposition "down" in this group means "away from 'the central platform'".

But what's "the central platform"? As we now know, it was originally a hill. In modern English, the exact meaning depends a little bit on what you're thinking about. Usually, the central platform is your current/starting location because you are the center of your existence and experience. It's like you're always on an abstract platform (in this case, an abstract "hill").

The dictionary will tell you that the preposition "down" means "away from" and the preposition "up" means "close to" in this kind of sentence. This is why it makes sense to use the preposition "up" in the example sentence that we saw earlier: "He walked up to me and punched me in the face". In other words, he walked "up the hill", meaning "closer to the central platform", which is my current location. The dictionary definitions are accurate, but the logic is deeper than that. Part of the problem is that this group is very abstract. The picture that's on the next page can help.

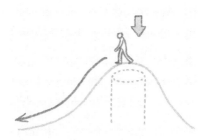

So, we can use the preposition "down" with the meaning of "away from" the hill, meaning the "central platform". In other words, away from the speaker's current location. But it's not just "away". It also kind of <u>feels</u> like the direction "down" in an abstract way, even if what you're talking about isn't at a lower position. In fact, if you look in the *Online Etymology Dictionary*, you'll see that this is "a sense development peculiar to English". In other words, native speakers feel and sense this use of the preposition "down" in time and space. As I said, the example sentences will make this clearer.

The last question is this: does this group have any connection to the ideas of a negative state/inactive state or a positive state/active state? Of course! We know that if you're <u>on</u> a platform, that's a positive state because the preposition "on" is always a positive state. If your current location is like a hill or a platform, then that's a positive state. When you go down the hill, your moving off of the hill, which means that you're moving off of the platform. So, you're going from a positive state (your current location, which is where you are currently existing) to a negative state (the location that is far away from your current location, which is where you are currently not existing). This might be a little difficult to understand because, just like we saw with the preposition "out", when one of these becomes positive, the other becomes negative and vice-versa at the same time.

Let's look at the example sentences. I recommend that you take a quick break first, but you can continue if you want to.

I'll meet you down at the park. Remember, wherever you start, that's the central platform. To make things simple, let's say that you're on a hill. When we say, "down at the park", it's because the park is not near this hill, meaning it's located some place that's far from the hill. So, (in order) to get to the park, you have to go down the hill and to the park. It doesn't matter if the park is to the north, south, east, or west. This is the feeling we get when we say "down at the park". It feels like we're on a hill or a central platform (our current/starting location) and we have to go from that platform/location and "down" to our destination (a location that is away from where we currently are).

Note: in real life, the park might be at a lower point than you, at the same elevation as you, or at a higher point than you. In all these cases, we can use "down at the park". That's because the main idea here is "away from". However, please note that if the park is at a higher point (like on a hill) and you're at a lower point, it's also possible to say, "up at the park". This is because the park is at a higher point than you are, so we can use the preposition "up" if we want. We can also use the preposition "up" if we're imagining ourselves already at the park, or if the person that I'm speaking to is already at the park and I'm imagining myself from their perspective. In your mind, you can put yourself into another location and "speak" from that point of view, which makes it feels closer. We do this often with the verbs "to go" and "to come", as well. This is what I mean when I say that it depends on how you're thinking about it.

I'm walking down Main street. This example is a little more complicated. We saw before that we can use "up the road/street". In fact, you can say this new example as either: "I'm walking down Main street" or "I'm walking up Main street". Both of these phrases mean the same thing. You might be surprised by that. How is it possible that we can use the prepositions "up" and "down" to mean the same thing? Because of the logic. The reason this example is a little more complicated is because it depends on what you're thinking and the exact details of the context. It's subtle, but let's see how this works.

349

In this case, the exact starting and ending points don't matter (this is very important!). Let's say that I'm walking from my house to the beach. I'm on Main street. You call me on the phone and ask me where I am. I say, "I'm walking down Main street". If I use the preposition "down", I'm not thinking about the "to the beach" part. I'm thinking about the "from the house" part, meaning where I came from (remember, I'm coming from my house, which is the "hill" in this case).

The purpose of the sentence is to say where I am now, which is on Main street. We don't like to say, "I'm walking on Main street" in this context (though we can) because the preposition "on" is more static. We're walking, which means we're moving and not staying in one place on that street like a house does. However, the prepositions "down" and "up" are usually not static. A big part of the logic of both of these prepositions is the movement between (to and from) negative states/inactive states and positive states/active states. In fact, if we use the preposition "on" in this context (giving your location while walking), it's much more natural to simply say, "I'm on Main street". You probably won't know if I'm going somewhere or where I might be going until I give you more details, but that still answers the question, "Where are you?" It's also possible that I'm still very far away from my destination, which means that the preposition "down" would feel more natural because it means "away from" in this context. It's like we're still walking down the hill at this point.

If I say, "I'm walking up Main street", then I'm thinking more about the destination and less about the place that I came from. Again, the exact start point and end point don't matter in this context. Also, just like the preposition "down" is more natural if I'm far from my location, the preposition "up" feels more natural if I'm getting closer to my destination (meaning more than half way). It's for all of these reasons that we can use both the prepositions "up" and "down". The meaning is basically the same (I'm walking somewhere and my current location is Main street). It's only when we look closely at the details that we can see how the logic explains the slight difference in exact meaning between using the preposition "up" or the preposition "down".

So, the most basic use of this group (the previous example sentence), isn't too complicated, but in a more complicated example like this, it might be harder to understand. This is because in this example, I'm not at the start point. Instead, I'm already moving from the start point to my destination, so it depends on the subtle feeling that I have in my mind.

"Where's the bathroom?" "Down this hall and to the left." Now that we've discussed all the information in the previous examples, the remaining three examples in this group will be easier. We say, "down this hall" because you and I are standing next to each other and the bathroom is farther away. In this context, the bathroom isn't "far away", but it is "away from" our current location, so the exact distance depends on the context.

In this context, you can also use the preposition "up", but if you do, it's most natural to also use the word "just": "Just up this hall and to the left". Remember that the preposition "up" in this type of sentence means "closer to" the speaker. That's why we use the word "just". The exact distance doesn't matter, but it's emphasizing that the bathroom is really close. But wait. If the preposition "up" means "closer to", why can we use it to say that something is away form where I am even if it's close? Remember that we can imagine ourselves from a different perspective. In this case, near the bathroom. This is like what we saw with "up at the park". The main point here is that the prepositions "up" and "down" in this context are just two ways of looking at the same thing.

The ring was passed down in his family for a hundred years. (given to each younger generation) We know that if we use the preposition "down" in this group, it means that we're talking about something moving from a starting point (the central platform) to another point that is away from it. We can also use the preposition "down" this way when talking about time. It's not very common, but we can use this way. In this example, "to pass down"

351

means to give something to your son or daughter, then they give it to their son or daughter, and so on. It can also be a relative (a niece or a nephew, for example), but it's usually a son or a daughter.

How does the preposition "down" work in this case? It's like you're passing something to someone or giving something to someone, but there's also chain from person to person. For example, it's like if I give you a ring and then you give it to your friend and they give it to their friend, etc... The only difference here is that instead of passing from person to person right now, it's passing from an older person to a younger person, then when that person becomes old, they pass it to another younger person, etc... As this process repeats (older to younger, older to younger, older to younger), it's like the item travels through time, constantly going down to the younger generation.

Depending on how you think about it, you might perceive this process as going "up" because of the past turning into the present. For example, the ring was bought in 1850 and the mother gave it to the daughter in 1900, then she gave it to her daughter in 1934, etc..., until today. It makes sense to think of it as going "up" through time, but we don't look at it that way in this context.

The legend comes down to us from the 2nd century. The logic applies to this sentence the same way as the previous example, but we have a few extra details that we can talk about.

Remember that we're talking about something moving from a starting point (the central platform) to another point that is away from it, but through time. In this case (and in the previous example), we're talking about a long period of time, meaning that the starting point is far away (in the past) from the present moment (now). This is why it's natural to use the preposition "down". The 2nd century was a long time ago and that's when the legend started or was created, but we're in the present moment, and the present moment is much closer to us in time than the 2nd century is. So, coming down through time until the present moment (now), the legend has survived and people still know about it. It's like the legend traveled down a big hill that's made of time, all the way into the present moment.

352

But wait. The preposition "down" is used for the idea of "away from", but the legend is coming closer to us. It's important to remember that we can look at things from two perspectives: the start point or the end point. In other words, when we're talking about the legend, we're not thinking about the end point (now). We're thinking about it from the perspective of the start point (the 2nd century). It moves away from that point as it gets closer to the present moment.

In these previous two examples, we used the preposition "down", but can we ever use the preposition "up" like this? Yes. For example, "Up to that moment/point, I had never been to the ocean." This sentence describes the first time that I ever went to the ocean. In this context, the starting point is when I was born. Then we have the moment when I went to the ocean. Then we have the present moment (now/today), which is when I'm saying this sentence to you. In this case, I'm thinking about things from the perspective of the point in time that I went to the ocean. So birth → going to ocean → now. We have a line through time that is coming closer and closer to the present moment, and I'm specifically talking about something that I had never done until a certain point in time. This means that my focus isn't on the start point (my birth), it's on the end point (going to the ocean).

D) Some verbs that often use the preposition "down"

Get down	Feel down	Go down
Fall down	Put down	Come down

E) **Phrasal Verbs.** Look up each phrasal verb and try to understand how the logic of the word "down" applies. Remember, a phrasal verb is basically a preposition put into action by a verb.

It's not nice to look down on people. "To look down on" someone means that you think that you're better than that person. This can be about being better at a skill, being morally superior, or having a higher social status that makes you a superior person overall. We use the preposition "on" because "people" (in this case) is the topic/focus. We use the preposition "down" because in your mind, you think that you're better than them, which means you feel that you are in a higher position or that you have a higher status. It's like you're standing on a platform that is higher than their platform and because of that you're better than them, which also means that when you look at them, you have to look downward from your platform.

He's been feeling down because his dog died. If you feel down, it means that you feel sad. Instead of a positive (good) emotion (happiness, excitement, etc...), you feel a negative (bad) emotion, specifically sadness or depression. Notice that when someone seems really happy and full of energy, we can say that they're feeling "upbeat". In this particular case, the prepositions "down" and "up" actually mean good and bad. However, let's say that you feel ok. You're not sad or happy, just ok. From that state (which is like "between a positive state and a negative state"), we can go "upward" to feeling happy or "downward" to feeling sad. However, note that because the prepositions "up" and "down" (or "on" and "off") don't usually mean "good" and "bad", we do say "upbeat" and "down", but we don't say "I'm feeling up". This is a rare case that might be an exception.

I never back down from a challenge. As you know, we can sometimes use some prepositions as verbs. In this sentence, the verb is "to back". Together, "back" + "down" means "to quit", "to stop" or "to not accept", depending on the context. But how does the logic work? Well, we know that the preposition "down" can

354

mean "away from" (the hill). The verb "to back" can be used with the preposition "away" to mean "to move backwards and away from something". For example, you see a bear, and instead of running (because you don't want the bear to chase you), you don't turn around. As you continue facing the bear, you slowly walk backward. You are backing away.

Before we continue, remember that we have phrases like "I'm up to the task" or "I'm up to the challenge". That means that you're willing and able to accept the challenge. Notice the preposition "up". In an abstract way, we have the idea of the central platform or hill. It's like you go up to the challenge (in order) to accept it, just like you can go up to a person (walk toward a person until you are close to/next to them). So, we have the idea of the verb "to back", plus the idea of the hill. We know that we can also use the preposition "down" with the hill idea. Combine the two, and you are either refusing the challenge or giving up after you try to complete the challenge because you decide to (abstractly) move backward/away from where the challenge is "located" (the hill). In other words, instead of physically backing away from a bear, you're backing away from the hill/challenge in your mind.

This example also has the idea of moving between a positive state/active state and a negative state/inactive state. If you are up to the challenge and accept it, the challenge is "active" and you are engaging it. When you back down from a challenge, you are moving from the positive state/active state of being up to it and into the negative state/inactive state where the challenge is "inactive" because you aren't engaging with it.

F) Examples of idioms that use the preposition "down", with detailed explanations.

You're going down! When we say this, it means that we're telling someone that we're going to defeat them in some challenge. It can be a fight, a video game, a sports match, etc... The idea is that there's a challenge (positive state/existence) and

355

both people or teams are actively engaging in the challenge (active state). If one side loses, then they are "down" because they lost (negative state) and the fight/game/challenge is over (negative state/inactive state). However, the winner is "still standing" (positive state/active state). This phrase probably comes from boxing.

"Do you want to go to the movies tonight?" "Yeah, I'm down". This is slang, but if you're under the age of 30 or 40 and you're not just learning (American) English for work, then it's something that you want to know. Not everyone uses it, but many people do. Either way, this is a good example of how the logic of a preposition can be applied in new ways.

If you say, "I'm down", it means that you want to do the thing that was mentioned. In this case, it's going to the movies. But why do we use the preposition "down" in this context? Because of the idea of "creation". I ask if you want to go, and that makes you think, "Yeah, I want to do that". In other words "let's make that happen" → "let's make that active/exist".

Also, remember the central platform/hill idea? Well, if you get off (of) that central platform (your starting point/where you are now) and <u>start</u> going to another location, that's also "creation".

ALTERNATIVES: "I'm up for it." This means the same thing, though these two phrases might be used in different contexts sometimes. We can see that, once again, the prepositions "up" and "down" are very similar in how we can apply the logic.

356

UNDER

A) Example Sentences. Remember to follow the instructions in section A from previous prepositions.

1)

Put the box under the table.
The submarine dove under the surface (of the water). (dove = past tense of "to dive")
If it rains, we'll get under my umbrella.
(Parent to child:) There are no monsters under your bed.
After the missile hit, the ship went under (the water). (the ship sank)

What does the word "under" mean in this group?

2)

My parents say that I can't get under 90% on any test or I'll be punished.
Wow! I can't believe that they sell something so great for under a dollar!
Anyone under the age of fifty can't participate in the program.

What does the word "under" mean in this group?

3)

(At the library:) Books on World War II are under "History". (in the history section)
You can find "account settings" under "profile". (Click on the word "profile" and you will see the words "account settings")
The military commander has 2,000 soldiers under him. (He is in charge of 2,000 soldiers)

What does the word "under" mean in this group?

4)

The terms of the contract are currently under discussion. (being discussed)
Under the terms of our contract, you're not allowed to do that.
(On a battlefield:) We're under fire! Take cover! (People are shooting at us.)
Early humans were under constant threat from nature. (always in danger)
He has difficulty working under pressure.
Many people are under the belief that human nature is bad.
We had to put the tiger under (sedation) (in order) to perform the surgery. (to sedate)

What does the word "under" mean in this group?

B) The Logic

Key Idea(s): 1) a downward force (usually 'restricting'; often 'negative' in some way); 2) lower than or less than (not in the picture)

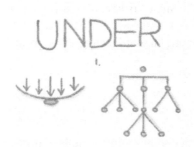

"under" is a one-way preposition

Explanation of the logic: "downward force" means a force that pushes something downward or in the direction of a negative state/inactive state. What's the difference between "down"/"downward" and a "downward force"? Unfortunately, there's no better word than "downward" to describe the logic, but when we talk about a "downward force", it's a specific application of the idea of "downward". This application very often involves the idea of "restricting" or "limiting", but it also includes the idea of organization (especially hierarchies) and the idea of using physical or abstract pressure. We know that when we're talking about the logic of prepositions, "positive state" doesn't mean "good" and "negative state" doesn't mean "bad". However, there are many sentences which use the preposition "under" that are about something "negative" with the normal meaning of "bad".

"Restricting" is the most common application of the "downward force" idea, but we have a similar word: "limiting". When we talk about "restricting" and "limiting", these two ideas are extremely similar. They're like how "path" and "way" are very similar, but sometimes one word is better than the other when trying to describe the logic. "Restricting" and "limiting" are simply more specific versions of a "downward force". We'll see specifically how they work in the explanations.

The relationship between "over" and "above" is pretty easy. The relationship between "under" and "below" is similar, but it's a little more complicated. The logic of the preposition "below" is not covered in this book because it's one of the prepositions that are easy to learn and it isn't used in a lot of different ways, but we'll compare these two prepositions in the examples. One thing to note is that we use the preposition "under" a lot more than the preposition "below".

Etymology notes: The preposition "under" is extremely old. In fact, if we look at Proto-Germanic (the language that Old English came from), the word for "under" was "under". It hasn't changed. Most of the meanings haven't changed, either: "beneath/below", "among", "in the presence of", "in subjection to/under the rule of", "inferior in rank/position", "by means of". The only one of these that has changed is "among" (which generally means "between" when talking about more than two people or things). We might still abstractly use the idea of

359

"among" in some cases, but Modern English does not use the preposition "under" as a synonym for "among" meaning "between". For example, we can't say "under the three of us" (if we mean "among the three us"). The use of the preposition "under" with the meaning "less than" started in the late 1300's. 20

Now, go back to the example sentences and try to apply the logic. Ask yourself: "How does 'under' describe a downward force or less than/lower than?"

C) Detailed explanation of the example sentences.

1) *below or similar meaning*

This group is the most basic meaning of the preposition "under". It means "below" or something similar. Unfortunately, these two prepositions aren't always interchangeable.

Put the box under the table. In this sentence, the prepositions "under" and "below" <u>are</u> interchangeable. We saw before how the prepositions "over" and "above" can mean the same thing. This sentence works the same way. "Under" is like the lowest point of a downward arc and below is a static point that is in a lower position than something else. So, "above" and "below" are opposites, and "over" and "under" are opposites. This sentence uses part 2 of the logic: lower than.

ALTERNATIVES: "Put the box below the table."

The submarine dove under the surface (of the water). (dove = past tense of "to dive") Here we can use either "below" or "under" because this is simply the position in relation to the surface ("on/above" the surface or "under/below" the surface; note that this is one of the very strange times when "on" is the opposite of "under" because of the context. If we say "over the surface", it sounds like the submarine is not in the water at all and it's hovering/flying, instead.)

ALTERNATIVES: "The submarine dove below the surface (of the water)."

If it rains, we'll get under my umbrella. Unfortunately, in this example and the next three examples, the prepositions "below" and "under" are <u>not</u> interchangeable. In this example, the reason is because if we say "below my umbrella", that sounds like you are just physically below the item that's called an umbrella and you're not using it. For example, let's say when I get home, I close the umbrella and place it on a shelf. I take my shoes off and put them below the shelf. You ask, "Where are your shoes?" I can say, "They're below the shelf" or "They're below my umbrella" (because we include everything that is at a lower point). We're talking about the physical, static point of where something is located in relation to something that is above it. Note that in this case, <u>if</u> umbrella is physically on top of something, we can also use the preposition "under" ("They're under my umbrella") because this context is like the first example about putting the box under the table. However, if we say "get under my umbrella" because it's raining or because you want shade from the sun, the umbrella is <u>open</u> and <u>is being used to protect you</u> from the rain or sun. So it's not about being

361

located below the umbrella, especially because you're probably walking around, which means that your location is changing (not static). The purpose of an umbrella is some sort of physical protection. So you are under the umbrella (in order) to have that protection.

ALTERNATIVES: "If it rains, we'll use my umbrella." Notice the word "use".

"If it rains, we'll open (up) my umbrella." Notice that "open (up)" in this case indirectly describes using the umbrella.

(Parent to child:) There are no monsters under your bed. The preposition "below" works here, but when we talk about "monsters under the bed", it's a set phrase that we use, so we don't say "below".

After the missile hit, the ship went under (the water). (the ship sank) This sentence is very similar to the submarine example, but here we cannot use the preposition "below". Why? Because the meaning of the sentence is completely different. When a submarine dives under the surface, it's still a fully functioning submarine. But "to go under" means to sink. "To go below" does NOT have that meaning. The submarine does physically go below the surface, and you can say that the submarine went below the surface, but the ship only goes below because it's sinking, so we don't say it "went below". Of course, after the ship sinks, you can say "it sank below the surface" (meaning that it sank and as a result it's current position is below the surface) or "it's below the surface", because now we're talking about the static position in relation to the surface, not the act of sinking. So here, again, we see that the preposition "under" is used to describe a specific purpose or action + a description that tells us that something is at a lower point/position than something else, but the preposition "below" is only a description that tells us that something is at a lower point/position than something else.

2) less than or lower than

"Less than" or "lower than" can be about a quantity/amount, an age, a price, etc... It won't work in every context, but it works in most contexts. This is the opposite of the preposition "over" when it means "more than".

My parents say that I can't get under 90% on any test or I'll be punished. This is simply talking about how many points you receive on a test, but measured in a percentage. If there are ten questions and you answer nine correctly, then your score is 90%. If eight questions (80%) or less are correct, my parents will punish me.

Wow! I can't believe that they sell something so great for under a dollar! Here we're talking about a price or an amount of money. In this case, 99 cents or less.

Anyone under (the age of) fifty can't participate in the program. Finally, we have an example with age. In this case, "under fifty" means "younger than fifty".

3) category/hierarchy (specific type of restricting or limiting)

(At the library:) Books on World War II are under "History". (in the history section) When you go to the library, books are organized based on topic or category. For example, history, religion, psychology, etc... If a book is about World War II, then you can find it in the history section of the library, which is where all the history books are located. So, the preposition "under" in this case is about categorizing, but categorizing is a more specific type of restricting or limiting.

You can also think of it as "narrowing". Let's say that there are 500 books in the library and of those 500, only 30 are about history. When we separate books based on topic or category, we are narrowing them by subject. So, we have the main heading "HISTORY" and then more specific books under that heading

(WWI, WWII, History of Japan, etc…). You won't find a book about psychology in the history section, so books about psychology are not allowed in that group (restricted), which also means that there's a limitation on what books can go in the history section.

If we take a step back and look at the bigger idea of a "downward force", the category forces all other books (books that aren't about history) outside, which puts them into a negative state for that category. Imagine you have a drop of water and you push your finger down on top of it. Part of the water is forced under your finger, but the rest of the water gets pushed to the side and is not under your finger. Remember that the preposition "down" connects to both a positive state/active state and a negative state/inactive state, so the books that belong to the category "HISTORY" are securely in that category (positive state/active/existing in that group), and the books that do not belong to that category are forced outside of the category (a negative state/inactive/not existing in that group). The downward force creates the restriction/category.

You can find "account settings" under "profile". (Click on the word "profile" and you will see the words "account settings") On a website, menus are usually organized in a hierarchical way using drop-down menus. This makes sense, because some pages of a website belong to the same section. For example, at the top of the web page you see "Profile". You move your mouse to the word and other words appear under it. These are links to specific pages that are related to your profile, such as "account settings" and "log out". Of course, different websites organize things slightly differently and there's no required or best way to organize things. This is just one possible example. You can see how this is very similar to the previous example. The idea is the same, but in this case the restrictions or limitations aren't as strong. The bigger "downward force" idea works the same way as in the previous example.

The military commander has 2,000 soldiers under him. (He is in charge of 2,000 soldiers) The military commander is like the top of a pyramid. He or she has <u>control over</u> 2,000 soldiers. In this context, the logic of the prepositions "over" and "under" meet and they mean the same thing from two different perspectives. The preposition "over" applies to the commander and the preposition "under" applies to the soldiers. The top of a pyramid is like a restriction point, because there's only one person on top (the commander), and there are always less commanders than soldiers. The higher the rank, the less people there are, which means more restriction/limitation. It works almost exactly like the books in the history section: we have the category "HISTORY", which is the top of the pyramid, and then all the different books that are in that category. Again, the general "downward force" idea works the same as before.

4) *restricting or limiting (includes the idea of a "process")*

This is the main group for the preposition "under". You can look at many sentences in this group as a process. However, the important thing to remember here is that the idea of a "process" is more of a surface meaning and not a direct part of the logic. I only mention this because it's useful to know.

The terms of the contract are currently under discussion. (being discussed) Two or more people want to make a legal contract. For example, maybe they want to start a business together and they need to make sure that if anything goes wrong, there are no disagreements. If there are still disagreements when something goes wrong, then the problem becomes a legal battle in court. In this example sentence, we're talking about what will be in the contract that everyone can agree with. Right now, those details are being discussed, which means that the people are trying to reach an agreement that they all accept. Though the meaning and the context is a little different, this is similar to the phrase "argue over" because there are two or more people that are going back and forth until they reach a final decision. The difference is

365

that when you argue over something, it's negative (not a negative state; actually negative) and you both are trying to be right. The result is we get the "volleyball" idea of an arc that goes one way and then back the other way between the two people. When you discuss the terms of a contract, you're trying to reach a final point that everyone <u>agrees on</u>. You're going through a process which applies a downward force and restricts/limits what will be in the contract.

Remember the water drop from earlier? That "point" (or points) that everyone agrees on is what you put your finger on top of. The restricting/limiting part applies because you have to remove or change the points that everyone doesn't agree on. Let's say person A wants three points (terms) to be in the contract and person B wants four other points (terms) to be in the contract. There are also two points (terms) that they both agree on. So, the two terms that they agree on will go into the contract. However, there are seven terms remaining. So they begin discussing: person A says that he accepts one of person B's terms, so it goes into the contract. Person B doesn't accept one of person A's terms, so they try to reach an agreement on how they can add it (maybe person B gets something extra, for example). And so on. So we have a process of adding terms, changing terms, and removing terms. You can see that we have a process that involves restricting/limiting until person A and person B agree on a final contract.

We have an interesting phrase related to this process that might make this easier to understand: "The terms of the contract are currently being hammered out". Now, you're probably wondering why we say "hammer out" and not "hammer down" or "hammer under". There's actually a very good reason, and it comes from the logic of these prepositions. In this case, "hammer under" doesn't make much sense and sounds more like "below" (I'm hammering under the table → I'm hammering something and I'm below the table while I do it). "Hammer down" sounds more like you're securing something physical (like furniture), and the emphasis is on the positive state (securing the furniture). However, "hammer <u>out</u>" sounds more like you're applying a downward/restricting force (in order) to <u>remove</u> things that aren't necessary or that aren't acceptable, and the emphasis is on the negative state. It's very similar to the process of taking a piece of wood and removing pieces of it with a knife (in order) to make a carving of a bird, for example. Remember that the preposition "out" deals with existence and non-existence. When you "hammer out" the details of something, you are trying to create a final result by removing (moving into non-existence) the things that aren't necessary or not acceptable.

This phrasal verb can be used for something physical, but it's usually not. An example of something physical is the hood of a car (the front part that's above the engine). Let's say the hood has dents in it. You can use a hammer to hit the dents outward and this will make the dents disappear because the metal returns to its original shape. So, you're "hammering out" the dents (using a hammer (in order) to remove them from existence; in this case, we also have an "outward direction"). When we apply this idea to something that isn't physical, like the terms of a contract, the only difference is that we're not using a physical hammer. The "hammer" is "discussion", because that's the tool that we're using (in order) to reach an agreement on the terms/details of the contract. So, we say that the terms "are under discussion".

ALTERNATIVES: You can change the sentence and use the preposition "over": "They're arguing over the terms of the contract". This doesn't mean exactly the same thing. In this case, it sounds more like the people are angry and they're having a lot of trouble agreeing on things. "Under discussion" sounds like a constructive (positive/good) process, but "argue over" sounds like a destructive (negative/bad) process.

Under the terms of our contract, you're not allowed to do that. In the previous example, we saw that the terms of the contract were under discussion, which is the process of creating the contract. It's interesting to note that the preposition "under" can be used for "creation" like the preposition "down" because their logic is very closely related.

367

In this example sentence, after the contract has been created, someone wants to do something that they can't do. The reason that they can't do it because of the contract. So, we can say, "Under the terms of our contract...". The difference between the first example and this one is that in the first example, we were making the contract by applying a downward force (in order) to narrow/restrict the terms and reach something that everyone agreed on. Remember that this is a process of restriction; only the terms that were accepted by everyone are in the contract. Now that the contract has been created, the terms *are* the restrictions and you can't do anything that is outside of those restrictions. In other words, the terms of the contract limit what you can do.

(On a battlefield:) We're under fire! Take cover! (People are shooting at us.) When we say "under fire", we're not talking about real fire. We're talking about shooting guns (or maybe arrows). One of the meanings of the verb "to fire" is "to shoot". Although there's not a literal downward pressure, you can easily see how there's some sort of abstract pressure that's negative (bad).

Also, you can't just walk around freely. Your movements are restricted because you don't want to get injured or killed. So there's definitely a threat, which is the "downward (negative) force". You can extend this idea a little more and think that if someone is shot and killed, then they're no longer alive, which means they're no longer existing/active (positive state; like a light bulb), so they were pushed down into a negative state/inactive state by the fire (gun shots).

Early humans were under constant threat from nature. (always in danger) This example is exactly like the previous example, except instead of s single threat (guns), there are a lot of possible threats in nature. Trying to survive in nature can be very difficult, even when you know what you're doing, so for early humans there was the constant threat of death (negative (bad/death) and negative state (non-existence)). Imagine that there's some downward force, like a giant foot, that's always trying to crush you. You have to hold it up, or you get crushed downward and into the ground.

This is obviously a form of restriction, as well, because you can't just do whatever you want. You're in a survival situation and have to prioritize certain things and make sure that you don't do anything that's too dangerous.

He has difficulty working under pressure. When we say "under pressure", we mean that it's difficult to focus because if he makes a mistake, there will be negative consequences (something bad will happen). For example, he might lose his job, someone might get killed, etc... It's very clear that we're talking about a downward force. Imagine he had to carry something very heavy. He would literally be under a lot of pressure (or, more specifically, "weight"). This example isn't about a physical thing that he has to carry, but it feels the same.

The pressure (downward force) is a threat that if he fails, something bad will happen. Let's say he loses his job. That means his status of having a job is now in a negative state/inactive state for him, just like someone turned off a light. So, if he wants to keep his job, he has to make sure that he doesn't make any big mistakes. This is the downward force of the word "pressure" in this context.

Again, we also see the more specific idea of restriction/limitation because he can't do the wrong things or make the wrong choices, which is causing the pressure. "Difficulty" is also a form of restriction here because he can't focus and easily do what he needs to do.

Many people are under the belief that human nature is bad. These examples haven't been too difficult, so let's look at one that might be a little more confusing. If you believe something, you can use the phrase "under the belief that...". We saw earlier in the book that we often use the preposition "in" with the verb "to believe" ("I believe in fairies"). However, we don't always use the preposition "in" with "believe". It depends on the structure of the sentence and exactly what you want to say. For example, another

369

way to say this example sentence is: "Many people believe that human nature is bad". That's the more common way to say it and it sounds less formal.

Here's the key: there's a difference between "believe" and "believe in". We use "believe" when you believe someone or something. For example: "I believe him". This means: "I think he's telling the truth". Another example: Person A says, "John said that he's going to California next week". Person B says, "I don't believe that." This means: "I don't believe that John is going to California". We use "believe in" when we want to express the idea of faith. In other words, something that you don't have any proof of, or someone that you have confidence in. For example: "I believe in fairies". I might have some experiences that make me think that fairies exist, but I don't have any good proof. Another example: "I believe in you". Obviously you exist, so this is a little different. This means that even if you've never done something before, I still confidently believe that you can do it. Specifically, let's say you want to write a book, but you've never written a book and you're not sure if you can do it. You talk to your friend about it and your friend says, "You can do it. I believe in you".

Okay, how does the logic of the preposition "under" apply to the example sentence? This one is more abstract than the other examples, but the logic still works. Basically, a belief is a restriction. If you believe one is true, then you believe other things are false. For example, if you believe that you're the smartest person in the world, then you believe that that's true, which means that if I say that I'm the smartest person in the world, you believe that that's false. So, we have two categories: "true" and "false". Just like the history section at the library, we put things that we think are true in the "true" category and we put things that we think are false in the "false" category. So, if fairies exist, then that's true and it can't be false, which means that it goes into the "true" category and is restricted from the "false" category. It doesn't matter if fairies actually exist because we're talking about beliefs. Let's say that monsters don't exist. Monsters go in the "false" category, which means that they are restricted from going into the "true" category. As you can see, a belief is like a downward force that creates restrictions on what's "real" or "true" based on a specific person. The belief (or belief system) pushes all "false" things out. In other words, all false things don't exist/aren't true (according to that person), so they're in a negative state/inactive state/non-existent.

We had to put the tiger under (sedation) (in order) to perform the surgery. (to sedate) This example is a little bit different than all the others, but the same idea applies. In fact, this sentence combines group four and group one, except not in a physical way. When we say "to put under" in this context, it means to sedate. The word "sedation" is optional because it's implied by the context. Of course, you can also say, "We had to sedate the tiger...". This is just another way to say it (because English speakers love phrasal verbs).

Group one applies here because when a person or an animal is sedated, they lose consciousness because the drug makes them go into a deep sleep. When you're awake and aware, your consciousness is active. It's like your consciousness is "above the surface". But when you're sleeping, your consciousness is inactive, so it's "below the surface".

You can also think of this like a light bulb that's either "on" (positive state/active state) or "off" (negative state/inactive state). Notice that when someone is sleeping, we can say, "He's out", for example. Or let's say I went to bed at 9:00 PM (21:00) last night. The next day, I tell you, "I was out at 9". This is because we're using the preposition "out" with the meaning of "negative state/inactive state".

How does group four apply? Well, we already know that we're talking about putting the tiger's consciousness into a negative state/inactive state. However, the idea of restriction or limitation also applies because the tiger is not conscious. In other words, the awareness/consciousness of the tiger is restricted/limited because it's sleeping. The idea of a "downward force" also applies because the drug that's used (in order) to sedate the tiger forces the tiger's awareness or conscious-ness downward

371

and "below the surface", or downward and into a negative state/inactive state, just like a light bulb that's off.

D) Some verbs that often use the preposition "under"

Be under	Work under	Dive under
Drop under	Fall under	

E) **Phrasal Verbs.** Look up each phrasal verb and try to understand how the logic of the word "under" applies. Remember, a phrasal verb is basically a preposition put into action by a verb.

Note: "Under" is not often used in phrasal verbs.

If we can't sell more products, the business will go under. This example is exactly like the sentence that talked about a ship going under, except in this case, it's not physical. It simply means that the business will fail and no longer exist (negative state).

She recently came under fire for some comments (that) she made. Here we have another use of "under fire", but this one isn't about physical shooting. It means "heavy criticism". The other way to say this is: "She was recently heavily criticized for some comments (that) she made". We're just applying the meaning in a figurative way so that it sounds strong, like she's actually being shot at, but she's not.

I think personality falls under the category of behavior. Lastly, we have another example that talks about a category. This use is a little more abstract because we're not talking about a physical section of a library or anything like that. The idea of "behavior" is a bigger and more general idea than "personality", and because "personality" is just one part of the general idea of "behavior", we can use "behavior" as a category that's inside the larger category of "psychology" and put "personality" inside the category of "behavior". So, "PSYCHOLOGY" → "behavior" → "personality". Instead of talking about books, we're talking about ideas or concepts. However, we can see that it works exactly the same: HISTORY → World War II → Allied Powers. We can keep creating more and more categories that are smaller and more specific (Allied Powers → Great Britain → Winston Churchill → etc...)

F) Examples of idioms that use the preposition "under", with detailed explanations.

Because of the scandal, he's trying to fly under the radar. (not be noticed) This is an idiom that comes from the idea of a plane flying so low that it's not noticed by radar, which is a device that's used to find planes. So this example is part of group one.

I took him under my wing. When you take someone under your wing, it means that you decide to guide, teach, and possibly protect someone. This probably comes from the idea of a bird caring for her babies. This example is similar to the phrase "under my protection" or "get under my umbrella".

Appendix A – Quick Reference for the Logic of All Seventeen Prepositions

ON – ALWAYS: positive state/active state; USUALLY ALSO: surface/platform

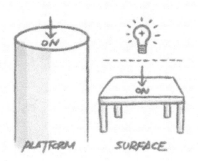

One-Way

OFF – ALWAYS: a negative state/inactive state; USUALLY ALSO: removed from/not on a surface/platform

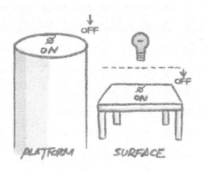

One-Way

UP – 1) an upward or northward direction; or an upward/upright position;
2) a forward/closer to direction;
3) moving to a positive/active state or onto a platform (including 'creation') OR moving to a negative/inactive state or off of a platform (including 'completion')

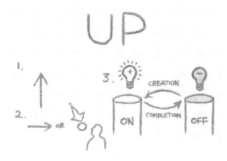

Two-Way

DOWN – 1) a downward or southward direction; or a downward position;
2) an away from direction (sometimes a backward direction);
3) changing to a negative state/off of a platform (including "completion") OR changing to a positive state/onto a platform (including "creation")

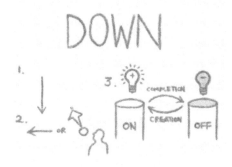

Two-Way

OUT – 1) an outward direction; 2) movement between existence and non-existence

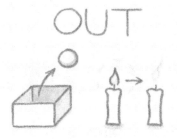

Two-Way

IN – a container

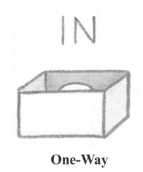

One-Way

AT – a specific point or "bubble"

One-Way

OF – 1) part; 2) content

Two-Way

378

TO – an end point

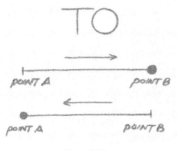

One-Way

FROM – origin point or start point

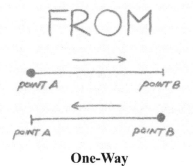

One-Way

379

FOR – 1) purpose; 2) basis/cause; 3) SPECIAL (1+2): distance/duration

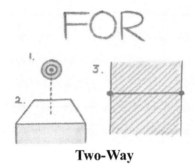

Two-Way

WITH – together

One-Way

BY – a path or a way

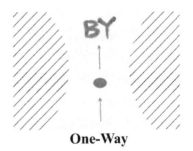

One-Way

AROUND – 1) a circle that's surrounding a specific point;
2) semi-circle that's surrounding a specific point;
3) within the general area of a specific point

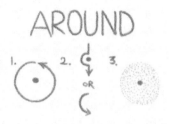

One-Way

ABOUT – a scope (the numbers are the surface meaning groups)

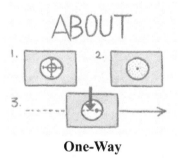

One-Way

381

OVER – 1) an arc shape (like a bridge) that goes from one point to another point (in order) to get to the other side of something;
2) a cycle or circular movement;
3) more than (like the top of the arc)

One-Way

UNDER – 1) a downward force (usually 'restricting'; often 'negative' in some way);
2) lower than or less than (not in the picture)

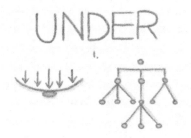

One-Way

Appendix B – The Cone of Existence: English Preposition Maps

<u>NOTE</u>: If you haven't read the whole book yet, you can look at the maps (in order) to see what's happening, but some things won't make sense until you know the logic of all or most of the prepositions.

One of the most amazing and useful things about the logic of English Prepositions is that we can actually make "maps" that show the relationships and connections between all the logic of the prepositions. This makes sense because if there's logic, we can say, "this goes here, that goes there, etc..." However, these maps show a general, top-level overview, so they can't possibly show every little surface meaning and detail. Instead, the maps only show the general relationship of each preposition's logic as a whole.

The first map shows the core of the Cone of Existence, which is the prepositions "at", "on", and "in". This is like a skeleton that the other two maps are based on. The second map adds more prepositions and is the main Cone of Existence. This is like a visual picture of the English language and it's the most important map. The third map adds the remaining prepositions.

Note: I didn't "create" these map, the logic did. I simply looked at the logic of all of these prepositions and saw that this is what it would look like if I put them on a map. The logic speaks for itself. I was actually very surprised to discover that these maps were even possible and when I realized that they were possible, I was fully convinced that what I had discovered about the logic of English prepositions was real and accurate.

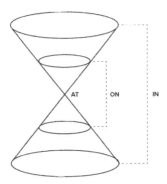

Explanation of the map: As we know, there's a special connection between the prepositions "at", "on", and "in". These three prepositions are extremely important because they're at the core of the English language and they're very closely connected. We've seen many examples where they touch, but they don't usually overlap. For example, we've seen that sometimes you can be "in" clothes, but usually you wear clothes "on" your body; we've seen "at" target "in" and "on"; we know that processes are usually containers ("in"), but they can be active and inactive ("on" and "off"); and many more. It just depends on exactly what we're talking about and the exact way that we're looking at things (within the boundaries of what the English language allows).

Look at the map above. Why is the preposition "at" the center and why are the prepositions "on" and "in" both above and below the preposition "at"? We've already seen the top half of the map earlier in the book. This is the idea of an increasing scale: "at 9:00", "on Monday"/"on the 5th", "in September", "in 1990", "in the second century", etc... We start very small and specific with a specific time, then it gets bigger and less specific with a day of the week or a date, and then it gets even bigger and even less specific with months, years, centuries, so these are containers. We saw the same thing with space: "at 123 Main street", "on Main street", "in Los Angeles", "in the US", etc... This is the top half of the map because the scale is getting bigger and less specific (less focused).

And the bottom half of the map? Find a pen and hold it in your hands. First, look at the pen. The pen is located at a specific point in space, and your eyes are targeting that space. Most of the time, when you look at a pen, you're also focusing on the pen. (Remember the difference between "look at the sky" and "look to the sky": if we use the preposition "at", it means that you're focusing on the sky itself.) However, if you're looking at the pen, that doesn't necessarily mean that you're focusing on the pen. For example, you might be looking at the pen, but you don't really see it because in your mind you're thinking about what happened yesterday. So there's a difference between the prepositions "at" and "on" in this case, but they're very closely related.

When you focus on the pen, you're looking at the pen more closely. Maybe you're analyzing the edges and the exact shape of the pen, for example. On the map, this is the "on" that's below the preposition "at". Why? Because we're looking more closely at the smaller details. In other words, the scale is getting smaller, so we're going downward on the map. Notice that the "in" that's at the top of the map is the biggest and least specific, then "on" is smaller and more specific, then "at" is even smaller and even more specific, but if we continue going down to the next "on", we're getting even smaller and even more specific than the preposition "at", but in a slightly different way.

We can continue going farther down and look in(side) the pen. Notice that when we look closer and closer at things that are smaller and smaller, we enter new little worlds that are big in comparison. From the perspective of the ink that's inside the pen, the case of the pen is big. In other words, when we go inside of something, we enter a new scale or environment where things that were small before become the environment for things that are even smaller. Let's make this clearer: think about the human body. Imagine that you're the size of a blood cell and you're inside a vein swimming with the blood cells. The environment that's around you is very large, but compared to the full size of our bodies, that environment is very small. Remember that the preposition "on" is usually about a surface or platform. Our skin is a surface, but if you go inside the skin to a smaller scale, now we're inside the body. Now the veins are containers, meaning that they become the "in" that's at the top of the map. When we look at the human body as a whole, the body is the container ("in" at the top of the map) and the space inside your veins is very small ("in" at the bottom of the map). In other words, there's a point at which the preposition "on" (that's under the preposition "at") turns into the preposition "in" because we're looking closer and closer at smaller and smaller things until we're inside a completely new environment that's big compared to the things that are inside of it. This is why the "in" that's at the bottom of the map is so big, because it represents a completely new scale/environment. *Don't forget, this also means that the "in" that's at the bottom of the map becomes the "in" that's at the top of the map when we enter the new environment. This is because what was extremely small and specific is now really big and not specific because the scale has changed.*

Ok, so we can look at a pen, focus on a pen and "go inside" a pen. This is the bottom half of the map. We can also talk about a specific place or time ("at"), go to a larger scale ("on Monday") and then an even larger scale that becomes a container because it's so big ("in Los Angeles"). This is the top half of the map. So the preposition "at" is the center, which is why the logic of the preposition "at" is "a specific point". This is also why the preposition "at" is the preposition that almost all other prepositions revolve around. From that center point, we can go "up" or "down" (increase the scale or decrease the scale), depending on what we're talking about. As I said, these maps don't cover every connection between every preposition, so you'll probably be able to find specific cases (surface meanings) where this map doesn't work. But remember that we're looking at things from a general perspective and we're talking about the core logic of each preposition, not all the surface meanings of each preposition.

386

The Main Cone of Existence

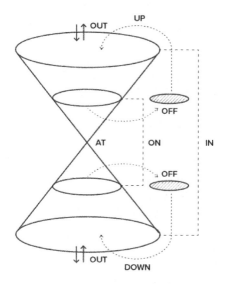

Explanation of the map: These seven prepositions ("at", "on", "in", "up", "down", "out", and "off") are the most important prepositions in English. If you can master these seven, you'll have a very good understanding of how the English language works and how the language feels to native speakers.

We've already talked about the prepositions "at", "on" and "in". Here, we're simply adding four more prepositions: "up", "down", "off", and "out". We've learned the logic of all of these prepositions, and this is what it looks like if you put them together on a map. Again, this is a general view of the logic of the prepositions. In the first map, we only talked about things that are inside the Cone of Existence. Now we're going to talk about things that are outside of the Cone of Existence, as well as the connections between the two.

OUT: The preposition "out" is about an outward direction, as well as the connection between existence and non-existence.

Remember that the idea of an "outward direction" is the basis for the idea of "movement between existence and non-existence". Why? Because something can go out of existence and into non-existence (like the flame on a candle) or something can go out of non-existence and into existence (like a book that's been written and published). As you can see on the map, there are two arrows next to the word "out". We can see this both at the top of the map and at the bottom of the map. The reason it's at the top and bottom is because the preposition "in" is at the top and bottom. So let's talk about this relationship.

A big part of the logic of the preposition "out" is the connection between existence and non-existence. Remember that existence is like a special container and non-existence is like a special container. If something is in existence, it's outside of non-existence and if it's in non-existence, it's outside of existence. Also remember that when something goes from one of these containers into the other, it means that that thing is going from being outside of one to being outside of the other at the same time. This is what the two arrows mean because the preposition "out" is the connection between the two containers of existence and non-existence. For example, if I want to write a book, that book is currently inside the container called "non-existence", meaning that it's currently outside of the Cone of Existence. After I write the book and publish it, the book has been created, which means that it now exists, so it's inside the container of existence, meaning that it's inside the Cone of Existence. Before: Book exists = no, book doesn't exist = yes. After: Book exists = yes, book doesn't exist = no. You can see how these ideas are closely related to a "positive state" and a "negative state", which we'll talk about soon.

But there's something else happening that's very interesting. The previous map shows us that the preposition "in" represents both the largest and smallest scale/environment. We also saw that when we reach the smallest scale, the environment at that scale becomes the new larger environment ("in" at the bottom becomes "in" at the top). For example, your veins are very small compared to the size of your body, but your veins are very large compared to the size of your blood cells. So, if we go into the human body, we're going out of the bottom of the map and into the top of the map because now we're in a new larger environment. In other words, we're at the scale of a blood cell, so the environment is big in comparison. Remember that the veins are the containers ("in" at the top of the map). When we look at the human body as a whole, the body is the container ("in" at the top of the map) and the space inside your veins is very small ("in" at the bottom of the map). So the preposition "out" isn't just the connection between existence and non-existence, it's about the connection between "levels of existence" or "scales of existence". When you go out of one scale (inside the body), you enter another scale (outside of the body). Or we can go from outside of the body to inside of the body, just like we can go from non-existence to existence. In other words, we've "created" or discovered a new environment/world by going inside the smaller scale.

OFF: We know that the preposition "off" is about a negative state/inactive state and it's usually also about moving off of a surface/platform or something that's removed from a surface/platform. The map shows us that the preposition "off" is outside of the Cone of Existence. This is what "negative state/inactive state" means. For example, if you turn a light off, it becomes inactive, but the light that's shining into the room also disappears. It literally goes out of existence. But what about the surface/platform idea? We can see that the prepositions "up" and "down" are the connection between the prepositions "on" and "off", which we'll talk about soon. First, imagine that you're on a stage. A stage is both a surface and a platform. When you get off of the stage, you're not existing on the stage (negative state/inactive state). In other words, you moved off of that surface/platform. Also notice that in this case, when you get off of the stage, you move downward, which also means that have completed the action of getting off of the stage (in relation to the stage, you've moved from a positive state/active state to a negative/inactive state).

UP and DOWN: We can't finish talking about the relationship between the prepositions "on" and "off" unless we start talking about the prepositions "up" and "down". Notice that

389

the preposition "up" is on the top half of the map and it connects to the "on" that's above the preposition "at". This is because we're increasing the scale (at 9:00, on Monday, in September). Also notice that the preposition "down" is on the bottom half of the map and it connects to the "on" that's below the preposition "at". This is because we're decreasing the scale (look at, focus on, go inside).

As you can see, there are two arrows connected to the preposition "up": one goes from the preposition "on" to the preposition "off" and the other goes from the preposition "off" to the preposition "on". But that's not all. The second arrow is going all the way up and then **in**to the Cone of Existence through the preposition "**in**". Also, the preposition "off" is **out**side of the Cone of Existence, so when the preposition "up" passes through the preposition "in", it uses the preposition "**out**" so that it can enter the Cone of existence, meaning that it goes from the container of non-existence into the container of existence. What does all of that mean? "Creation". Something is coming into existence (or becoming active). Remember that the phrasal verb "bring up" means "to mention". Let's say I start talking about going to the beach and my friend says, "I'm glad you brought that up. I wanted to ask you if we could go on Saturday." The topic of the beach was inactive ("off"), or we could say that it wasn't "existing" (remember, these ideas are very similar), so the topic of going to the beach was "outside of existence" in an abstract way. But when I bring it up, I'm bringing that topic into the conversation by speaking about it. This makes the topic "active" ("on") and now it's "existing" in an abstract way. Also notice that we were **off** of the topic of going to the beach, I brought that topic **up**, and now we are **on** that topic. Off → up → on = "creation"

The first arrow that connects the preposition "on" to the preposition "off" is "completion". Let's say that we're talking about something, but I have to leave soon, so I say, "Let's wrap this up because I have to leave soon." The phrasal verb "wrap up" means "to finish" (we can also say "finish up" in this context), so we're talking about ending the conversation ("completion"). The conversation is currently active/existing ("**on**"), but I have to

390

leave, so we have to wrap it **up**, and then the conversation will be finished ("**off**"). On → up → off = "completion" (Note: the line of the first arrow looks like it's going "down", notice the end of the arrow. It's pointing upward to the preposition "off".)

The preposition "down" is the exact opposite. If you look closely, you'll see that even the arrows are going in the opposite direction. We know that the preposition "down" also uses the "creation" and "completion" ideas. Do you remember the sentence, "I put $300 down on a new car"? That means that you made the first payment so that you start using the car and you will pay for the rest of it over time. First, you couldn't use the car, meaning that your access to the car didn't exist or was inactive. If you put $300 down on the car, you can start using it and you have started to pay for it ("creation"). This means that your access to the car does exist/it's active. Off → down → on = "creation". If you look at the map, you'll see that this "down" arrow goes from the preposition "off", then down and into the Cone of Existence. Just like the preposition "up" did at the top, the preposition "down" passes through the preposition "in" using the preposition "out", meaning that your access to the car was outside of existence (it didn't exist) and now it has come into existence.

The Full Cone of Existence: A Complete Map of Seventeen English Prepositions

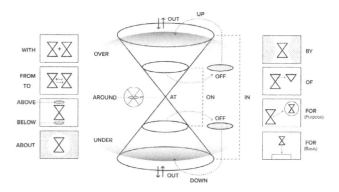

391

Explanation of the map: There isn't a lot of explanation for this map because we've already talked about the most important details. Notice that the preposition "around" is surrounding the preposition "at". We have the arc-shapes of the prepositions "over" and "under", which are "over" the preposition "at" and "under" the preposition "at". In other words, they're over and under a specific point. I added the prepositions "above" and "below" in one of the boxes that's on the left. It looks like they're outside the cone of existence, but in reality, they're not. The problem was that I couldn't fit them on the map because there was already too much on it and if I added them it would make the map harder to read. Some prepositions are in boxes that are on the side because they don't work well with the map, especially since most of them are very abstract. If the images in the boxes are confusing, you can ignore them. Don't forget that all of the prepositions have individual pictures that show their logic in Appendix A.

References

1 Jackson, Steven B. "Masculine or Feminine? (And Why It Matters)." *Psychology Today*, Sussex Publishers, 21 Sept. 2012, www.psychologytoday.com/intl/blog/culture-conscious/201209/masculine-or-feminine-and-why-it-matters.
2 https://www.etymonline.com/word/of
3 https://www.etymonline.com/word/a-
4 https://www.etymonline.com/word/to
5 https://www.etymonline.com/word/have
6 https://www.etymonline.com/word/in
7 https://www.etymonline.com/word/for
8 https://www.etymonline.com/word/at
9 https://www.etymonline.com/word/ease
10 https://www.etymonline.com/word/by
11 https://www.etymonline.com/word/from
12 https://www.etymonline.com/word/bag
13 https://www.etymonline.com/word/with
14 https://www.etymonline.com/word/about
15 https://www.etymonline.com/word/over
16 https://www.etymonline.com/word/around
17 https://www.etymonline.com/word/off
18 https://www.etymonline.com/word/off-limits
19 https://www.etymonline.com/word/down
20 https://www.etymonline.com/word/under

Made in the USA
Columbia, SC
19 May 2023

16996433R00215